Engineer in Gray

Engineer in Gray

*Memoirs of Chief Engineer
James H. Tomb, CSN*

Edited by R. Thomas Campbell

McFarland & Company, Inc., Publishers
Jefferson, North Carolina, and London

Frontispiece: James Hamilton Tomb

The present work is a reprint of the illustrated case bound edition of Engineer in Gray: Memoirs of Chief Engineer James H. Tomb, CSN, *first published in 2005 by McFarland.*

Library of Congress Online Catalog Data

Tomb, James H. (James Hamilton)
Engineer in gray : memoirs of chief engineer James H. Tomb, CSN / edited by R. Thomas Campbell.
p. cm.
Includes bibliographical references and index.

ISBN 978-0-7864-4926-2
softcover : 50# alkaline paper ∞

1. Tomb, James H. (James Hamilton)
2. Confederate States of America. Navy — Biography.
3. United States — History — Civil War, 1861–1865 — Personal narratives.
4. Marine engineers — Confederate States of America — Biography.
5. Confederate States of America. Navy — Sea life.
6. United States — History — Civil War, 1861–1865 — Naval operations.
7. United States — History — Civil War, 1861–1865 — Technology.
8. Torpedo-boats — Confederate States of America — History.
I. Campbell, R. Thomas, 1937–
II. Title.
E596.T66 2011   973.7'57'092 — dc22   2004029507

British Library Cataloguing Data are available

© 2005 R. Thomas Campbell. All rights reserved

No part of this book may be reproduced or transmitted in any form or by any means, electronic or mechanical, including photocopying or recording, or by any information storage and retrieval system, without permission in writing from the publisher.

On the cover: James H. Tomb; the *David*, near Charleston *(courtesy of Dan Dowdey)*

Manufactured in the United States of America

*McFarland & Company, Inc., Publishers
Box 611, Jefferson, North Carolina 28640
www.mcfarlandpub.com*

Acknowledgments

The publication of Tomb's memoirs would not have been possible without the help and encouragement of many individuals. In any endeavor of this kind, however, the danger of omitting a reference to a person or an institution that helped in the preparation always exists. I am now running that risk, and I apologize profusely to those whom I may have forgotten.

First and foremost my thanks to Rachel Canada of the Wilson Library at the University of North Carolina, Chapel Hill. Over 300 pages of material in the Tomb Family Papers were reproduced by her staff and forwarded to me. Without her cheerful assistance, this work would never have seen the light of day.

My thanks also to Mr. Harvey Arche of Joplin, Missouri, the great-great-nephew of James H. Tomb. Mr. Arche was instrumental in providing numerous photographs and personal letters of Tomb from his family's collection. His many accounts of his father's remembrance of "Uncle Jimmy" brought a sense of intimacy to the work.

Thanks also to Mr. Kevin Spargur, Commander of the 6th Brigade, Florida Division of the Sons of Confederate Veterans, who relentlessly pursued and photographed the final resting place of James H. Tomb and his family. His many emails were filled with information and encouragement.

Appreciation must also be given to the following individuals and institutions: Leslie Sheffield and Miriam Gan-Spalding of the Florida State Archives; M. Pugh, of the Florida Department of State; Joan A. Pickett of the Jacksonville Historical Society; Thomas DiGiuseppe of Lynnfield, Massachusetts; Jason D. Stratman of the Missouri Historical Society; Eliane Perez of the Divisao de Informacao Documental/Biblioteca Nacional, Rio de Janeiro; Craig Symonds of the U.S. Naval Academy at Annapolis; Bob Holcombe of the Columbus Civil War Naval Museum; and Jewell A. Dalrymple of the Georgia Historical Society.

Last, but certainly not least, a note of deep appreciation to my wife and proofreader, Carole, whose patience, endurance, and encouragement never seem to falter. To all these mentioned above, and to others whom I have failed to mention, I am humbly grateful.— R.T.C.

Contents

Acknowledgments v
Preface 1
Introduction 7

1. The CSS *Jackson* 11
2. The CSS *McRae* 25
3. Prison Life at Fort Warren 42
4. The CSS *Chicora* 53
5. The CSS *David* 65
6. The CSS *Juno* 76
7. More Torpedo Attacks 83
8. The CSS *Leesburg* 91
9. Badly Used Up 101
10. The Cause Is Lost 108
11. Various Official Documents—Part A 115
12. Various Official Documents—Part B 126
13. To South America 133
14. Loss of the *Rio de Janeiro* 145
15. Adiós South America 159

Appendix A. Submarines and Torpedo Boats, C.S.N., by James H. Tomb, Chief Engineer, CSN 169

Appendix B. Manuscript of James H. Tomb 173

Appendix C. Reminiscences of Torpedo Service in Charleston Harbor by Commander William T. Glassell, CSN 178

Appendix D. Torpedo Service in the Harbor and Water Defenses of Charleston by General P.G.T. Beauregard 186

Chapter Notes 197

Bibliography 201

Index 203

Preface

Much has been written concerning the American Civil War. A great portion of this material concerns the massive armies of both North and South and the commanders who used them to wage conventional land warfare. In many respects this conflict differed little from wars of previous centuries. Comparatively few works have been published relating to the naval aspect of the war. It was, however, on the naval front that the most intriguing technological advances were made. This was particularly true of the Confederate effort. Most notable of these developments were armored warships, floating mines, submarines, and torpedo boats. The memoirs you are about to read were written by an individual who was cast into the center of this era of naval innovation. His account of these tumultuous years deserves our close attention, for much of what he experienced has shaped our world today.

James Hamilton Tomb devoted almost 12 years of his early life to wartime naval service—first in the Confederate States Navy during the American Civil War, and later in the Marinha do Brasil (Brazilian Navy) during the War of the Triple Alliance. A steam engineer by profession and a torpedo expert by circumstance, James H. Tomb was at the forefront of naval weapons technology during the mid- to late nineteenth century. His innovations, courage, and perseverance in the face of overwhelming obstacles brought him accolades and promotions from grateful nations, but more important, contributed immeasurably to the defense of one and to the victory of another.

Tomb was born in Savannah, Georgia, on March 16, 1839, one of seven children born to William R. and Sarah Tomb, both of whom had emigrated from England to the Georgia city. There the elder Tomb provided for his family by working as a painter. In addition, his oldest son, Robert, contributed to the family's support by working as a clerk in a local business establishment. Early in 1852, when James Tomb was only 13, his father moved the entire family to Florida, sailing down the St. Johns River in their own schooner. Passing New Berlin just east of Jacksonville, William Tomb liked what he saw and the family decided to stay. According to family

Wartime map of the Jacksonville area including the location of New Berlin, in the Yellow Bluff area (*Official Records Navy*).

lore, it was William who named the area around their home "Yellow Bluff" because of a 40-foot high precipice of "sand as yellow as an egg yolk." The area is still known today by this name. A house (which burned in 1907) was built, and Tomb constructed a sawmill that produced planks that can be seen in some of the houses still standing. In addition to operating the sawmill, William Tomb became the postmaster and a federal magistrate of New Berlin.

It was here, along the banks of the lazy St. Johns, that young James Tomb began to learn about steam engines and how to care for and operate them. In addition to the education he derived from his work at the steam-driven sawmill, Tomb also learned steam technology from Leonard Freeland who had married his sister, Cecilia. Freeland was a steamboat captain and undoubtedly took James along on many excursions on the St. Johns River. It was only natural, then, that he should mature with a keen interest and a flourishing knowledge of marine machinery. By 1861, as war clouds gathered, Tomb had amassed a decent comprehension of the duties required of a marine steam engineer.[1]

During the decade that the Tomb family went about their family business along the banks of the St. Johns River, they and their fellow citizens of Florida watched with growing apprehension the turmoil that seemed to engulf their sister states to the north. Like others in slaveholding states, the citizens of Florida shuddered at the thoughts of a slave uprising following the aborted raid by John Brown on Harper's Ferry in Virginia. Furthermore, they shared the common Southern concerns about

An early photograph of New Berlin, Florida, as seen from the St. Johns River (Florida State Archives).

Northern oppression, unfair taxation, and states' rights. Florida's electoral votes were cast for John C. Breckinridge in the presidential election of 1860, but the success of the "black Republican" party's candidate, Abraham Lincoln, was the last straw. Like South Carolina, Florida's legislators began laying the groundwork for the state's withdrawal from the Union.[2]

On December 20, 1860, South Carolina became the first state to leave the Union. The Palmetto State's actions were followed quickly by Mississippi, which passed its Ordnance of Secession on January 9, 1861. A week before Mississippi's action, delegates had gathered in Tallahassee to discuss what Florida would do. Emotions were high. Word soon came that local Florida militia units had seized Fort Marion in Saint Augustine and the arsenal at Apalachicola. Other Federal installations around the state were being threatened. On January 10, the delegates passed Florida's Ordnance of Secession by a vote of 62 to 7. The crowd that had gathered outside the statehouse received the news with joyous shouts and cheers. Torchlight parades were staged and politicians clamored for stump time to exhort the crowd and fuel the spirit of their newly declared independence. Soon Alabama, Georgia, Louisiana, and Texas followed. For better or worse, Florida's fate, and the fate of her citizens, were indelibly linked to the yet-to-be-formed Confederate States of America.[3]

On February 26, 1861, the delegates to the secession convention reassembled in Tallahassee and unanimously adopted the Constitution of the Confederate States. Governor Madison S. Perry immediately ordered state militia units to seize all remaining Federal property in Florida. The arsenal at Chattahooche was soon occupied as well as Fort Clinch at Fernandina, but Federal troops remained at Fort Pickens on Santa Rosa Island in Pensacola Bay and in Fort Taylor at Key West. Fort Taylor remained in Union hands throughout the war.[4]

On April 16, 1861, six days after Federal forces had surrendered Fort Sumter in Charleston Harbor, President Abraham Lincoln declared a naval blockade of the Southern coastline. At first this had little effect on Florida, for the number of ships available for blockade duty were few, and the state was not considered of much strategic importance by the Federal high command. This began to change toward the end of the year, however, as more war vessels were added to the Union Navy, and soon Federal warships began to appear off the east and west coasts of Florida.[5]

After spending several short tours on the USS *Keystone State* as an engineer apprentice, Tomb went before the examining board seeking an appointment as a third class engineer in the United States Navy. On April 24, 1861, after a successful review by the examining board, and against the ominous backdrop of national events, James H. Tomb was appointed third assistant engineer in the U.S. Navy. One week later, on May 1, he declined the appointment.

Instead, he offered his services to the newly formed Southern government in Montgomery, and on June 21, he was commissioned a third assistant engineer in the infant Confederate States Navy. It would prove to be a momentous assignment — one that would define the remainder of his life and change forever the course of modern naval warfare.[6]

In the age of steam propulsion, the position of engineer in the ranks of the world's navies was a relatively new one. Although ships powered by steam had been around since Robert Fulton's early experiment in 1807, many "old salts" looked with disdain upon the upstart engineer with his sooty clothes and noisy smoking engines. Most, however, had come to accept his presence as a necessary one, and ever-increasingly important as the age of sail began to give way to steam. The Confederate Navy, similar to the U.S. Navy, had not yet clearly defined the role of engineer. Because of this relatively new position, there were no laws or standing customs to go by. In some instances, engineers seemed equivalent in rank to paymasters, constructors, or medical officers, but in other circumstances, such as Tomb would find himself, they acted in the same capacity as masters or lieutenants in command. Much depended on the type of ship to which the engineer was assigned. Obviously the responsibility of an engineer on a Confederate ironclad was greater than that of an oceangoing cruiser. For while the cruiser could be propelled by sail, steam, or a combination of the two, the ironclad's sole source of propulsion was the steam engine — which was, in turn, dependent upon the engineer's ability to keep it running.

Recognizing the importance of this position, the Confederate Navy established four grades of engineers: a commissioned officer known as chief engineer, and first, second, and third class engineers (three grades of warrant officer). All of the twelve chief engineers subsequently appointed by the Confederacy were former officers in the old navy with between 7 and 18 years of experience, with the exception of Tomb who was promoted for gallantry. The successful completion of a formal examination was required before engineers could be promoted to chief engineer. Assistant engineers, who were warrant officers, could be appointed by the Secretary of the Navy, or in many cases, such as with the cruisers, could be appointed by the officer in command subject to the approval of the Naval Secretary.[7]

It was in light of his experience with marine machinery and his positive review from the U.S. Navy examining board that Tomb had been given the appointment as engineer in the Confederate Navy. He still had much to learn, however, but being a bright young man he would quickly amass not only the necessary knowledge required of a steam engineer, but also the courage and capacity to assume important positions of command. Within days of his commissioning he was on his way to his first assignment — that of third class engineer attached to the CSS *Jackson* at New Orleans, Louisiana. Because of the strategic importance of New Orleans, every effort was being made to strengthen Southern naval forces on the Mississippi River. It is here, amid a tightening blockade and a growing fear of a Federal attack from the Gulf, that Tomb's memoirs begin.

Introduction

At the approximate time of Tomb's appointment as an engineer in the Confederate Navy, officials in Richmond began to notice a decided increase in the number of Federal vessels blockading the mouth of the Mississippi River below New Orleans. In addition to this news, there arrived almost daily persistent rumors of Union ironclads being constructed along the upper Mississippi Valley near Cairo, Illinois. As a result of this information, Confederate thinking began to concentrate more and more upon the defense of this vital area.

For some time before the war New Orleans had possessed facilities for the construction and repair of small rivercraft, but no warship had ever been constructed there from the keel up. Time was of the essence, however, and even though the government—first in Montgomery and now Richmond—placed considerable faith in the land fortifications below New Orleans, Secretary of the Navy Stephen R. Mallory was convinced that only a strong naval force would be able to eventually stop the enemy's advance. With these factors in mind, Mallory instructed Captain Lawrence Rousseau, a distinguished veteran of the War of 1812, to go to New Orleans and purchase and outfit as many steamers as he could locate.

In response, on May 9, 1861, the elderly captain purchased the tug *Yankee*, a side-wheel steamer that had been built at Cincinnati in 1849. Strengthened and outfitted with two 32-pounders on pivots, one fore and one aft, she entered Confederate service on June 17 as the CSS *Jackson*. The *Jackson* was to be Tomb's first assignment, and with the converted tug painted black and her two large guns mounted prominently on deck, she looked every inch a warship. Her noisy high-pressure engines, however, were a disadvantage, for the enemy could hear her coming from miles away. In addition, Tomb often worried about the vulnerability of her boilers to enemy fire, for they were exposed on the main deck.

In addition to the *Jackson*, the navy purchased two privateers: the *Ivy* and the venerable old *Calhoun*, each mounting four and five guns, respectively. Also added to the Confederate fleet during this time frame were the *Oregon*, a wooden

Secretary of the Confederate Navy Stephen R. Mallory (Library of Congress).

Left: Chief Naval Constructor John L. Porter. *Right:* Commander John M. Brooke photographed after the war while a professor at Virginia Military Institute (Naval Historical Center).

side-wheeler, and the steamer *Arrow*, both of which had been seized by Governor Thomas O. Moore of Louisiana. It was a start, but it would take more than these converted riverboats to defeat the rumored ironclads of the enemy.

About the time that Tomb reported for duty at New Orleans, the news reaching Richmond concerning the building of a powerful Federal ironclad fleet near Cairo, Illinois, was no longer a rumor. In Washington, General Winfield Scott was busy implementing his Anaconda Plan. First proposed by the aging but famous general, the Anaconda Plan involved the establishment of an effective blockade of the approximately 1,700 miles of Southern coastline coupled with a strong naval force and army thrust down the Mississippi Valley from Cairo to the Gulf of Mexico. An additional recommendation involved a naval expedition that would capture and hold the city of New Orleans and then advance northward up the river. A successful execution of this plan would result in splitting the Confederacy in half.

In June 1861, Scott ordered the army to begin construction of a fleet of armored, shallow-draft gunboats, and in August, James B. Eads, a Missouri engineer, was granted a contract to construct seven ironclads in just 64 days. This ambitious order would have been unthinkable in the South, but the mighty industrial complex of the North made it possible for the Union. Eads traveled to St. Louis and marshaled every shipyard and manufacturing facility there that he could find. The net result was that by the beginning of 1862, the Union fleet on the upper Mississippi included nine heavy ironclads, each displacing from 500 to 1,000 tons and mounting a total of 129 guns. If such a formidable fleet should succeed in forcing its way south past the land fortifications, the Confederate Navy had nothing with which to stop them.[1]

With information concerning these ironclads now reaching Mallory's desk, the seriousness of the situation was not lost upon the Navy Department. On July 30, the naval secretary convened a conference with a group of officers to discuss what steps should be taken in the west to meet this danger. Present at the meeting, in addition to Mallory, were Captains Duncan N. Ingraham and George N. Hollins, Constructor John L. Porter and Commander John M. Brooke. Mallory presented a plan that he had drafted that called for the construction of ironclads along the Mississippi that could not only defend the river but could also be taken to sea and attack the blockade. Brooke strongly supported Mallory's plan and quickly drafted an organization and operational plan for the armored warships. If the Federals could not be defeated, at least they could be thrown on the defensive. The next day, Mallory replaced the aged and ineffectual Rousseau at New Orleans with Captain Hollins. The reckless and aggressive Hollins appeared to be the right man to carry out Mallory's plan in the Mississippi Valley. Sadly, events would soon prove otherwise.[2]

George N. Hollins was born in Baltimore in 1799, and was, like Rousseau, a veteran of the War of 1812. He entered the U.S. Navy as a midshipman in 1814 and served on the USS *Erie* during that ship's attempt to raise the English blockade of the Chesapeake Bay. After being transferred to the USS *President*, Hollins was captured at Bermuda and remained a prisoner of the British until the end of the war. After serving on various U.S. vessels and being elevated to lieutenant in 1828, to commander in 1841, and finally to captain in 1855, he submitted his resignation on June 6, 1861. Like many who resigned after the firing on Fort Sumter, his resignation was not accepted, and he was instead dismissed from the navy. He traveled south and offered his services to the new Southern nation and was appointed a captain in the Confederate Navy on June 22. Now, amidst an impending crisis at New Orleans and warnings of an enemy buildup to the north, Hollins was taking on the most critical assignment of his long naval career.

When Hollins arrived to assume command of all Confederate naval forces in the area, he proceeded with his usual bluster and enthusiasm to squander more than $250,000 on the purchase of seven Mississippi riverboats that he intended to have converted into gunboats. These were not the quality of warships that Mallory was anticipating, for they were all wooden side-wheelers and would stand little chance of success against the ironclads of the Federals. Still, they were better than nothing. In addition, and compounding the financial situation at New Orleans, Lieutenant Beverly Kennon, chief of the Ordnance Department at New Orleans, spent $146,000 on ordnance supplies even though he was allocated only $40,000.[3]

It was in the midst of all this frenzied preparation and financial chaos that Engineer Tomb arrived in New Orleans to assume his duties as third assistant engineer on the CSS *Jackson*.

1

The CSS *Jackson*

Having passed a satisfactory examination before a board composed of Chief Engineers W. H. Shock, President; Long and Garvan, U. S. N. members, I was appointed a 3rd Assistant Engineer in the U. S. N., from Florida, May 1, 1861, but declined the appointment, not wishing to serve against the South in case of war between the two sections.

> [Delegates appointed by the Florida legislature met in Tallahassee on January 3, 1861, and on January 10, passed an Ordinance of Secession taking Florida out of the Union. That night, joyous crowds surged through the streets of Tallahassee in celebration of the news.—Editor]

The feeling was very strong through the South in regard to the election of Lincoln as President, as it was felt he would represent the radical element of the Republican party and [be] unfriendly to the South. I was too young, perhaps, to understand all the points at issue, and, while feeling badly at Lincoln's election, yet thought we should wait and see just what his course towards the South would be, as he was not like Seward or Stevens, but of the people and plain and honest.[1] This was not, however, the trend of opinion [in the] South, and my expression of regret at giving up the federal service was not to my credit with my friends; yet it was not a pleasant thing to do, and it was only from a sense of duty that I did it.

I realized, as time passed, that it was not the most radical and extreme advocates of secession that did the best fighting. The conservative element, while slow to secede, were also slow to give up, after years of suffering and defeat.

June 21, 1861, I received my appointment as 3rd Assistant Engineer in the Confederate Navy, and was ordered to report to the Commanding Officer, at New Orleans, for duty aboard the C.S.S. *Jackson*. After a round about trip by rail, I reported for duty July 4, 1861, aboard the *Jackson*, Captain Washington Gwathney in command; McCreery, Executive [First Lieutenant Charles P. McGary]; Midshipmen Holt [Acting Midshipman Henry C. Holt], Phil Dougherty

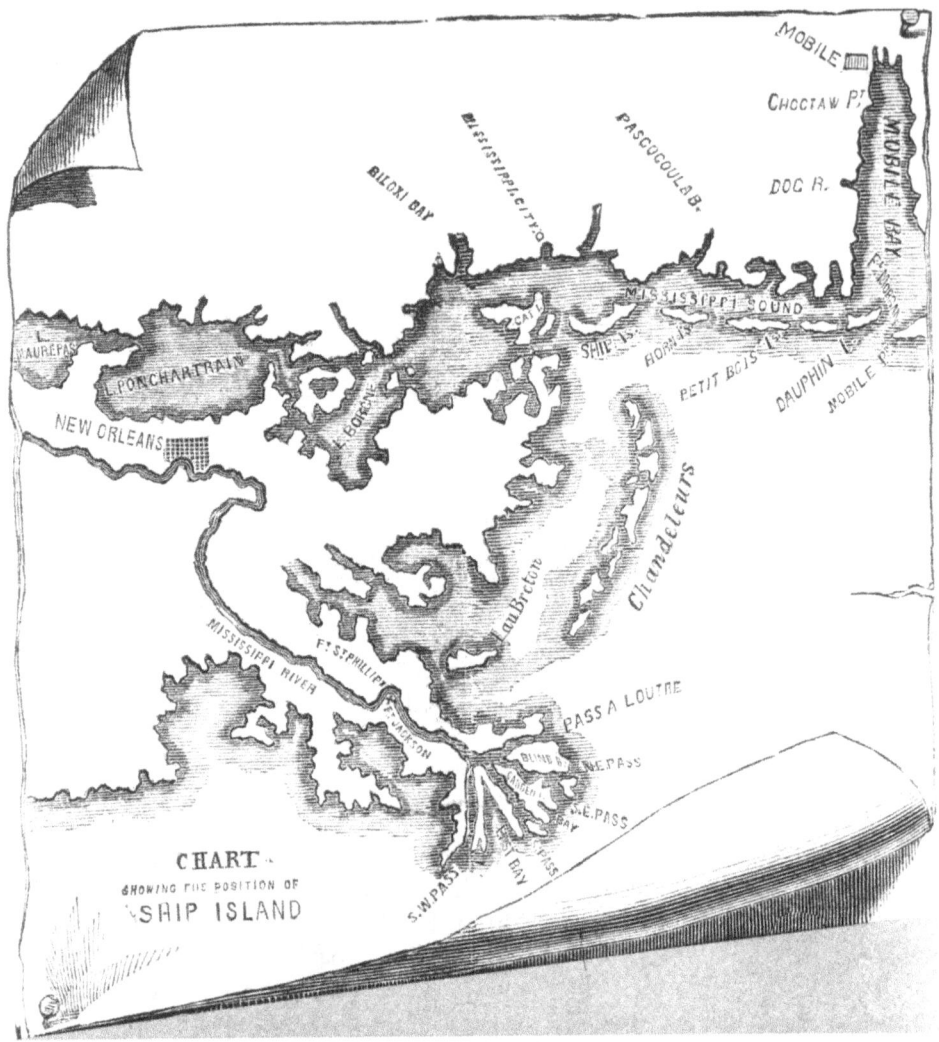

Chart of the Mississippi River from New Orleans to the Gulf of Mexico (Naval Historical Center).

[Acting Midshipman H. H. Daugherty] and Telfair [Acting Midshipman David A. Telfair]; Surgeon I. Ward [Surgeon John Ward]; Assistant Engineer C. Williams [Acting Second Assistant Engineer George Williams], in charge.

> [First Lieutenant Washington Gwathney was born in England but was a resident of Virginia by the beginning of the war. He had resigned from the U.S. Navy on April 17, 1861, and was appointed a first lieutenant in the Confederate Navy three days later on April 20, 1861.—Editor]

At this time, the C. S. N., at New Orleans, consisted of the *McRae*, the *Ivy*, the *Jackson*, the *Calhoun*, and the *Manassas*, none of them being ready for active service.

1. The CSS *Jackson*

The CSS *Manassas* (Naval Historical Center).

The *McRae* was a barque-rigged propeller, a sister ship of the C. S. S. *Sumter* that had succeeded in running the blockade, and passing out to sea on June 30, 1861. The *McRae* mounted six 32-pounders, one 9-inch smooth-bore Dalghren amidships, pivot, and one 12-pound Howitzer on the poop, and was commanded by Captain Thomas B. Huger. The intention was to send her to sea also, but later the spars were sent down and she was made flagship of the station, under Commodore Hollins.

The *Ivy* was a side-wheel steamer, mounting one 30-pound rifle, but not ready for service, commanded by Lieutenant Joseph Fry.

The *Jackson* was a large high-pressure steamer, with four boilers on the main deck, and was formerly the towboat *Yankee*. She mounted two 8-inch smooth bore guns, one forward and the other aft, on pivots.

The *Calhoun* was a side-wheel steamer, but not in commission or ready for service.

The *Manassas*, iron-clad ram, mounting one 24lb smooth bore forward, and the upper works covered with 3/4 inch iron, commanded by Lieutenant W. A. Wharley [First Lieutenant Alexander F. Warley], was so constructed that no one could stand at the gun to load it. She was a ram, but lacking in power as well as armor.

> [The *McRae* was the former Mexican bark *Marqués de la Habana* whose crew had mutinied. She was captured by the USS *Saratoga* in March 1860 and taken to New Orleans. Thomas B. Huger was from South Carolina and had resigned from the U.S. Navy on January 11, 1861. His appointment in the

First Lieutenant Joseph Fry, commander of the CSS *Ivy* (Scharf, *History of the Confederate States Navy*).

Confederate Navy was dated March 28, 1861.

The *Ivy* had been given a letter of marque and reprisal as a privateer on May 16, 1861, but a few months later was sold to the Confederate Navy. Joseph Fry was from Florida and had resigned from the U.S. Navy on February 1, 1861. He was appointed a first lieutenant in Confederate service on March 26, 1861.

The *Jackson* was a fast river tug that had been built at Cincinnati in 1849 and was one of the purchases made by Captain Rousseau at New Orleans on May 9, 1861.

The *Calhoun*, like the *Ivy*, was a former privateer that had been chartered by the Confederate Navy. She was under the command of Lieutenant Jonathan H. Carter from North Carolina, who had resigned from the U.S. Navy on April 25, 1861, and was commissioned in the Confederate Navy two days later.

The CSS *Manassas* was formerly the powerful towboat *Enoch Train*, built at Medford, Massachusetts, by J. O. Curtis in 1855. She was purchased and converted to an ironclad by New Orleans commission merchant James A. Stevenson for the purpose of privateering. Before she could go to sea, however, she was seized at gunpoint by Confederate authorities in September 1861. Lieutenant Warley was from South Carolina and had resigned from the U.S. Navy on December 24, 1860, being given a commission as first lieutenant in the Confederate Navy on March 26, 1861. He served briefly as executive officer on the *McRae* before being given command of the *Manassas*.—Editor]

New Orleans was full of active workers who were anxious to contribute money to defend the city, or volunteer for the war, and, up to the time of its surrender, always impressed me as being a fine city with fine people. The surrender was no reflection on them, but reflected rather on the Army and Navy for not being in better shape to defend them. Both branches of the service might have been under better heads.

When the *Jackson* was ready for service, she was sent down the river and was at the Head of the Passes and at the forts, Fort Jackson and Fort St. Philip, some 75 miles below the city. Our duty consisted in watching out for the Yankees, and fighting mosquitoes—the largest I ever saw or felt.

Left: First Lieutenant Alexander F. Warley, commander of the ironclad CSS *Manassas* (*Battles and Leaders of the Civil War,* Johnson and Buell, eds.). *Right:* First Lieutenant Thomas B. Huger, commander of the CSS *McRae* (Scharf, *History of the Confederate States Navy*).

> [The Head of the Passes was a section of the river about 70 miles below New Orleans and 15 miles from where the river empties into the Gulf of Mexico where the Mississippi separates into three channels leading to the open sea: Pass A Loutre, South Pass, and Southwest Pass. Forts Jackson and St. Philip were the main bastions guarding the entry of the Mississippi River.— Editor]

The duty was anything but desirable, but it was not as bad as that of the fellows blockading outside.

Forts Jackson and St. Philip were strong forts facing each other in a bend of the river, and St. Philip had a water battery of 32-pounders that extended along the whole front, and between the two forts, anchored in the river, was a large raft of logs reaching from Fort Jackson to within some hundred feet of Fort St. Philip, leaving a channel for the passage of vessels. At this time the forts were in better condition to prevent the Yankees from passing than they were when Farragut [Admiral David G. Farragut] arrived, as it was a solid obstruction, and his ships never could have broken through.

The driftwood coming down the river had accumulated above the raft until it was about as heavy as the raft itself. Captain Gwathney called this to the attention of the officers in charge of the forts. He said if it were not removed it would soon carry away the raft, but it was not attended to. After a while the drift became so heavy that the raft was broken up. It was some time before officials at the fort replaced it by four old hulks anchored in the river with chains passed between and

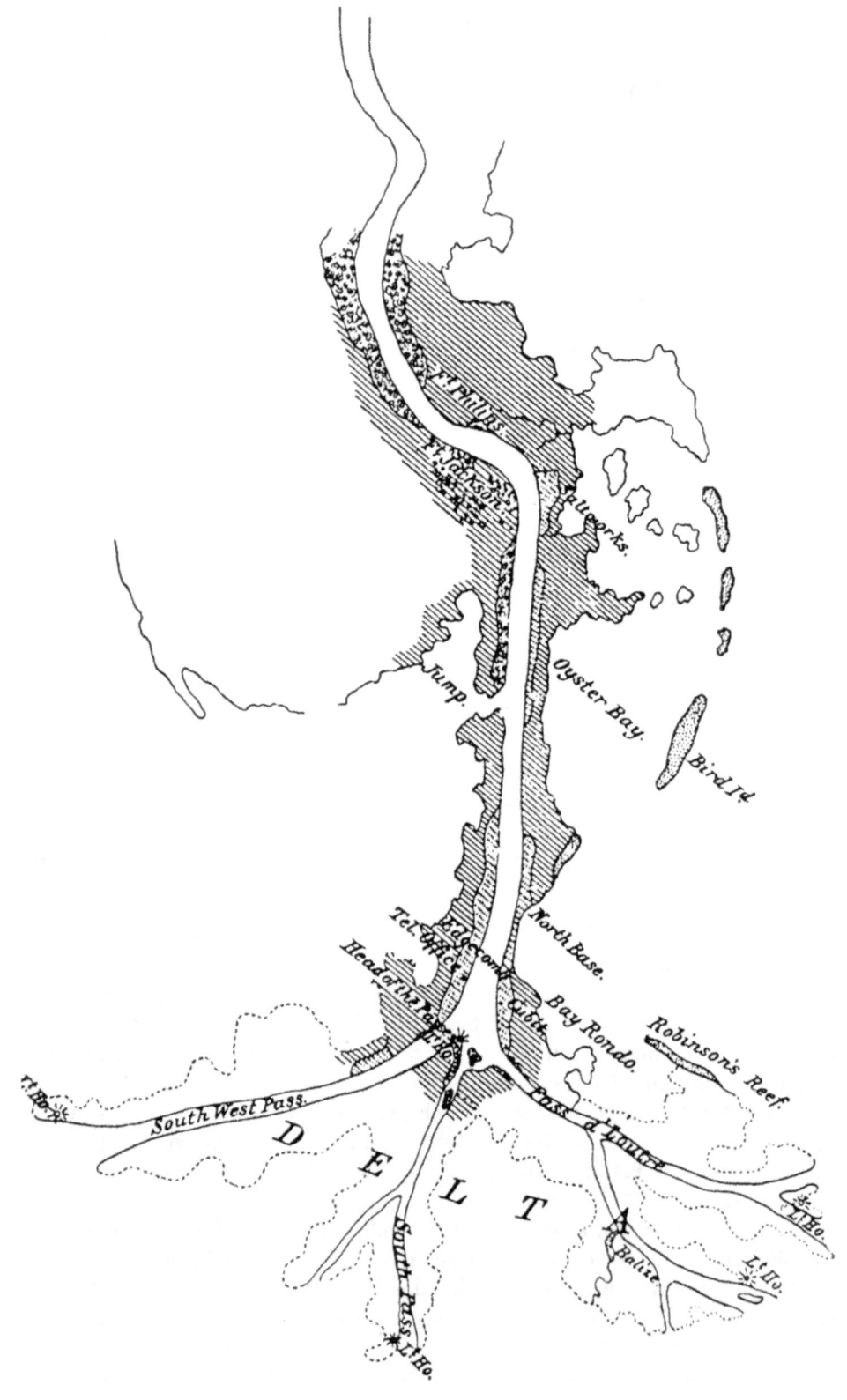

1. The CSS *Jackson*   17

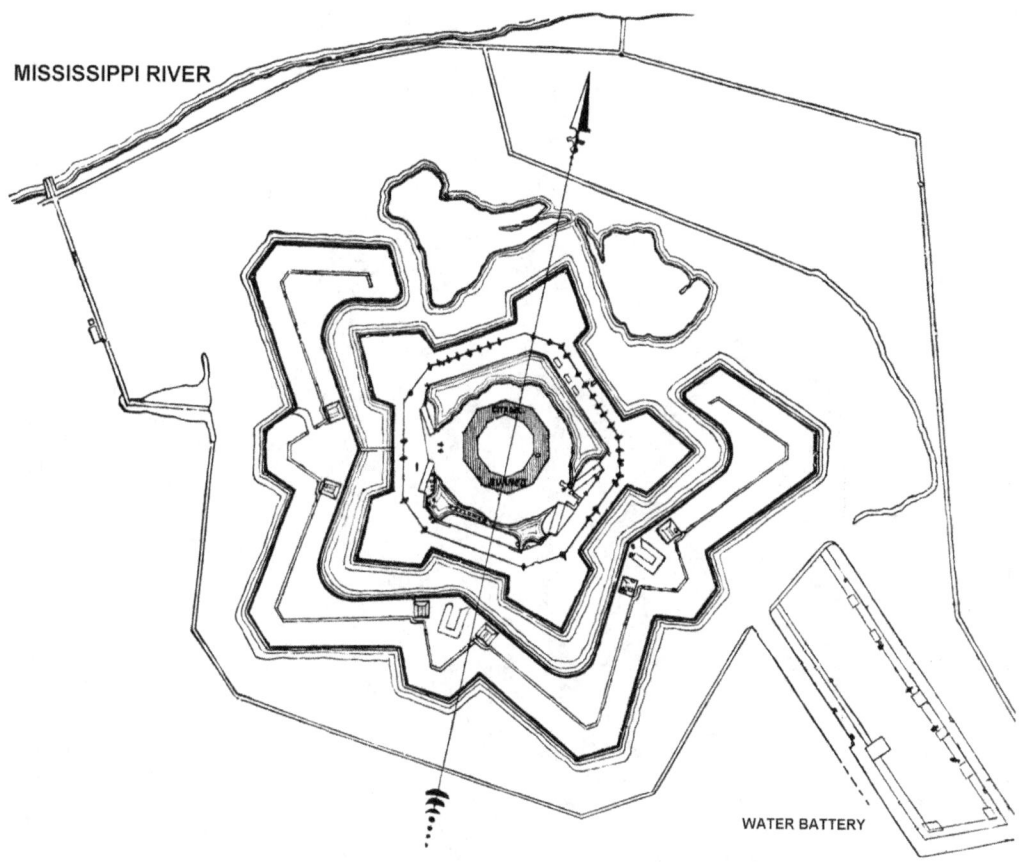

Plan layout of Fort Jackson (*Battles and Leaders of the Civil War*, Johnson and Buell, eds.).

over decks. This was a poor substitute for the raft of logs that had been there before.

The *Jackson* was below the Head of the Passes one day bringing up some families that had been ordered to move above the forts; and as we were watching the sailors run down a lot of hogs, the lookout, who was at the top of a long ladder behind the stack, reported two Yankee gunboats coming up South East Pass.

All hands came aboard when we blew one whistle, and leaving the hogs and chickens, we started up the river with orders to make all the steam we could, as Captain Gwathney felt that we should have a short trip should one of the shells reach our boilers. We were all interested and the *Jackson* did her best to get away, since this was a case for discretion not fighting.

The Doctor went to all parts of the ship looking for a safe spot. When a Yankee shell passed over the boiler deck, he took a look at the steam gauge and furnace, and concluded he would go to the bow. He stuck there until we got out of range.

Opposite: Map of the Head of the Passes (*Gulf and Inland Waters, 1883*).

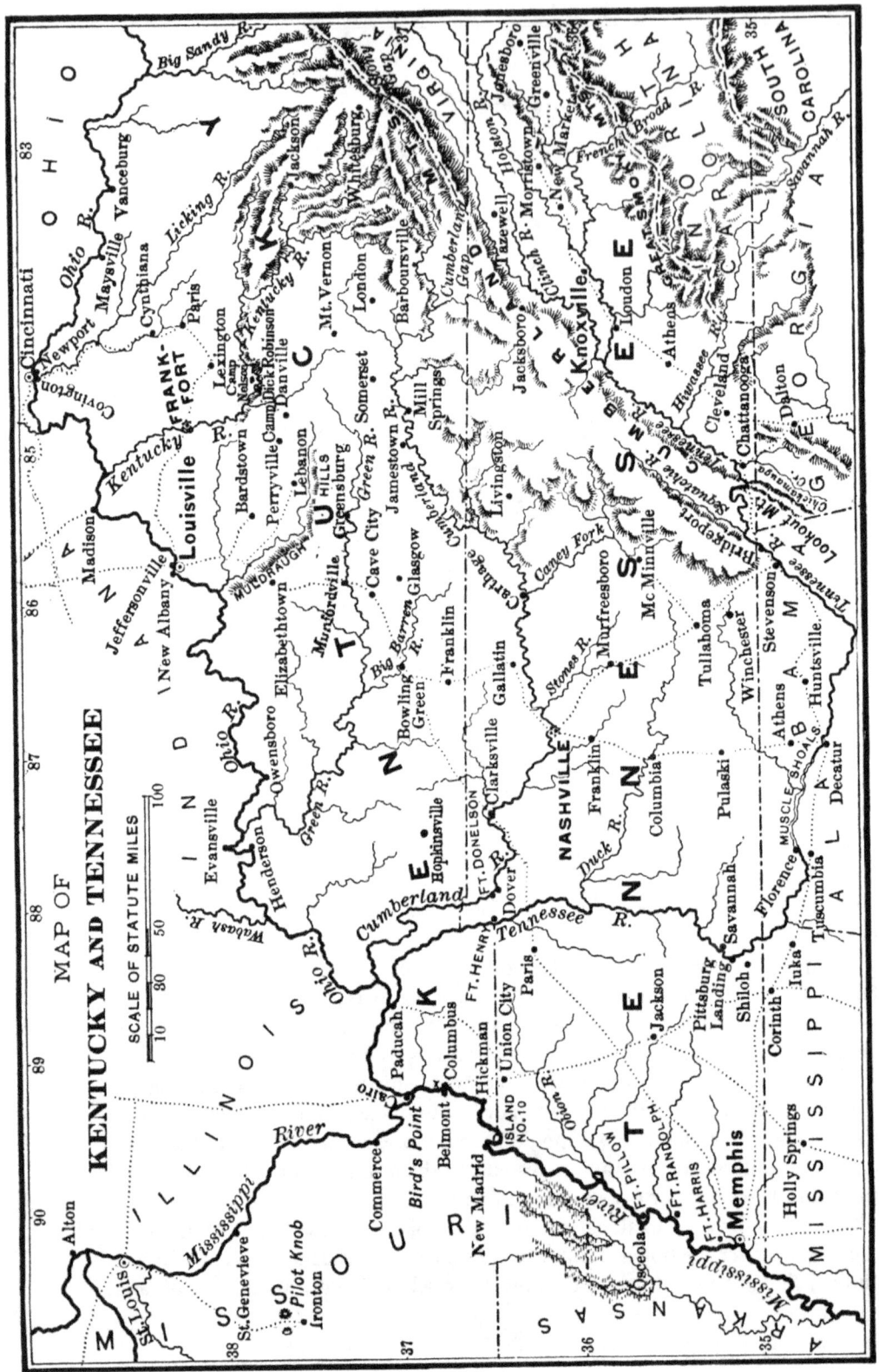

1. The CSS *Jackson* 19

The USS *Lexington*, which engaged the CSS *Jackson* at Hickman, Kentucky, on September 4, 1861 (Naval Historical Center).

The USS *Tyler*, which, along with the *Lexington*, exchanged shots with the CSS *Jackson* at Hickman, Kentucky (Naval Historical Center).

Opposite: Map of the upper region of the Mississippi River (*Battles and Leaders*).

The USS *Conestoga*. This vessel, along with the *Lexington*, engaged the CSS *Jackson* at Lucas Bend, Missouri, on September 10, 1861 (Naval Historical Center).

Dougherty, who was as cool as could be under the circumstances, said, "It would go hard with us if we were wounded as Dr. Ward would be as apt to cut a head off as a leg, in the condition he was in."

The *Jackson* certainly could run if she could not fight.

After we returned to the fort, things went along about as usual, and at the table one day it was said Col. Duncan [Johnson K. Duncan], who was in charge of these two forts, had expressed a wish that the Navy would keep away and let the forts get a chance at the Yankee fleet. Captain Gwathney said that they might have that chance some day.

Up the River

When it was decided to fortify Columbus, Ky., just below Cairo on the Mississippi River, the *Jackson*, under the command of Captain Gwathney, was sent up the river from New Orleans, to cooperate with the Army, and hold it while the guns were being mounted.

> [In September 1861, prompted by the Federal occupation of an area opposite Columbus, Kentucky, Major General Leonidas Polk had ordered Brigadier General Gideon J. Pillow to occupy the town. In retaliation, two days later, General Ulysses S. Grant seized the Ohio River town of Paducah, Kentucky. Confederate

forces now pushed into the neutral state and established a defensive line that stretched 400 miles from the Cumberland Gap in the east, through Bowling Green, and on to Columbus, which was on the Mississippi River opposite Belmont on the Missouri side.—Editor]

When we arrived at Memphis we were out of rations, and, what was more serious, out of funds. When this was understood by the people of Memphis, there was no lack of either, and considering that the C. S. N. was represented by such a powder magazine as the *Jackson*, the attention shown us was most gratifying; but as her hull and upper works were painted black, she made quite a formidable appearance with her two 8-inch guns, one forward and one aft.

We made a short stop here to take on coal end provisions, also taking in one or two entertainments, in each of which Dougherty said there were more pretty girls then in the whole distance up from New Orleans. I was quite of his opinion, but would not include New Orleans, as there were lots of them there.

Brigadier General Johnson K. Duncan, Confederate Army commander of Forts Jackson and St. Philip (*Battles and Leaders of the Civil War*, Johnson and Buell, eds.).

Proceeding up the river, and reaching Hickman, [Kentucky] September 4, 1861, we made fast to the bank, as it was reported that two gunboats were on the way down the river from Cairo.

There was a small company of artillery on the shore with a small Napoleon rifle. They took position just above the town, and when the two Yankee gunboats came in sight, we moved out from the bank into the river, and headed for them.

When within range, we opened fire with the forward gun, and they both returned our fire, at the same time turning their heads up stream, making use of their after guns.

About the time we were getting each other's range, the little Napoleon also opened, and that caused the Yankees to fear, no doubt, that there were more behind us, for the way they made tracks up stream reminded us of the time the *Jackson* was doing her best below South West Pass, when the two gunboats were after us.

While some of our shots seemed to strike near them, and one of them went over the deck, I do not think we did them any injury.

They passed up the river and out of sight. If the rest of the officers felt as I did, they were not disappointed at the change of base on the part of the Yankees. I was thinking of those boilers all the time the engagement was going on.

Captain George N. Hollins, commander of the Confederate squadron at New Orleans (Scharf, *History of the Confederate States Navy*).

The two steamers were the *Lexington* and *Conestoga*. They were painted black, and were steamers like the *Jackson*.[2]

Just before dark we continued on our way up the river, and from the speed the Yankee gunboats made when last we saw them, they must have left us well behind, as we did not show any special desire to keep up with them. When we arrived at Columbus and made fast to the bank, there were no signs of troops and guns; but a few days later General Pillow and troops arrived, and things began to look more active for us.

There was a large pile of coal on the bank, the property of a Union man, and his agent would not accept an order on the C.S.N., so Captain Gwathney gave me orders to take it, or as much as Engineer Williams wanted. The agent was hot and said things not the most polite; but when two sailors came up with guns, he was as mild as any man could be under the circumstances.

There being no signs of mounting any guns, we were in rather a bad position, as the report was that the Yankees had the *Lexington* and *Tyler* ready for service, and those were great odds for us to think of contending against in an engagement without a gun on the bluff to assist us.

As it was reported that there were two or three gunboats on the way down from Cairo, Captain Gwathney very wisely decided to run up above the bluffs, make fast to the bank, let fires go down, and work both guns as a broadside facing up stream. After we made fast and let steam go down, the crew were called to quarters, and we waited for the Yankee gunboats to come down. There were two of them, and as they came down from Cairo, it looked as if New Orleans was to be their next stopping place.

When they got near our position, they were evidently at a loss to understand it; but it cleared up when they let us have a shot from each forward gun, and we let them have two, — one from the forward and one from the after gun. As this was

The USS *Richmond*, the Federal warship rammed by the CSS *Manassas* at the Head of the Passes on October 12, 1861 (Naval Historical Center).

not what they had been expecting, they turned at once and headed up stream, at the same time firing their after gun.

Our shots came near them, but neither the Yankees nor the *Jackson* did good shooting. Not one shot from either of the gunboats struck us, and, while it was reported that one of our shells had struck the ship nearest us, I could not see any signs of it.[3]

Dr. Ward was not nervous while preparing for the wounded. We all felt more satisfied as to results, had a shell struck either of the boilers.

When the gunboats started for Cairo, we remained fast to the bank. After nightfall, getting up steam again, we proceeded down below the high bluff, end made fast to the bank, as Captain Gwathney thought they might try to take the ship by boarding if she lay above the port after dark.

Shortly after this, a battery of light artillery was brought up and placed in position, and then a large gun called "Lady Polk" was mounted on top of the high bluff commanding the river some miles above, and the *Jackson* was ordered back to New Orleans, and Fort Jackson.

The First Action

October 11, Commodore Hollins was placed in command of an expedition which was started down the river from the forts to drive out Commodore Pope [Captain John Pope, USN], who was at the Head of the Passes in command of the U.S.S. *Richmond*, and other ships, and who was going to build a fort at that point.[4]

We left the forts about midnight with the *McRae*, the *Jackson*, the *Ivy*, the *Livingston*, the *Manassas* and the *Tuscarora*, and with another tug towing a large coal barge loaded with cotton, tar, turpentine, and other stuff, as a fire ship.

When Lieutenant A. Wharley, in command of the *Manassas*, ran for the *Richmond*, he struck a schooner [*Joseph H. Toone*] that was alongside discharging coal, and so made a failure of it. The *Manassas* was disabled and stuck in the marshes.

The fire boat went down the river all in a blaze, and made a most magnificent sight to us, who were behind her, but to the Yankees it must have been the reverse, as the way they slipped their cables, and went down South West Pass was interesting to us, following close after them.

The U.S.S. *Vincennes*, commanded by Captain Handy [Commander Robert Handy], was stuck in the mud, and as we found out afterwards, had been abandoned by the crew, and a slow match placed near the powder magazine; but as it did not explode, the crew returned to the ship.

All we got out of the expedition was the capture of the schooner holding the coal, and the pleasure of giving a scare to the "Yankees." The old Captain who had charge of the lighthouse at this point did not show up for a couple of days. This man was a character. He gave a good bit of information about the Yankees, but Captain Gwathney thought it just as likely that he gave as much to the Yankees in return, and it would not do to believe his account as to what was doing while the firing was going on, and rockets going up from the *Richmond*.

> [An amusing incident happened when the *Manassas* struck the *Richmond*. It had been prearranged that the *Manassas* would fire a rocket when she struck the enemy as a signal to the rest of the Confederate fleet. In the midst of all of the confusion when she rammed the *Richmond*, a midshipman clambered out onto the shield and lit the fuse of the promised rocket. Unfortunately, he held it incorrectly, and it burned his hands, causing him to drop it. Like a Hollywood cartoon, it happened to be pointed at an open hatch and down it whizzed into the interior of the *Manassas*, hissing and sputtering like some angry demon. Thinking it was an enemy shell about to explode, Confederate sailors bowled over each other in trying to get out of the way and attempted to hide behind any protective bulkhead they could find. Sheepishly, the midshipman got it right on the second try and the signal rocket arched into the blackened sky.—Editor]

2

The CSS *McRae*

February 4, 1862, I was detached from the *Jackson* and ordered to the Flagship *McRae*, Commodore Hollins, Captain Huger in command, Lieutenant [Charles W.] Read, Executive Officer, Lieutenant [Thomas D.] Fister, Assistant Engineer [Samuel] Brock in charge of Engineer Department, with assistants [Henry] Fagan, [Charles W.] Jordan, [James H.] Tomb, and [John H.] Dent.[1]

The *McRae*, *Livingston* and *Ivy* were ordered up the river to Columbus about March, 1862.

> [The vessels that accompanied the *McRae* up the river have long been the subject of mystery. The various participants, including Read, give different accounts, but it would seem most appropriate to trust the testimony of Hollins, which was given to a navy review board after the fall of New Orleans. According to him, the *McRae* was accompanied by the *Livingston*, the *Maurepas*, the *General Polk*, and the *Ivy*. Additional reports indicate that the floating battery *New Orleans*, *Pontchartrain*, and *Calhoun* were also present. The ironclad *Manassas* had developed problems on the way up and had been sent back to New Orleans.—Editor]

When Columbus was evacuated, the Confederate troops fell back to Island No. 10, and New Madrid, and we were sent to New Madrid to protect the few troops at that point, and prevent General Pope from crossing the Mississippi at Commerce, a short distance below New Madrid. The troops, some 2,500, were under the command of General Gantt of Arkansas, and the breast-works were all made of sacks of corn and dirt. There was very little artillery.

> [Midshipman James Morris Morgan left a descriptive and somewhat amusing account of the *McRae's* trip up the Mississippi:
> "On the way up the river our first disaster happened, when on a dark and foggy night we rammed the plantation of Mr. Jefferson Davis, President of the Confederacy. For this heroic performance, it is needless to say, none of us were

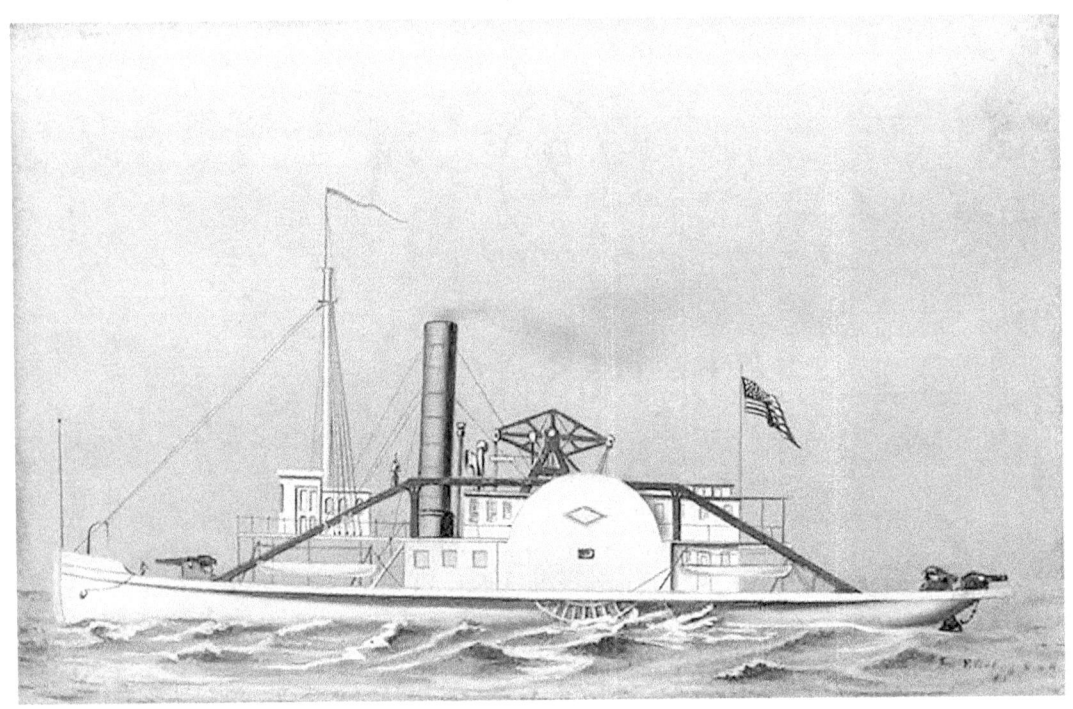

Top: The CSS *Calhoun* (depicted after her capture by U.S. forces). *Bottom:* The CSS *McRae*. (Naval Historical Center.)

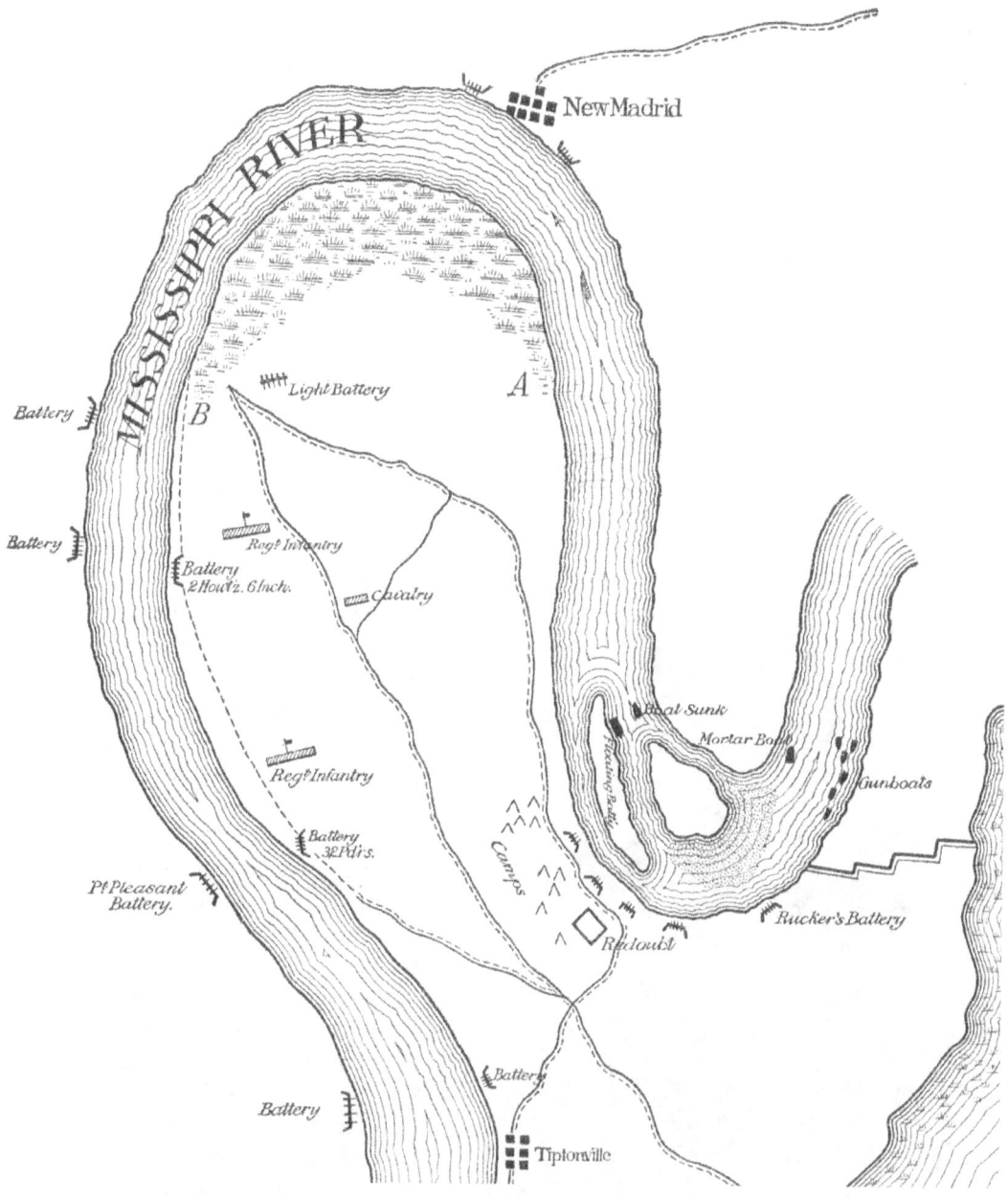

Island No. 10 and surrounding area (*Official Records Navy*).

promoted, and we lay ingloriously stuck in the mud until we were pulled off by a towboat. Disaster number two came when we were passing Helena, Arkansas—the *Tuscarora* caught fire and was destroyed.

"Day after day, with our insufficient power and great draft, we struggled against the mighty current of the Mississippi, occasionally bumping into a mud bank and lying helpless there until we were pulled off. At the cities of Vicksburg and Memphis we received ovations. The dear people were very enthusiastic, and knowing nothing about naval warfare, they felt sure we could whip the combined fleets of the universe.

"When we finally arrived at Island Number 10, we found a lively bombardment going on. It was, however, decided that we should drop down to New Madrid to assist in the defense of that city."[2]—Editor]

General Pope was a short distance back of New Madrid with a large army, and we had to protect our small detachment from being captured. Pope could have taken them at any time had our ships been away.

There was a large public road running directly out of town right abreast of the *McRae*, and a good sized fort was built, mounting a number of dummy guns made of logs and painted black. It gave quite a good face to the enemy, who, no doubt, counted each gun, as they were mounted at night, and looked for all the world like large 8" S.B. [smoothbores]

There was a flagstaff and, by day, a sentry on duty, but after dark a poor dummy only was left.

In line of this road was a large dwelling, and as it gave Pope a good chance to approach the earthwork, it was decided to burn it and a party was sent for that purpose.

There was a large piano in the house and it was brought out and put aboard one of the transports and sent down the river.

A few days later, while the *McRae* was alongside the bank, two women came down and asked to see the Captain.

Lieutenant Read, who was officer of the deck at the time, said he would attend to them and asked what was wanted. They said the piano taken from the building was their property, and they wished it restored to them. As Lieutenant Read had found quite a number of treasonable letters under the lid of the piano, this fact showing how a good deal of information had

Midshipman James Morris Morgan of the CSS *McRae* (Naval Historical Center).

been sent to the Yankees, he gave them to understand that if the piano was theirs, it was also clear that they themselves were liable to arrest for treason. This was something they did not look for, or expect, and both said it was not their property and they did not want it. It evidently did not belong to them, but they thought it was a good chance to get a piano.

An interesting incident took place aboard the *McRae* while at New Madrid, in which I had a part. The Asst. Engineer in charge, Mr. Brock, was a most disagreeable man, and most arbitrary. He had taken every opportunity to make things disagreeable for Fagan, Dent, and myself. He began to burn the midnight oil reading up Navy Regulations aboard ship—"When in face of the enemy, etc." Finding he could work a hardship, he gave orders that while on watch and under banked fires, we should not read or sit in the engine room, Dent and I seemed to be a constant nightmare to him.

Lieutenant Charles W. Read, executive officer of the CSS *McRae* (courtesy of Blanshard and Evelyn Maynard).

One afternoon Fireman Kendrick came aboard with a small pig under his arm and reported to Engineer Fagan and the Officer of the Deck, Fister, that while on shore the pig had run at him and that he had to kill it.

This being satisfactory to these officers, he proceeded to carry it forward. Shortly afterward the report was received that the Federal army was about to advance on New Madrid and we immediately beat to quarters. The report was not correct, however, and we were cooling off when Brock, looking down the fire room, espied a pig in front of the furnace, where Kendrick had placed it to be out of the way while at quarters. Brock asked the fireman to whom it belonged and he, thinking it best, said "to the Engineers and Midshipmen."

Brock became very indignant, said his orders were supreme, and to throw the pig into the furnace; so in it went, and all the pork chops that the mess had been counting on for a few days, went up in smoke and smell. Brock gave us a look that impressed us with the idea that it would please him to have us go with the pig.

A couple of days after this, coming into the engine room a few moments before his watch was off, 8:00 A.M., I caught him reading a large volume, and, seeing me, he put it inside the log desk, and waited for me to leave, but I was there to stay and watch the book. As soon as he left the engine room, I went over to the desk and, taking out the book, called Fireman Kendrick. I asked him if it was his book, or if he knew the person who had disobeyed Mr. Brock's orders about books, etc.

Not getting any information out of Kendrick, I handed the book to him and said, "You put this book the way the pig went, and don't be long about it either, as I intend to carry out Mr. Brock's orders."

Kendrick went down the ladder to the fire room so fast that he came near landing on his head, but the book went into the furnace just as the pig had gone. I could see a genuine expression of pleasure in the faces of the men when Kendrick told them what it was.

About 8:30 A.M., Mr. Brock came into the engine room with a rather pleasant expression about the weather, and passed over to the desk, remarking, "Mr. Fister has a book here." But not finding it, the smile left his face, and turning to me, he asked if I had seen it.

"Yes," I said, I had found it, and remembering his orders, had called up the men to see if any of them had put it there, but getting no satisfaction, and having his orders in my mind, I had ordered them to place it where the pig had gone, in the furnace. That was the last of the book, and I felt that it would have been for the good of the service, if Brock had followed the pig and the book.

[For ten days the Federal forces inched closer and closer to the Confederate fortifications. While Tomb sweated in the engine room, Lieutenant Read paced the deck of the *McRae* while directing the fire of the 9-inch Dahlgren and the three 32-pounders. Gradually the Confederate land defenders were forced back and took shelter in the two forts leaving the space in between to be covered by the *McRae*. Pope's heavy guns finally arrived, and the struggle became hot and heavy. The almost continuous roar of the guns was deafening. The *McRae* shuddered and vibrated with every discharge. Smoke and dust obscured the targets as Read went from gun to gun encouraging the men to load faster and shoot straighter. Midshipman Morgan remembered one particular discharge well:

"I was standing by the commodore on the poop deck watching the firing when we saw a light battery enter the other end of the main street. Our nine-inch gun was trained on them, and when it was fired the shell struck the head of the column and burst in about the middle of the company. To see horses, men, and guns cavorting in the air was a most appalling sight. Flushed with success the officer in charge of the gun reloaded and tried another shot, when the gun exploded, the muzzle falling between the ship's side and the river-bank, while one half of the great breech fell on the deck beside its carriage. The other half went away up into the air and coming down struck the rail between the commodore and myself and cut the side of the ship, fortunately glancing out instead of inside. The commodore coolly remarked, 'Youngster, you came near getting your toes mashed!'"[3]

On March 13, a massive bombardment from the heavy guns that Pope had been able to assemble convinced Hollins to withdraw his warships out of range lest they be destroyed. Major General John McCown, commander of Confederate forces, now had few options.

"On the night of March 13th it was decided to evacuate New Madrid," Read wrote. "A darker and more disagreeable night it is hard to conceive; it rained in torrents, and our poor soldiers, crowed on our gun-boats, leaving behind provisions, camp equipment and artillery."

Midshipman Morgan remembered that night:

"At midnight the gunboats were brought alongside the bank, gangplanks were put out, and we had not long to wait before the terrified troops, every man for himself, rushed aboard the smaller gunboats in the greatest disorder. They at once rushed to the side farthest from the enemy, and in doing so almost capsized the top heavy and cranky little *Ivy*.

Major General John P. McCown, Confederate Army commander at Island No. 10 (Library of Congress).

"But it was a different thing with the *McRae*, where they found a sentry at the gangway who ordered them to halt. They raged and swore and openly threatened to rush the sentry, but at that moment the gentle Read appeared on the scene and told the men that if they came on board it would have to be in an orderly manner as soldiers, and not as a mob. At this the men commenced to threaten him, but he only asked them where their officers were, and was told that they did not care a rap where they were, but that they were coming aboard. By this time Read had gone ashore and was standing amongst them. He quietly asked them to be silent for a moment, and then inquired who was their head man. A big fellow, with much profanity said he 'had as much to say as any other man.' Instantly Read's saber flashed out of its scabbard and came down on the head of the mutineer, felling him to the ground, as in a thunderous voice the usually mild Read roared, 'Fall in!'— and the mob ranged themselves in line like so many lambs and were marched quietly across the gangplank and on to the ship.

"We carried the frightened creatures across the river to the Tennessee side and put them ashore at Point Pleasant, some two or three miles below New Madrid, and near Tiptonville. That was the last we saw of them."[4]— Editor]

Island No. 10 was evacuated April 7, 1862, but the troops did not succeed in crossing a large lake back of the island, Reels Foot Lake, and most of them were captured.[5]

Those at Madrid, along with the munitions of war, were placed aboard ship and taken down to Fort Pillow, and Pope's Army took what was left.

Two men, who could not speak a word of English, were brought aboard by our picket one night. They said they had been landed one day and enlisted the next, getting more money than they ever could have earned in Germany. They were strong looking fellows. No wonder the Yankees had troops when they could get them for prices ranging from $80 to $500.

Top: Confederate fortifications at Island No. 10 (*Harper's Weekly*, May 1, 1862). *Bottom:* The surrender at Tiptonville of Confederate forces from Island No. 10, April 8, 1862 (*Frank Leslie's Illustrated*, May 3, 1862).

[The *McRae* and the rest of the flotilla now had a new danger to face. They had been at anchor only a few days at Tiptonville when early one morning the cottonwoods that lined the opposite bank of the river suddenly fell forward and numerous enemy artillery pieces opened fire. Fortunately the Confederate vessels had steam up, and immediately the signal gong rang in the *McRae's* engine room. The call to quarters was sounded, and men rushed to their guns. As the *McRae's* head swung into the stream, one, then another, 32-pounder thundered away, sending their loads of canister whistling through the cottonwoods. The *Maurepas*, the *General Polk*, and the *Pontchartrain* also opened fire, but before

The Confederate position at Fort Pillow, Tennessee. The *McRae* stopped here on her way down the river to New Orleans (***Battles and Leaders of the Civil War**, Johnson and Buell, eds.).

they could close on the enemy the Federals had limbered up and galloped off. Not before some serious damage had been done, however, for flags run up on the *General Polk* indicated that she had been struck near the waterline and was leaking badly. Hollins ordered the squadron to withdraw several miles downstream, but the enemy followed and soon the same episode was repeated over and over.[6] — Editor]

The Yankee gunboats followed us down to Fort Pillow, but as neither side seemed anxious for a fight, we came to anchor below the fort without an engagement worth mentioning.

While at "Pillow," Dent and I, together with Lieut. Read, who, by the way, was one of the best officers we had on board ship, went ashore to see about a lot of cotton, ginned and unginned, belonging to a southern woman. She said she would rather burn it than have the Yankees get it, so Lieutenant Read gave her a receipt for it, and set on fire about 200 bales. She was a remarkable old lady and full of fire.

The ground was low, and had been under water. The old lady seemed to take a fancy to Dent and me and gave us a lot of preserves. She said she did not want the Yankees to get her preserves.

When we were on our way to the boat, we saw a number of young turkeys up in the trees, and she went for her son, a slim looking young, fellow, who had a stock of chills at the time. He brought his gun and soon had four large turkeys to add to the preserves.

The Engineer's and Midshipmen's messes were the center of attraction, and the only regret was that Brock, being in the ward room, would also get his share of the booty,—but no jam.

After a short stay at Fort Pillow, we continued on our way down the river to New Orleans. We felt that perhaps Fort Pillow might check the Yankee fleet for an indefinite time, and give us a chance to protect the rest of the lower river.

When we left "Pillow," Porter's boats were throwing 11 and 15 inch shells into the fort. At first most of them passed either beyond the fort or fell into the river, but they were gradually getting the correct range of the battery.

As we passed Memphis, we saw no signs of guns being mounted on the bluff, but at Vicksburg there was apparently active work going on above the hills.

When we reported at Fort Jackson, the old raft was not in evidence, and it was a long tune before pontoons were moored in place of the rafts. There was no sign of any movement on the part of the Yankee fleet, and our duty was not pleasant.

The ironclad *Louisiana* came down the river and made fast to the bank, just above fort St. Phillips so that the guns from the fort were unobstructed from that side. She looked quite formidable, but we did not know what was inside.

[The *Louisiana* was designed for four engines, driving two paddle-wheels in a center-well and two propellers, with twin rudders. Her casemate, all four sides sloping sharply at nearly a 45-degree angle and extending her full length (less 25 feet at each end), was covered by "T" railroad iron in two courses, while its top was encompassed by sheet iron bulwarks nearly four feet high. She was still incomplete, her propellers not being connected, and she had insufficient power to maneuver as a warship in any naval action. Captain John K. Mitchell, commanding naval forces in the lower Mississippi, decided that she should only be operated as a floating battery. Accordingly he had her tied to the eastern bank of the Mississippi a half mile above Fort St. Philip. With mechanics on board working furiously night and day to prepare her batteries for action, the *Louisiana* lay just clear of the line of fire of Commander Porter's mortar boats that continued bombarding the forts. The *Louisiana*'s armament consisted of two 7-inch Brocke rifles, three 9-inch shell guns, four 8-inch shell guns, and seven 32-pounder rifles.[7]—Editor]

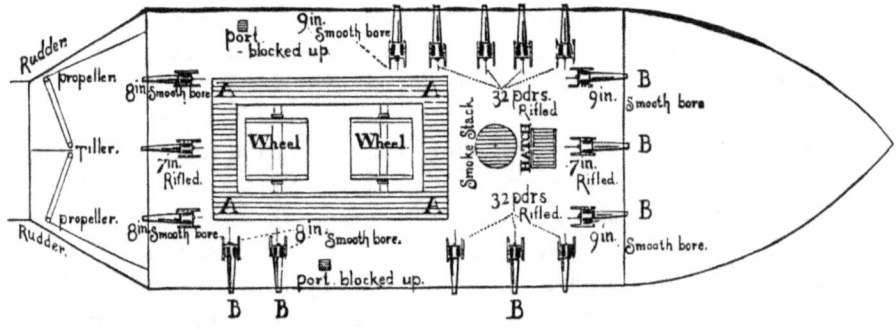

The Confederate ironclad CSS *Louisiana* (*Battles and Leaders of the Civil War*, Johnson and Buell, eds.).

Commodore John K. Mitchell was now in command of the station, Commodore Geo. Hollins having been detached, upon our arrival at New Orleans, and sent to Richmond.

> [Hollins had essentially abandoned the upper river to the enemy. Believing, rightly so, that his wooden ships were no match for the ironclads of the enemy, and convinced that the greater threat was from the Federal warships in the Gulf, he sailed south with the *McRae* and the *Ivy* without gaining authorization from the Navy Department. Mallory was furious and relieved him from command.[8]— Editor]

Commander John K. Mitchell, who succeeded Hollins at New Orleans (Scharf, *History of the Confederate States Navy*).

It was reported that Commodore Hollins wanted to send a lot of fire rafts down in Farragut's fleet, just as he had done with Commodore Pope. It might have been a success, but the chances are Farragut would have captured the best part of what was left of our fleet when the fire rafts had passed, as there never was in any Navy, a braver or more able officer than Farragut.

The guard boat on duty below the forts was reported as having deserted to the enemy. I can't say whether it belonged to the Navy or to the fort.

When the Yankee mortar fleet under Commodore Porter came up the Mississippi, above the Head of the Passes, the mortar schooners were made fast just below the bend near the forts on the west side of the river, and it was not long before the 15-inch shells began to come at regular intervals. The intervals seemed very short, and soon the pontoons holding the chains began to disappear. It reminded me of what Captain Gwathney had said about the raft, and the chance of the forts to get at the "Yankees." The old raft could have stood it all and would have been in good condition when Farragut's fleet came up. When he did come there was little left of chains or pontoons, as they did not amount to much at best. We paid for being over-confident when Farragut's fleet passed the forts and found a clear channel.

The ships of the Confederate Navy now at Forts Jackson and St. Philip were the *McRae, Jackson, Manassas,* and *Louisiana*, all others being above New Orleans and at Fort Pillow.

> [Mitchell's naval forces were woefully inadequate to the task ahead. In addition to the vessels recorded by Tomb, there were available two steam launches with a small howitzer each, along with half a dozen tugs, fire-rafts, and unarmed vessels. Two gunboats, the *Governor Moore* and the *General Quitman*, carrying two guns each and belonging to the state of Louisiana, had placed themselves under Mitchell's orders. There were also six gunboat-rams of the "River Defense Fleet," manned by steamboat men from New Orleans, but they refused to take orders

Federal mortar schooners firing on Fort Jackson. For six days, at 2,859 yards, the schooners fired 16,800 shells into the fort (*Battles and Leaders of the Civil War*, Johnson and Buell, eds.).

The Louisiana gunboat *Governor Moore* (Naval Historical Center).

from the navy and would give little account of themselves. In all, Mitchell could count on six vessels mounting approximately thirty guns.[9] — Editor]

The *Louisiana* mounted six guns, in poor condition. She was built on the lines of a shoe box, and was a decided failure in every respect. Her engines were in the combination class. She had two wheels working in the center and a propeller on each quarter. When these were all working and she had a hawser out to the bank, she might be depended upon to hold her own, but nothing more. She was a nondescript. Her Commanding Officer was Captain Charles F. McIntosh.[10]

To these ships could be added the State Navy, but it did not amount to much, and with the exception of the *Governor Moore*, disappeared about the time Farragut made his appearance. (The *Governor Moore* was commanded by Lieutenant B. Kennon, a fine officer, who had resigned from the U.S. Navy, and, also, from the C.S. Navy.)[11]

The morning of the 24th of April, 1862, I

Lieutenant Beverley Kennon of the Louisiana State Navy (*Battles and Leaders of the Civil War*, Johnson and Buell, eds.).

was on duty in the engine room of the *McRae* when the quartermaster reported some ships moving up from below the bend. It was about 3:30 a.m. We could not see the hulls, but could see the spars with brush apparently lashed to them. Without orders I had the fires spread and sent a messenger to call Engineer Fagan.

There were 15 pounds of steam on at that time, but it was dead steam, and by the time the first ship came around the point, we had twenty pounds of steam, and all hands at quarters, with Mr. Fagan in charge of the engine room. The engines were worked ahead and when the first ship came up we were going slow.

Captain Huger was in command, and there was no time for him to address the crew.

At the first shot was from the 9-inch Dalghren, it burst just forward of the trunions, leaving only the 32 and 12 pound howitzers.

We were well into the engagement by this time. The report of the guns was terrific. You could not hear the bell or gong at times. We worked out into midstream, and almost between two large ships of the enemy.

The order was given to repel boarders, just as the engine became hot, due to the injector choking, and we shut off steam, causing the *McRae* to drop back down stream. They passed on up the river, which no doubt saved us for the time being at least, as we never could have held the ship against them.

The *McRae* was badly riddled, some of the shells going in on one side and out on the other, leaving holes above the water line large enough to crawl through. The stack was torn away as well as all the rigging; one 11-inch shell passed right through the engine room, while another burst overhead, taking off about half of First Class Fireman Kendrick's head. He was standing a few feet from me. Another portion of a shell nearly amputated Captain Huger's leg. He was directing the fight and the ship's course from a position just above the engine room. He died a few days later in New Orleans.

When the Captain was taken below, Lieutenant Read took command, following the enemy right up to the point, then one of our rudder chains was shot away, and we ran into the bank.

> [In Read's official report he described the *McRae's* horrific battle with Farragut's ships: "On the *McRae*," he wrote, "we had little trouble to find something to fire at, for as we were out in the river the enemy was on every side of us, and gallantly did our brave tars stand to their guns, loading and firing their guns as rapidly as possible. Our commander, Lieutenant Huger, was what we all expected—cool and fearless, and handled the *McRae* splendidly. One of the enemy's shells, fired from one of the howitzers aloft, went through our decks and exploded in the sail-room, setting the ship on fire; and as there was only a pine bulkhead of 2-inch boards between the sail-room and magazine, we were in great danger of being blown up."
>
> As Tomb and Read have both described, the *McRae* was now in a desperate strait. The fire was burning fiercely and the engine and deck pumps were started. Crewmen struggled to drag the fire hoses through the smoke and flames to where they could fight the fire. If the flames burned through the pine bulkhead, the *McRae* would explode in an instant. Huger ordered the burning vessel into the

The Battle of New Orleans. Note the *Louisiana*, bottom left, and the *McRae*, bracketed by two Federal warships, center right (*Battles and Leaders of the Civil War*, Johnson and Buell, eds.).

riverbank so that the men might jump ashore while Read hastened to the scene of the fire. Using the fire hoses, buckets of water, and scraps of sailcloth, Read and several of the crew were finally able to smother the flames.

"Just then," Read continued, "one of the large sloops-of-war ranged alongside and gave us a broadside of grape and canister, which mortally wounded our commander, wounded the pilot, carried away our wheel ropes and cut the signal halyards and took our flag overboard. New tiller ropes were rove and soon we were at close quarters with a large steamer."

Huger was savagely wounded: shell fragments tore through his groin area and another inflicted an ugly wound on the side of his head. He was carried below deck but died several days later.

"Two large ships and three gunboats were now engaging us at a distance of about 300 yards," Read continued. "We backed off the bank with the intention of dropping down nearer the forts, when the *Manassas* came up to our relief. She steered for the enemy's vessels, and as soon as they discovered her they started up the river.... I now directed the course of the vessel across and up the river, firing the starboard guns as rapidly as possible, and I think, with much accuracy. We soon reached a position which furnished a view around the first bend above the forts, where I discovered eleven of the enemy, and not deeming it prudent to engage a force so vastly superior to my own, I determined to retire under the guns of the forts."[12] — Editor]

Top: The destruction of the CSS *Louisiana* (Naval Historical Center). *Bottom:* The Louisiana gunboat *Governor Moore* fires through her own bow into the USS *Varuna* (*Battles and Leaders of the Civil War*, Johnson and Buell, eds.).

At this time all the ships had passed beyond the point and were nearly up to the quarantine station. Lieutenant Read certainly was a good successor to Captain Huger who was one of the best officers in the service.

While we were repairing the chain, Dent went over to one of the state ships that was stuck in the bank, with all steam up, but no one aboard. They had all taken to the woods over her bow, and Fagan remarked that if they had rammed a Yankee ship half as well as they did the bank, they would have sunk it. There was a great lot of stores aboard for eating and drinking. Dent brought a lot of it back for our mess. They evidently did not have fighting whiskey aboard, as she was not injured in the least, either above or below decks.

The repairs being made, we returned to the flagship at the forts, and reported our condition, and also as being ready for action. Our casualties were 19 killed and wounded.

As we still held the forts, Commodore Mitchell decided to move the *Louisiana* below the forts, by towing her, and drive Porter's fleet away. He called for volunteers to man the *Landers*, a large steamer abandoned by the state. Lieutenants Whittle, Harris, Fagan, Dent, and I volunteered, but when this was decided upon and before it could be executed, a white flag was raised on the flag staff of the fort, and we heard that the forts had surrendered.

Commodore Mitchell and the other officers decided to blow up the *Louisiana* and not have her pass into the hands of the enemy, so she was set on fire.

The *McRae* had been sent up to New Orleans with sick and wounded, [by flag of truce] and as we heard afterwards, was so badly injured that she sank shortly after the wounded were taken off.

When the *Harriet Lane* came up to accept the surrender of the forts, Lieutenant Whittle was sent down in a cutter, to inform her commander that the *Louisiana* was on fire, and the magazine might explode at any time, so she returned below the point.

When the fire reached the guns, one after the other would go off, and when the fire reached the magazine, there was a terrific explosion, and the casemate went up in every direction. The general expression of our officers, was that as the *Louisiana* could not be propelled through the water, the only way was to send her upwards. It would have been a reflection upon our Navy, to have such a combination called a C.S. Ironclad ship.

When we took into consideration all that we had done in this engagement, the action of Lieutenant B. Kennon, in command of the *Governor Moore*, a state ship, was the most gallant as he followed up the fleet above the point and rammed the *Varuma*, and finding he could not depress the forward gun enough to reach the hull of the *Varuma*, he fired a shell right through the bow of the *Moore* and into the hull of the *Varuma*. She sank a short time afterwards, and so did the *Governor Moore*, Lieutenant Kennon and the remainder of the crew being captured.

Lieutenant Warley did good work with the *Manassas* and had she had the power, would have sunk some of the fleet. No doubt he did save the *McRae*, when he saw how badly pressed she was, by making for one of the ships alongside of us. The last we saw of her, was when she passed down the river in mid-stream in a sinking condition, and she soon went to the bottom.

> [Warley wrote in his report: "Steaming slowly up the river — very slow was our best — we discovered the Confederate States steamer *McRae*, head up-stream, receiving the fire of three men-of-war. As the *Manassas* forged by, the three men-of-war steamed up the river, and were followed, to allow the *McRae* to turn and get down to the forts, as she was very badly used up."[13] — Editor]

3

Prison Life at Fort Warren

When the *Louisiana* blew up, we were all on the *Burton*, a small river steamer. Commodore Porter was not feeling in the best of spirits about the *Louisiana* going up and no prize money, and for that reason, no doubt, felt that we would be better off as prisoners than paroled.

> [Captain Mitchell, believing that he was not bound by the surrender of the army command at the forts, had set fire to the *Louisiana* on the east bank of the Mississippi near Fort St. Philip to keep her from falling into Union hands. He and his men, realizing that capture was inevitable, retired to the opposite shore with the unarmed tenders *W. Burton* and *Landis*. After three Federal gunboats fired at them, *W. Burton* and *Landis* surrendered to Commander Porter.[1] — Editor]

When we heard that the *McRae* had sunk, and had not fallen into the hands of the Yankees, Fagan, Dent, and I expressed the hope that Engineer Brock had stuck to her, and also gone to the bottom, where no doubt he would start some new invention. All of our wardrobe went to the bottom with her, as we had left everything on board at the time of our surrender.

> [After delivering the sick and wounded under a flag of truce, Read tried strenuously to save the *McRae*: "I anchored the *McRae* off Julia Street," he wrote, "as near inshore as possible and landed the sick and wounded without delay. At 8:30 P.M. the ship commenced to drag; the cable was veered its entire length, 50 fathoms. I had no other anchor to let go, and it was found impossible to bring her up. I accordingly started the engines and sheered over to the point near the second district ferry landing, where the water was shoaler. In going across the river the ship rested on something under the water, and swung entirely around several times, when she drifted off and brought up a short distance below. I soon ascertained that the ship was leaking badly. The donkey and bilge pumps were immediately started and kept going. At 11:20 the water had gained such a height as to put the fires out in the furnaces, thus stopping the donkey pump. I sent a

boat onshore to ask the assistance of the police or citizens. A lieutenant of the police with ten men came on board and assisted us in working the pumps. At 6 A.M. the water was 6 feet in the hold and gaining on us, the vessel was settling rapidly, and the water on the outside was only 2 inches below the shot holes in the ship's sides. The leak was not confined to any particular place, but the water appeared to come through all her seams. My men were exhausted, and I felt confident that further exertions were useless. I directed her injection pipes to be cut, so that she might sink as soon as possible, and got all hands ashore without delay. At 7:00 A.M., the ship went down."[2]—Editor]

I had nothing of my uniform on but trousers and waistcoat, as the coat was uncomfortable, so I was not in the best condition as far as appearances went.

The position of Forts Jackson and St. Phillip was so strong that Farragut must have thought over it for a long time before deciding to run the forts and supposed obstructions. Had the raft that was there at first been attended to, as Captain Gwathney had suggested, he could not have passed.

There was a splendid iron clad ship with three propellers near completion at New Orleans, mounting over 8 heavy guns, and with a clean gun deck, except where the stack passed through. The casemate was 22 inches thick, had five inches of iron over them, and she was expected to make 8 or 9 lots. This ship was evidently in his mind, for had she been ready for service Farragut's fleet would have been out-classed in every way, and the Mississippi cleared of them.

[The CSS *Mississippi* was built by N. and A. F. Tift in a shipyard erected for that purpose in Jefferson City, Louisiana, just beyond the city limits of New Orleans. Construction was started on October 14, 1861, and she was launched on April 19, 1862. A fast, triple-screw steamer, she was far from complete at that time, having neither her 20 guns nor ammunition on board. She would have indeed been an overpowering vessel. As Commander Arthur Sinclair described her: "A formidable ship—the finest of the sort I ever saw in my life, she would, in my opinion, not only have cleared the river of the enemy's vessels but have raised the blockade of every port in the South."

It was only at the last minute that Sinclair, her commanding officer, attempted to take her up the river when the Federal fleet under Farragut appeared from below Forts Jackson and St. Philip on April 25. His objective thwarted, Sinclair fired her to prevent capture.—Editor]

We felt that it was a great pity we did not have the *Mississippi* instead of that nondescript *Louisiana*, for in that case Farragut would never have reached New Orleans.

From New Orleans, we were sent to Fort Warren, Boston Harbor, via Key West, as they would not parole any of the naval officers, after the destruction of what was left of the fleet.

We stopped at Pensacola, and found things in bad shape, as the Yankees were in full possession. We also stopped at Key West and while there, Mr. Fagan's mother and sister came aboard the *Rhode Island* to see him, and we were about to sail when they parted. They said the war would soon be over and that he would be home again, but it was not to be, as Fagan, along with some twenty others, was killed in the explosion of the boilers on board the C.S.S. *Chattahoochee*, on the Chattahoochee River, May 27, 1863.

> [The CSS *Chattahoochee* was a gunboat built in 1862–1863 at Saffold, Georgia, by D. S. Johnson under the supervision of Lieutenant Catesby ap R. Jones, CSN.* The *Chattahoochee* was plagued by machinery failures, one of which, a boiler explosion which killed 18, as she prepared to sail from her anchorage at Blountstown, Florida, in an attempt retaking the Confederate schooner *Fashion*, captured by the Union. On June 10, 1864, she was moved to Columbus, Georgia, for repairs and installation of engines and a new boiler.—Editor]

Leaving Key West, we arrived at Fort Warren and took up our term of imprisonment, being in messes of 25 or 30 to each casemate.

> [Construction of Fort Warren had begun in 1833, and the bastion was initially intended as part of the maritime fortification and defense system of the east coast that emerged from the War of 1812. The fort, however, was never combat ready during the Civil War and was not officially completed until 1866. Thus, initially it was used as a training camp and garrisoned the 14th Massachusetts Infantry.
>
> At the outbreak of the war, Fort Warren imprisoned several smugglers, and, in a controversial move by the Lincoln administration, a few political prisoners—some of whom were Maryland legislators—arrested for contemplating secession from the Union.
>
> After the Federal capture of North Carolina's Cape Hatteras in 1861, prisoners began arriving at Fort Warren. One hundred Confederate prisoners were expected as the first arrivals, including transfers from Governor's Island in New York. Hundreds more arrived, for whom there were no provisions and inadequate facilities.
>
> In spite of this, however, conditions at Fort Warren were far better than any other northern prison. Only 12 of the 2,307 prisoners died at the prison from illnesses contracted before or during confinement.—Editor]

The accommodations were substantial consisting of tiers of bunks, one above the other, having a solid spring of planks and some straw, with one blanket marked U.S.A. Col. [Justin] Dimick, as well as his staff, were as considerate of the prisoners as they could be under the orders of the government. We were put on parole inside the fort, but with permission at certain times to pass out on the open terrace. After our imprisonment and the humane treatment received from Col. Dimick, we decided that any hardship suffered at other prisons was due more to the disposition of the officers in charge of the prison than of meanness on the part of the government, for our rations were good enough.

---

*The designation "ap" was a Welsh convention indicating "the son of." Thus "Catesby ap R. Jones" indicates that Catesby was the son of Roger Jones.

Fort Warren, Boston Harbor, as it appears today.

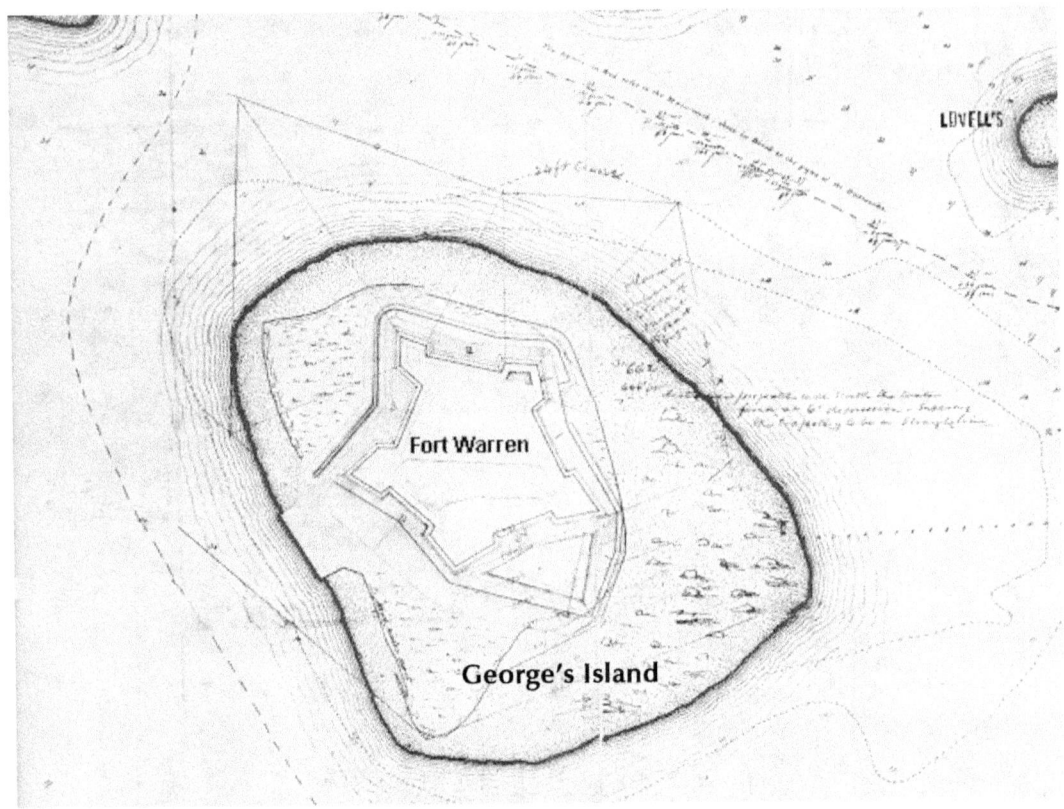

Chart of George's Island and Fort Warren, Boston Harbor (National Archive).

[Colonel Justin E. Dimick was transferred from Fortress Monroe to command at Warren. A professional soldier, Dimick was given orders as to the conduct and to the deportment of the prison and prisoners in October 1861.

Contingents of prisoners were sent to Warren after captures at Hatteras Island, North Carolina, and prisoners held at Fort Columbus in New York Harbor were transferred in. Political prisoners were brought from Fort Lafayette, many held without formal charges. Political prisoners were held on the south side of the fort, to the left of the salleyport; military prisoners to the north, or right side.

Prison fare was contingent on the prisoner's ability to pay. Those with resources were very well fed from the restaurants of Boston. The city also provided bedding, hospital supplies, food, etc., to those in need. Lawrence Sangston, a political prisoner from Maryland, stated, "Money will enable you to live anywhere, especially where there is a Yankee near and he wants it, as he usually does." Gifts and packages from outside were permitted with discretion.

Enlisted men did not fare particularly well and were crowded in the small rooms of the fort. Large cooking pots were located outside the barracks where they cooked what food they had. These cooking areas had no protection and were used year-round regardless of weather. — Editor]

I felt the cool fog at night as I had not succeeded in adding to my slim wardrobe after that little trouble at New Orleans. This did not, however, stand in the way of my promotion, for I was made a water commissioner, and along with another officer, took away all slops from our mess, and brought back fresh water, and after the required service was promoted to assist H. K.

There was something, however, that Grant and I never understood, and that was we took away 25% more slop water than we delivered clear water, and after my promotion, Grant was working it out, but with little satisfaction.

After a short time as assistant to Dunkel, I was voted a failure and promoted to second cook. This seemed fine as my duty consisted in peeling potatoes and seeing that they went into the soup pot in time to cook. I was a little absent minded one day and did not put the potatoes into the pot until it was nearly time to serve the soup. The result was a lot of hard potatoes; and harder words, that ended in my being forced out and left without office.

Then our commissary had became so slow that he was the last man to drew rations each morning and that resulted in our getting what was left. I proposed that I be made assistant commissary, stating that I would be about the first there to draw rations, and I was.

A group of Confederate prisoners at Fort Warren (*Miller's Photographic History*).

The commissary sergeant was from Ireland, and we soon became good friends. I told him that my ancestors came from the north of Ireland, and, on chance, told him the truth. The Sergeant was a fine fellow and was a good assistant to his superior officer.

Major McPherson, up to the time he left the fort, did all he could to make our position comfortable, especially in the way of rations. There were none among the officers, from Col. Dimick down, but showed consideration, and when the time came for them to go to the front, when McClellan fell back to the James, there was not an officer or man among the prisoners in the fort that did not feel it was a loss to each and all of us, yet nothing was ever done that was not correct.

There were quite a number of political prisoners there, mostly from Baltimore, and they were all very generous in having the ladies of Baltimore send clothing and funds to the Confederate prisoners.

> [In order to prevent the Maryland legislature from voting for secession, Lincoln had many of the legislators arrested and thrown into prison. Those at Fort Warren included representatives Severn T. Wallis, Henry M. Warfield, William G. Harris, and T. Parkin Scott. Also imprisoned were Charles Howard, the mayor of Baltimore, and Frank K. Howard and George P. Kane, two officials of the Baltimore City Police Department. Several newspaper editors were also held at Fort Warren. Other legislators were incarcerated at Fort McHenry in Baltimore Harbor.[3] — Editor]

There was one fine fellow, Dr. Magill, who gave us pills; "scrapers" they were called, and they were about the size of a small cannon ball, and stuck all the way "down and out." That was what Lieutenant Jones said when I gave him one while sitting up with him one night. I think he put them in the water jug, at least I never found them. Jones got well just to avoid the pills.

Mr. Fred Harris and some others, every one a credit to the state, had quite a lot of clothing sent us, but as I was looking for funds from friends [in the] North, I did not care to accept any. For that reason I went without comfortable clothing longer than I should, as I had quite a time with chills. At last my funds came, and

Left: Marshal George P. Kane of the Baltimore Police Department. Kane was imprisoned at Fort Warren during the same period as Tomb (National Archives).

through the quartermaster, I had a suit made at Oak Hall, Boston, of gray with Maryland buttons. That was as near as they would go for buttons, and I was as proud as a turkey-cock at the change in my appearance. Clothing does not make the man, but it goes a long way towards it, as I realized at the time that I put mine on.

> [In 1913, Tomb penned an article for the *Confederate Veteran* magazine entitled "Prison Life at Fort Warren, Boston Harbor." While much of it was taken from his earlier memoirs, there are sufficient differences to warrant reproducing part of the article here:
>
> "We were sent to Fort Warren, Boston Harbor, on the *Rhode Island*, and while laying at anchor the opportunity was given those who wished to desert the Confederacy for the United States to do so, and I regret to say that a few did so. When we landed at Fort Warren, we were assigned quarters in casemates, our bunks being of pine boards three in a row, one above the other, having a supply of straw and one blanket. Our rations were good and sufficient. I was fortunate enough to secure a position on the water commission, and along with another Reb each day we would march back and forth with a large barrel supported on side bars, a Yank with a gun acting as an escort, who frequently ordered us to 'hump ourselves.' We would rest the barrel on the ground and make a rough estimate as to the water consumed by each fellow in the casemate. I was promoted from the water to the swill department, and again my partner and I failed to get a clear idea of what was doing, as we found that we had to carry more swill away than we had brought water. I lost this position also, and was made housekeeper. I was again promoted to second cook, and was doing well; but becoming interested in hearing about the Yanks being cleaned out by Lee, I failed to put the potatoes in the soup in time, and the result was that I was fired again. After thinking over this, 1 decided that I was best adapted to the duty of assistant commissary; and as it called for little work and any amount of rest, I held it with credit to myself and profit to the mess.
>
> "Colonel Dimick, who was in command of Fort Warren, was a regular army officer, as were also all of his staff, and they were as considerate in their treatment of the prisoners as we could wish for. The privates were also regulars; and as I had reason to find out before the war was over, there was less sectional feeling with them than with the volunteers. After a time Colonel Dimick put us on parole and let us go out on the ground outside of the fort, and we certainly appreciated it.
>
> "Major McPherson, who was quartermaster, was a fine officer and most accommodating. There was an order not to pay a Reb more than $5 at one time from any funds in his hands; but when I had a suit made at Oak Hall, in Boston, for $35, he gave me the money. I was very much in need of clothes, and the good people of Baltimore sent a lot to the fort. I had been waiting to buy them myself."[4] — Editor]

When the news came that General Lee had defeated General McClellan, and he had fallen back to the James River, we all felt as if it were Christmas and wanted to celebrate. It was hard to get any news, but as all the men and officers of the gar-

The interior of Fort Warren as it appeared during the time of Tomb's incarceration (*Harper's Weekly*).

rison looked very blue, we felt very good. There was no way to get correct information, since no papers came into the fort.

Lieutenant Harris, who had the bunk just above me, succeeded in getting one gallon of gin at a good price, through the Sutler office, and when all lights went out at 9 o'clock, the gin went out also. I am sorry to say that the casemate was not a Quaker meeting house; excepting, as I found out before morning, the spirits did move things, yet I did not take a drop of it myself.

The time for our exchange came just about the time I received a very kind invitation to attend a strawberry festival in Pennsylvania, but I was at a loss to understand how I was to get there at the time.

While a prisoner here, a good friend of Senator Cameron, of Pennsylvania, wrote me that he regretted the position I was in, and if I wished, he would see about my leaving the C.S.N., and perhaps could have me reinstated in the U.S.N., as Third Assistant Engineer. I appreciated his kindness, but wrote him that I was satisfied with the position I had taken, and had no desire to leave the service of the C.S.N. Then he wished to have me paroled; but, while appreciating his kindness, I thought best to decline the offer.

Leaving Fort Warren on a steam transport, we reached Hampton Roads, [Virginia] and found a large, body of Confederates there, who were to go up the James River above Harrison's Landing, the present base of the Union Army, under McClellan.

We were put on board the *Knickerbocker* along with a lot of other Confederates and found that we were the best conditioned ones of the whole lot. We were all clear of any sickness, and in good condition, while some poor fellows from Fort

Delaware and other prisons looked terribly and could not hope to reach home alive.

There was so much anxiety on the part of the Yankees to get the munitions of war and provisions to McClellan's Army, that they overlooked the rations for us Confederates. While each transport under a flag of truce was loaded with Confederates and provisions, no rations were served out to us until Lieutenant Parry, who was in charge of the prisoners, demanded that the quartermaster break open the boxes and serve out provisions. I paid the cook 50¢ for a cup of coffee water and some hardtack for three of us. The other fellows had more appetite than money.

Lieutenant Parry could see no distinction between a hungry Confederate and a Yankee, and he was certainly a good officer.

I got another cup of coffee and some soft bread for a poor fellow from Tennessee, who, I understood, never reached Richmond alive, much less his home in the upper part of that state.

The old cook was a generous chap. When I requested a little more coffee and, some milk, on an imaginary lump of sugar, he filled it up with an additional lump of sugar. It cost him nothing, but how those fellows enjoyed it.

There was quite a fleet of us proceeding up the James River, and as we moved, the position of the army would come into view. There was much confusion above and below the [Union] army, but there was no sign of retreating further. No doubt the army felt most grateful that there was such a thing as a gunboat or an ironclad, for it looked to us as if it was all that saved them.

It was a great disappointment that Lee had not captured the whole army, but McClellan showed that he was a good General, when he could save his Army after such a defeat as he had had at the hands of General Lee. How that name brought a cheer from these poor fellows who might never see the ranks again.

Reaching Aikin Landing, [August 5, 1862] we made fast to the bank and the work of disembarking the Confederates began. Then came the sick and wounded, who could not in many instances walk the gang plank to the shore they were so anxious to reach. As one was brought on shore, he said he would rather die there than exist longer in prison. The more I saw of the condition of some of these men, the more I appreciated the treatment at Fort Warren.

I understood that Henry Borchert, brother of my friend Lieut. George Borchert, C.S.N., died here also, but did not know what ship he was brought up on. Had I but known, the chances are I would have been able to do something for him. He had been a prisoner at Fort Delaware.

There was no transportation for us to Richmond, and the sick and wounded had to wait for wagons. Fagan, Dent, myself, and others started for Richmond afoot, passing quite a large Yankee troop on the way to the landing, having been exchanged for our party that had just landed at Akin. They all seemed in better condition than our men, except those from Fort Warren, and a great many were eating soft bread holding the loaf under their arms, and it seemed to be relished. There were frequent exchanges of good-natured jokes. They no doubt felt as we did, glad to be on their way home.

Arriving in Richmond about midnight, we were more fortunate than those who got in the next morning, for by doubling up we got a room at the Exchange Hotel, and, after a bath, got to bed about 1:00 a. m. The clean sheets were such a luxury that Dent could not sleep.

The next morning the rest of the party got in, but having lain down to camp a few hours, did not make another start before sunrise; and the road was so deep in dust all the way from the landing, that they all looked alike as they came staggering into Richmond.

After reporting at the Department, we got thirty days leave to visit our homes, also back pay. When we got to the train there was a guard at each entrance to the coaches, and about five applicants for each seat. Not wishing to be left out, Fagan was put through one of the windows, and we soon got inside, and each secured a seat, as privates, captains, or colonels all had to take equal chances, there being no distinction along that line. There was not one women in the crowd.

When we reached Florence, we found there was a hotel or eating house, and as it was dinner time, supper time, and breakfast time, with most of us, we made for the hotel entrance, only to find a line that could never get into the building, much less the dining room.

Dent, Fagan and I passed around to the rear, and while doing so saw Landushine from Camp Chase, lying on the ground with his head against the tree. Landushine was in very bad condition and could not walk without assistance. I made him comfortable and promised to bring him something to eat if we got inside. A colored woman was doing some washing nearby and we made it interesting for her to lend us the tub and bench. With this assistance, Dent was able to enter the dining room, and we soon followed, finding the table set for a meal, and about half full of hungry vets, who were hard at work on the spread, consisting of bacon, corn bread, sweet potatoes, rice, and "sweet-potato-coffee," or other mixture. When Captain Cook opened the inside door to let those in who had paid, he was upset at the sight of the table as there was not a vacant seat to be seen. When we got through and I had put away a good lunch for Landushine, we passed out, handing a $5.00 Confederate bill to Captain Cook as we did so.

The way Landushine put away that fine lunch of corn bread and sweet potatoes was a sight, and he said he had about starved since leaving Richmond. As there was no regulation for moving the trains, we lay on a side track about half the time.

We passed through Charleston to Savannah, and from there I went to Florida, but after a disappointing trip, not being able to see my relatives, returned to Savannah. George Borchert had just gotten back home, after resigning from, the U.S.N.

> [Unknown to Tomb, however, his family had been forcibly "resettled" from New Berlin on July 8, 1862, to Fernandina, Florida, which was under tight Federal control. This probably accounts for his failure to see his family.[5] — Editor]

The CSS *Chicora*

After a short tine, I received orders to report to Captain John R. Tucker, in command of the *Chicora* at Charleston, and was glad to receive my orders, for I was anxious to be in active service once more.

> [Tomb fails to mention the fact that, according to Confederate Navy records, he was promoted to second class engineer on September 5, 1862. This was probably about the time that he reported to the *Chicora*. Not only was this a promotion in rank, but it increased his annual salary from $750.00 to $1,000.00.[1] — Editor]

Savannah was not looking very lively, the wharves were deserted of all shipping, and the grass was growing in many of the streets that had little traffic on them. When I reported to Captain Tucker at Charleston, it was for service as Third Assistant Engineer on board the *Chicora*, an ironclad being built by James Eason for the State of South Carolina, and not yet ready for commission, so we all took up quarters at different hotels, and reported for duty each morning.

> [Born in Alexandria, Virginia, in 1812, John Randolph Tucker was one of the ablest officers to ever wear the gray of the Confederate Navy. On June 1, 1826, at the age of 14, he was appointed acting midshipman in the U.S. Navy. After a long and distinguished career, he submitted his resignation on April 18, 1861, after his home state of Virginia had seceded. As with many others who submitted their resignations after the start of the war, his resignation was refused and he was unlawfully dismissed from the navy. He was commissioned a commander in the Confederate Navy on June 6, 1861, and served distinctively as commander of the CSS *Patrick Henry* during the two days' battle in Hampton Roads, Virginia. Under Tucker's direction the Charleston Squadron became a model of Confederate naval ingenuity, fielding such advanced weapons as mines, torpedo boats, ironclads, and the submarine *H. L. Hunley*. When Charleston was evacuated, Tucker commanded the naval batteries on the James River below Rich-

A rare photograph of the Confederate ironclad CSS *Chicora* (Naval Historical Center).

mond. When Lee's lines were broken below Petersburg in April 1865, Tucker's Naval Battalion of some 400 sailors and marines became the rear guard of the Army of Northern Virginia as they retreated toward Appomattox. At the Battle of Sayler's Creek, the battalion fought furiously before being forced to surrender. After the war, Tucker went to Peru where he became a rear admiral in the Peruvian Navy. He introduced Confederate naval technology to both Peru and Chile whose combined fleets he commanded in their long and bloody war with Spain. Tucker died at Petersburg, Virginia, on June 12, 1883.[2]—Editor]

Commander John R. Tucker, captain of the CSS *Chicora* (Naval Historical Center).

The hotels were not hurting their guests by over feeding nor by rich diet, otherwise things were as comfortable as any young officer could want after the little experience since the fall of New Orleans.

The *Chicora* was built with about 14 inches of wood in her casemate, four inches being oak on the inside, and a covering of four inches iron at an angle of 45 degrees, was to have four guns, not yet mounted.

The engine was single acting and was taken from a tug. While the engine was lacking in power, she was a good ship, after so many tinder boxes and cook shops we had had. She was thought to be able to make eight

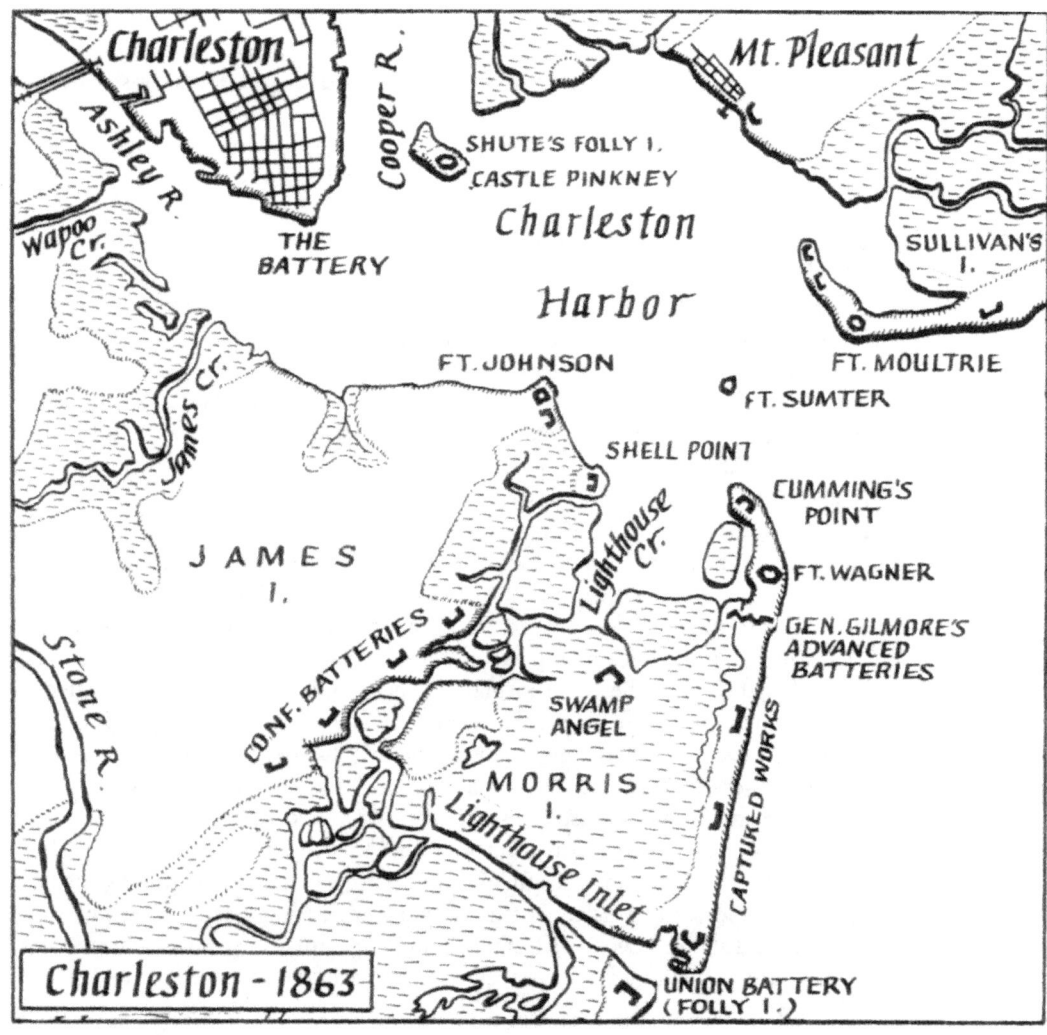

Wartime chart of the approaches to Charleston (*Battles and Leaders of the Civil War*, Johnson and Buell, eds.).

knots without forced draft, but when completed, could not under the most favorable circumstances make over seven.

> [Two ironclads, *Chicora* and *Palmetto State*, had been under construction at Charleston throughout the spring and summer of 1862. By June, both vessels were ready for their armor, but the army refused to relinquish the scarce railroad flatcars that were required to transport the heavy iron plates. Throughout the summer, the badly needed armor arrived sporadically, and it was not until the end of August that a sufficient supply was on hand to sheath both vessels.
> Although construction of the *Palmetto State* had begun earlier, the *Chicora* was actually the first to be launched, sliding down the ways on August 23. She

was built using the same dimensions as her sister vessel, which was 150 feet in length, 35 feet abeam, with a draft of approximately 12 feet. Although fully loaded, she probably drew more than this. Her slanted casemate was constructed of 22 inches of oak and pine, and over this, two layers of 2-inch iron plates were laid. Extending five feet below the waterline, these plates then swept forward to protect her pointed bow that was designed for ramming. Five hundred tons of iron was required to sheath her casemate, and she had cost the state of South Carolina $263,892.00. After launching, as per agreement, she was sold to the Confederate government, and the proceeds were used to begin construction of another ironclad. The *Chicora*, unlike the *Palmetto State*, was propelled, as Tomb points out, by only one engine taken from an old steamboat. This engine of inadequate power for a vessel the size and weight of the *Chicora*, turned via a long shaft, a single propeller of eight feet in diameter. Reports differ, as does Tomb's, but most evidence indicates that the *Chicora's* battery consisted of two 9-inch smoothbore guns mounted in pivots, and four 32-pounders mounted in broadside, two on each side, which had been banded and rifled in the Brooke design configuration to fire 60-pound shot.[3]

The next to be launched was the CSS *Palmetto State,* which slid into Charleston Harbor on October 11. Built with the typical John L. Porter design, which was similar to the original CSS *Virginia* of Hampton Roads fame, she also was 150 feet long, 35 feet abeam, and drew 12 feet of water. The *Palmetto State* was armored with four inches of iron plate on her sloping casemate that turned inward at the waterline forming a "knuckle," which was designed to protect the vessel in the event of being rammed by an enemy. The roof and the forward and after decks were sheathed with two inches of iron, and her hatchways were covered with heavy iron gratings. Unusual for most Confederate ironclads was her armored pilothouse, which was located behind the single smokestack. As with the *Chicora*, there is some confusion concerning her armament, but most accounts list her battery as consisting of two 7-inch Brooke rifles mounted in pivot fore and aft, and two 9-inch smoothbore shell guns, one per side, mounted in broadside. Her engines worked well, and she could do seven knots if pushed to the limit.[4]— Editor]

The CSS *Palmetto State* of the Charleston Squadron (Naval Historical Center).

4. The CSS *Chicora*

There was a good deal of rivalry between this ship and the *Palmetto State*. The *Palmetto* was called the ladies' gunboat, as they had raised a generous sum towards her construction, but nothing like what she cost.

When the time came to fix up our quarters, there was a great lack of funds among the engineers, and, in fact, among all the officers. As I was elected caterer of the Engineer's Mess, it was up to me to see about the arrangement of our quarters. After stating the condition of our finances to Mr. Eason, he generously gave me authority to go ahead and fix up our steerage to suit myself.

I did so, and, when ready for furnishing, our quarters were said to be as perfect as the space would permit. Then I had another talk with Mr. Eason, and after some hesitation on his part, he gave me permission to furnish it just as I wished. After I got through, there was everything in the way of furniture, damask curtains, spreads, and a pantry with everything but provisions.

While this was going on, neither the Midshipmen nor Wardroom officers had done a thing towards fitting up their quarters, and when they saw how the Engineer's steerage was fixed up, were anxious to find out who was going to pay for it. I told them the state was going to through Mr. Eason. Lieutenant Harris, after seeing me, went to Mr. Eason who decided that it was more than he had expected, but said that they could all have the same, the Midshipmen joining the Wardroom Officers and doing nothing to their steerage.

When the officers of the *Palmetto State* saw what we had, they started in to duplicate it, but were informed it must come from their own pockets, and a lot of stuff had to be sent back. We decided, on the *Chicora*, after going into commission, that the *Chicora* was the "Ladies Gunboat."

Captain [Duncan N.] Ingraham was Flag Officer, and, while a fine officer in his way, was not as active as the younger officers felt he might be.

> [Duncan N. Ingraham was from South Carolina and, as a captain, had resigned from the U.S. Navy on February 4, 1861. He was commissioned a captain in the C.S. Navy on October 23, 1862, to rank from March 23, 1861. He commanded the Charleston station from 1862 until its evacuation in 1865.[5] — Editor]

Captain John R. Tucker, who commanded the *Chicora* was everything an officer should be to command the love, respect, and confidence of officers and men. Up to the fall of Charleston, he

Captain Duncan N. Ingraham, flag officer of the Charleston Squadron (Scharf, *History of the Confederate States Navy*).

retained it, and at all times was as considerate in his treatment of the men as of the officers.

After the ship went into commission it was decided to make an attack on the blockading fleet off Charleston. January 30, 1863, we all had steam up, and about midnight proceeded over the bar, the *Palmetto State* leading and followed by the *Chicora*. We made about seven knots and I think the *Palmetto State* could make eight.

About daylight on the 31st, we started for the blockading fleet. The intention was for both ships to ram, as it was felt we could hope to do nothing with them if they had a chance to get away. The *Palmetto State* rammed the *Mercedita* and she surrendered to Commodore Ingraham. He paroled all hands through the officer who gave up the ship. The *Palmetto State* started for another ship, and in the meantime the *Mercedita* got away.

[Lieutenant William H. Parker, executive officer of the *Palmetto State*, wrote:
"Lieutenant T. Abbott, the executive officer of the *Mercedita*, had come in a boat. I conducted him through the port to the presence of Commodore Ingraham. He must have been impressed with the novel appearance of our gun deck; but his bearing was officer-like and cool. He reported the name of the ship and her captain, said she had 128 souls on board and that she was in a sinking condition. After some delay Commodore Ingraham required him to 'give his word of honor, for his commander, officers and crew, that they would not serve against the Confederate States until regularly exchanged.' This he did — it was a verbal parole. He then returned to his ship."[6]

From the description given by Parker, it seems evident that Ingraham was having difficulty deciding what to do with the stricken Union vessel and her crew. There was certainly no room on board the crowded ironclad for over 100 prisoners, and the number of small boats was inadequate. By this time the two vessels had drifted apart, and Ingraham's procrastination exasperated his younger officers who saw daylight fast approaching and wanted to continue their attacks on the other blockaders. It became obvious that the Federal officers had prematurely panicked, and the *Mercedita* was in no immediate danger of sinking. Amid the confusion and indecision, the damaged *Mercedita* was able to limp away into the darkness. — Editor]

First Lieutenant William H. Parker, executive officer of the *Palmetto State* (Naval Historical Center).

The *Chicora* also headed for a ship and we in the engine room were waiting for the signal to back full speed, when fire was opened on the *Keystone State* with the forward gun, under Lieutenant William T. Glassell, and we were told we would not ram. Mr.

4. The CSS *Chicora*

The *Palmetto State* rams the *Mercedita*, while to the right the *Chicora* attacks the *Keystone State* (*Illustrated London News*).

[Hugh] Clark, engineer in charge, and Chief Pilot [Thomas R.] Payne had advised Captain Tucker against it, as the ram, was of cast iron, and the back end projected some six inches above the deck. They feared the *Chicora* would not have power to back clear again.

The *Keystone State* received a shot in the steam drum and was in bad shape. She hauled down her flag and surrendered and we ceased firing. Lieutenant Glassell was ordered to take charge as prize officer and I was ordered to take charge of the engines.

When we were about ready to start for her it was noticed she was headed directly away from us, and gradually getting out of range. Before this, Lieut. Glassell had asked permission to open on her again, but the Captain said she had surrendered and not to fire. When we saw she had no intention of surrendering, the order was given to open fire on her.

> [Instead of ramming, Tucker ordered the ironclad rounded to and her broadside guns opened fire. The Confederate aim was excellent. One shell entered the Federal vessel's berth deck, "tearing the hammock racks...to pieces, setting fire to some of the woodwork, rudely disturbing the watch asleep in their hammocks and wounding and killing several men."[7]
>
> With the *Chicora*'s explosive shells continuing to smash into her, the Union vessel's head was turned out to sea and into the wind in an effort to extinguish the flames. From the pilothouse on board the *Chicora*, Tucker could see the Fed-

eral vessel turning away, and he quickly rang the bell in the engine room ordering "all ahead full." The best the *Chicora* could do, however, was only about six knots. At 12 knots, the *Keystone State* rapidly pulled away from the ponderous ironclad and made good her escape.[8] — Editor]

By this time the *Keystone State* was well down to the S. E. and out of range, and, not having the speed to follow her, we returned over the bar and came to anchor in the harbor.

There was great rejoicing on shore where it was said we had raised the blockade, but there was a general expression on board ship that we would rather have raised----, and sunk the ships. We were all disappointed as we had neither captured nor sunk a ship, at least we did not bring one into port.

[Tomb's report in the *Official Navy Records* — Editor]

C.S.S. *Chicora*
Charleston, S.C., Friday, January 30, 1863.

We had orders to have our department in good condition for active work for some time. Tonight we had steam, and it looked like we were going to do something. As we steamed down the harbor we knew it was an engagement outside, and from constant talk felt the sooner it came the better. The intention is to ram the first ship we come to. Chief Engineer Clark gave me orders to that effect and to be ready to back without delay.

January 31. — It must have been about 5 A.M., after crossing the bar, that the *Palmetto State* struck the first ship, but our ship, for some reason we who were waiting for the signal did not understand at the time, did not ram, but depended upon our guns. Chief Engineer Clark afterwards informed me that himself and Chief Pilot Payne did not think that the *Chicora* had power enough to back out in case we rammed the enemy's ship, and for that reason Captain Tucker decided not to make the attempt. There was no reason why we should not have rammed and every reason why we should have done so. The blow we should have struck, while sufficient to sink the enemy, would not have passed beyond the incline of the heavy cast-iron prow or ram on our bow. We could not hope to catch them once we were sighted, and, unless disabled with our guns, [it] would get away from us. We fired into the *Keystone State*, and they evidently were not prepared for us. From what we could learn below, she was heading away from us when a shot from our bow gun, under the command of Lieutenant W. T. Glassell, struck her steam pipe or drum and another her wheel. At this time she was within close range, and our shots told on her. The *Keystone State* hauled down her flag and did not change her course any. Her engines were working right along. The signal was made to us to stop our engine. Chief Engineer Clark took my station in the engine room, and I was ordered to take my crew of firemen and, along with the officer who was to take charge of the *Keystone State* as a prize, to take charge of the engine department. When we got ready to take the second cutter to go aboard the *Keystone State*, Lieutenant Glassell requested permission to fire on her again, as she was passing out of range. Captain Tucker said, "No; she has lowered her flag and surrendered."

Shortly after this, realizing that she was only getting away and had no intention of surrendering, Captain Tucker gave orders to run the cutter up and for Lieutenant Glassell to open on her again; but she had got well down to the southeast and well out of range.

The upshot of the engagement was a good bit of glory, but not a prize or ship destroyed, and when we passed back over the bar and back to Charleston we all felt disappointed at the night's work. We did not accomplish as much as our sister ship, the *Palmetto State*. They say we raised the blockade, but we all felt we would have rather raised h—l and sunk the ships. There was quite a heavy fog at the time we went out, but cleared up at the time we came into the harbor and anchored.

JAMES H. TOMB[9]

Had we rammed the *Keystone State*, as Captain Tucker intended, she would have gone to the bottom, and we would have come out safe, as the projection above the shield was not over a few inches, and it is doubtful if the *Chicora* could have gone beyond it.

As I had made a few trips on the *Keystone State* as Assistant Engineer, while preparing for my entrance into the U.S. Navy, I was much disappointed. Being selected to take charge of her as prize engineer, I would have felt perfectly at home in the engine room, and, am sure would have been considerate of the officers who had charge of that department, for I have felt, more than ever, since my own experience as a prisoner of war, that a prisoner gets very little at times.

The next day our friends, the blockaders, began to show up again, but did not seem very anxious to come close in.

It was something to us of the Navy to see how the good people of Charleston took it, as you would imagine we had about finished the Yankees for all time.

When the Swamp Angel first opened fire on Charleston, we would not believe that the first shells exploding in the lower section of the city came from the battery near Morris Island; but as the shells began to explode higher up in the town, it was evident that they had the range.

[The "Swamp Angel" was a huge 8-inch Parrott rifle that the Federals had mounted in the marshes of Morris Island. Its sole purpose was to lob its 150-

The "Swamp Angel" fires into Charleston on a moonlit night (National Archives).

The citizens of Charleston under artillery fire from the "Swamp Angel" (*Illustrated London News*).

pound projectiles into the city of Charleston four and a half miles away. It first opened fire on the night of August 22, 1863.—Editor]

I took up my quarters at the corner of Market and Meeting Streets, thinking it was out of range, but one Sunday morning there was an explosion like an earthquake as a shell passed through the building and exploded in the Market. Not wishing to wait for another such visit, I packed my valise and selected safer quarters, and in passing out advised the family to move out also, but they said it was seldom a shot struck twice in the sane place, and while upset, they would not change just then.

We found that the section of the City, from the Battery up to Tradd St. was about the healthiest spot in the City to avoid Yankee shells from the "Swamp Angel."

I heard some shells explode uptown, and when I went back to pack everything that I had left in my room, I saw them bringing the old gentleman and his wife from the building, both severely injured, and the upper part of the building wrecked by the explosion of a shell, which must have struck just after I left. It was a very sad sight, as they were both well advanced in life, and I suppose they hardly knew where to go when the shelling began.

There was a combined attack about this time [September 8–9, 1863] on Fort Sumter by the Army and Navy, but for some reason the Army failed to make connections with the boats of the Fleet that made a landing at Fort Sumter. The garrison made such a splendid fight that it was a failure, and the best part of those landed were taken prisoners.

4. The CSS *Chicora*

The failed Federal attack on Fort Sumter, September 8–9, 1863 (*Battles and Leaders of the Civil War*, Johnson and Buell, eds.).

The *Chicora* was at anchor above Sumter and had a good chance to work her guns on the boats of the landing party.

> [Major Stephen Elliott, Jr. was the Confederate commander of Fort Sumter, and a portion of his official report of the night action pays tribute to the services rendered by the *Chicora*:
>
> "At 1 A.M., while observing a monitor that had taken position near the fort, I saw the enemy pulling up from the eastward, in two columns; the head of the one directed upon the northeast, that of the other upon the southeast angle of the fort.
>
> "I ordered up three companies within supporting distance, and reserved our fire until they had deployed and commenced to land. The outer boats replied rapidly for a few minutes. The crews of those that had effected a landing sought refuge from a galling fire under the projecting masses of the wall, whence grenades and fireballs soon dislodged them.
>
> "The fire of the *Chicora*, lying at a short distance to the northward of Sullivan's Island to the northwest, and of Fort Johnson to the westward, encircled the work and effectually assisted to prevent any reinforcements from coming up.
>
> "The enemy, with some of his boats disabled by hand grenades and masses of masonry, convenient weapons to the ready bands of our garrison, and overwhelmed by our own and the fire of our supports, called for quarter, and were ordered, in detail, to make their way to the gorge, whence they were transferred to a place of security. Not one of our men was injured.

"The whole force engaged on our side consisted of 80 riflemen and 24 men detached for service of the grenades and fireballs. The remainder of the garrison was ready for action and remained in position.

"The force of the enemy exceeded, according to the statement of captured officers, 400 men. Captured papers would indicate it to have been 870."[10]—Editor]

5

The CSS *David*

[At this point in his memoirs, Tomb relates his experimentation and involvement with torpedoes (mines) and torpedo boats. It would be this service for which he would be most widely known. To fully appreciate his accomplishments, some background information is essential.

The first acid chemical fuse designed as a firing mechanism was developed by Professor Moritz Hermann von Jacobi, an eminent Russian chemist and philosopher. This fuse arrangement saw extensive service in Russian torpedoes at Sebastopol and Cronstadt during the Crimean War.[1] Captain Francis D. Lee of the Confederate Army developed the spar arrangement to carry the torpedo, and improved upon the original Jacobi-type fuse. Whether Lee had knowledge of the Russian fuse is unknown, but his design closely resembled that of the Professor Jacobi.

Prior to the war, Lee had been a well-respected and much sought-after architect in Charleston. Born in 1827, into one of the city's most wealthy families, Lee was assigned as an engineering officer in 1862 to the staff of the military commander of Charleston, General Pierre G. T. Beauregard. While designing and aiding in the construction of many fortifications surrounding Charleston, Lee had become interested in underwater explosives and in developing a means of delivering them to the side of an enemy vessel.

His first consideration was to design a reliable fuse mechanism to explode the torpedo underwater. While other devices had depended upon some form of lanyard, which, when snagged by part of a ship, would pull a trigger, Lee set about developing a fuse that would explode upon impact. Encouraged by General Beauregard, Lee began experimenting with the idea of a chemical type fuse. After extensive testing, he settled upon an ingenious yet simple mechanism. It consisted of a small lead tube approximately three inches in length, the head of which was capped with a very thin hemispherical piece of metal. Inside the tube Lee carefully placed a hermetically sealed glass vial containing sulfuric acid. Between the glass vial and the inner wall of the tube, he packed a composition of chlorate of potassium, powdered sugar, and very fine rifle powder. The lower part of the tube, which was screwed into the body of the torpedo, was sealed with oiled paper and was protected against leakage by brass couplings and rubber washers. With several of these screwed into the head of a torpedo it became an extremely dangerous and formidable weapon. When contact was made with the side of an enemy vessel, the impact would dent the end cap enough to break the glass vial, releasing the acid. The sulfuric acid, acting upon the composition, would ignite the rifle powder, which in turn caused the entire torpedo to explode.[2] — Editor]

Captain Francis D. Lee, CSA (courtesy of the South Carolina Historical Society).

Lieutenant William T. Glassell, C.S.N., and I had been experimenting for some time with the first and second cutters of the *Chicora*, with a spar torpedo attached to the bow of the cutter, in an effort to reach and blow up one of the monitors off Morris Island, but it was always a failure, as we would pass out by Sumter in good shape on the last of the ebb-tide, and that was about all we did, as neither Glassell nor I ever got near the monitors. The nearer we got to them, the less headway our boat made, and when striking the first of the flood, it was a tie, and then we lost out. As we both had the same trouble we reported to Flag Officer Tucker that we could do nothing unless we had other means of propelling the boats.

[Lieutenant Glassell was born in Virginia but was appointed from the state of Alabama when he entered Confederate service. He had served as a lieutenant in the U.S. Navy and was in China when the Southern states seceded. Returning home onboard the USS *Hartford* (later to become famous as Admiral Farragut's flagship) Glassell was informed upon reaching Philadelphia on August 5, 1862, that he must take a new oath of allegiance. The young lieutenant refused because he considered the new oath inconsistent with the one that he had taken when he entered the navy. Arrested and thrown into prison at Fort Warren in Boston Harbor, Glassell was confined as a prisoner of war for eight months, even though he was a civilian and held no position in Confederate forces. Finally exchanged, he was offered a commission as a first lieutenant in the Confederate Navy, his appointment being post-dated to the same day as his incarceration. Sent to Charleston, he reported aboard the ironclad *Chicora* where he performed the duties of deck officer in charge of the first division.[3]

Glassell sought permission from his superior, Captain Ingraham, to equip several small steamers with Lee's spar torpedoes, but the crusty old sea captain did not believe in what he called "new-fangled notions" and refused permission. Lee and Glassell, though discouraged, remained determined to prove the effectiveness of their new weapon. With the help of financier George A. Trenholm, Glassell secured a collection of rowboats and equipped them with Lee's torpedoes, but Ingraham refused to assign the necessary officers and men. Unwilling to accept defeat, Glassell borrowed one of the cutters from the ironclad *Chicora*, and Lee attached a 50-pound torpedo to the boat. Ingraham had not refused permission for Glassell to attack the Federals alone, so accordingly, at about 1:00 a.m. on the night of March 18, 1863, with six volunteer seamen from the *Chicora* manning the oars of the cutter, Glassell headed for the open sea.

Lieutenant William T. Glassell (courtesy of the Orange Public Library).

The moon had set and the sea was calm as Glassell steered toward the USS *Powhatan,* whose lights were clearly visible from Fort Sumter. "The bow of the ship was toward us and the ebb tide was still running out," Glassell wrote. "I did not expect to reach the vessel without being discovered, but my intention was, no matter what they might say or do, not to be stopped until our torpedo came in contact with the ship. My men were instructed accordingly. I did hope that the enemy would not be alarmed by the approach of such a small boat so far out at sea, and that we should be ordered to come alongside."[4]

At a distance of 200 to 300 yards, they were discovered by the deck watch aboard the Federal vessel and ordered to halt and not come any nearer. Glassell ignored the order, and giving evasive "and stupid" answers to their questions, quietly ordered his men to pull for all they were worth. When within 40 feet of the *Powhatan*, and only seconds from striking her, one of the men, from "terror or treason," backed his oar, stopping the boat's headway. The other crewmen now gave up in despair, and the cutter drifted with the tide past the Union vessel's stern. With the *Powhatan* beginning to lower a boat to go in pursuit, Glassell drew his revolver, ordered the torpedo cut loose, and directed his men to pull away with all their strength. No shots were fired, and soon they were out of sight and headed back into the harbor.[5]

Tomb does not mention whether he was along on this first attempted attack using a cutter, but it is probable that he was. Later attempts would involve both the first and second cutters from the *Chicora* with Glassell commanding one and Tomb the other.—Editor]

At this time there was a small cigar shaped boat designed by Dr. [St. Julien] Ravenel, built by Theodore Stoney and others of Charleston. It was requested of Flag Officer Tucker, that Lieutenant Glassell and Engineer Tomb, take the boat and fit her up as a Torpedo Boat, and attempt the destruction of the U.S.S. *New Ironsides*, off Morris Island.

[One of the first steps taken by Dr. Ravenel in constructing the *David* torpedo boat, was to enlist the aid of David C. Ebaugh who was superintendent of the niter works at Ravenel's plantation on the Cooper River. The account of the design and construction of the *David* is a story in itself, but suffice it here to quote from a postwar letter written by Ebaugh:

"I laid out the boat full size under a niter shed at Stoney Landing. It was 5 feet in diameter and 48½ feet long, 18 feet of the middle of the boat was the same size tapering to a point at each end. The ends were made of large pine logs turned off with a grove to receive the ends of the planking, the timbers were made of 1½ inch oak doubled and riveted together, they were placed about 15 inches apart, the planking was the whole length 1½ inches thick hollowed on the inside to fit the timbers and rounded on outside, the planking was riveted to the timbers, the whole was put together at Stoney Landing, chalked and launched. It was sent to Charleston to have the machinery put in. It was there hoisted out of the water by a crane on the Northeastern Railroad wharf, put on a car and carried to the railroad shop."[6]— Editor]

David C. Ebaugh, builder of the original CSS *David* (Naval Historical Center).

Lieutenant Glassel took command, and I made the attachment for torpedo spar and torpedo. Our first arrangement was 8-½ feet below the surface, but finding a defect in the boiler tube furnished us by Frasier and Co., we had to bring it up to 6-½ feet below the surface.

The boat was built in the shape of a cigar, 50 feet long and 6-½ feet beam, had one propeller, and steaming in good condition could make about 7 knots.

The torpedo was made of copper, by Captain F. D. Lee, Eng. Dept., C.S.A., and held about 65 pounds of powder. At the head of the torpedo were 4 tubes containing fulminate of mercury. The spar was so attached that it could not be raised or lowered after leaving the dock.

The night of October 5, 1863, we decided to make the attempt on the

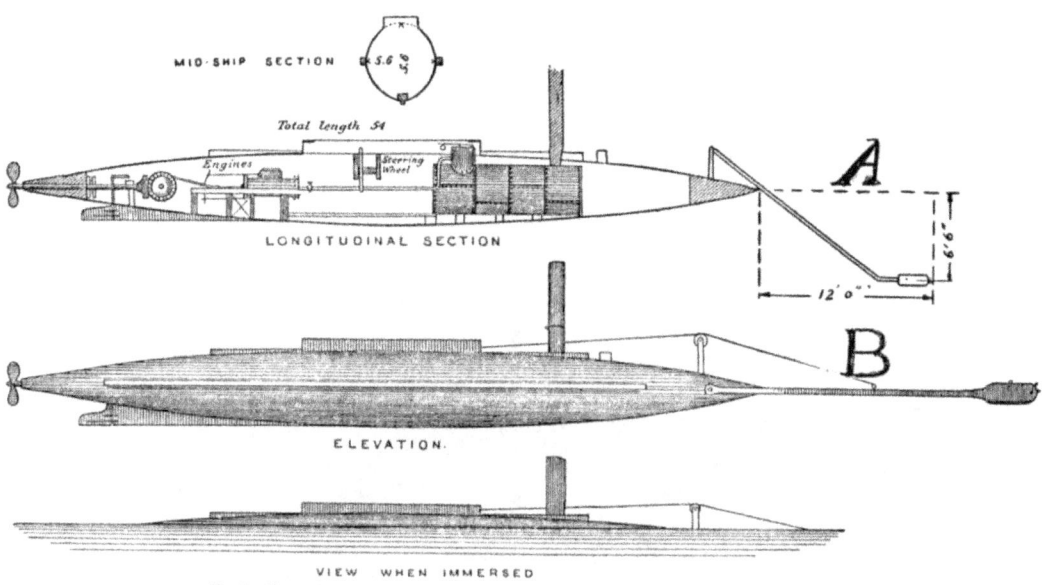

Top: Plan drawing of the CSS *David*. Sketch "A" shows the torpedo arrangement when the *David* attacked the *New Ironsides*. Sketch "B" illustrates the torpedo arrangement after modifications were made (Tomb Family Papers). *Bottom:* A "David" torpedo boat photographed at Charleston at the end of the war. Some historians believe that this may be the original *David* (Naval Historical Center).

The USS *New Ironsides* (*Official Records Navy*).

Ironsides, even while not satisfied with the depth of the torpedo. There was a slight haze over the harbor as we started down about 7:30 P.M. The intention of Lieutenant Glessell being to strike the *Ironsides* on the turn of the tide, or first of the flood, so that we would have a little chance to get back to the harbor.

We arrived abreast the *Ironsides* about 8:30 P.M., and found her swinging down stream. We stood off and on until about 9 P.M.

When, all being ready, and a good head of steam on, the little *David* was headed for the frigate that even at that distance loomed up like a powerful ship just as we felt she was. When within a short distance, we were hailed from her quarter deck, and the only reply was from a double barreled shot-gun in the hands of Lieutenant Glassell. He felt that a torpedo attack was an innovation in naval warfare, and that if we did not give warning of our approach we might, if captured, get a short shift. He thought best to fire, not with the particular intention of killing someone, but for our own benefit.

The *David* struck the *Ironsides* about 15 feet on the starboard quarter, and the torpedo some 6-½ feet below the surface. The *David* was going full speed when she struck, but the engine had just been reversed. The concussion was severe; so much so that along with the volume of water thrown up and into the *David* the engine was disabled, and would not work. I reported this to Lieutenant Glassell, who then gave orders for us all to abandon the *David*, as she was apparently sinking. The *Ironsides* kept up a severe fire with small arms, for at the time we were so close to her quarter, she could not use her large guns. While hanging on to the *David*, and trying to keep away from the bullets, I noticed that a great many struck a large iron buoy, that was a great distance off the bow of the *Ironsides*. Sullivan, the fireman, did not leave the boat until I told him to, and then Lieutenant Glassell and he, each having a life preserver, swam away in the direction of the Yankee transports. As the flood of water had taken the rest of the preservers, I also went overboard, but without a life preserver, and started to swim in the direction of Morris Island; but looking back and seeing that the *David* was still afloat, concluded to swim back and make another effort to save her. On reaching her, I found that Pilot Cannon was hanging to the life lines, as he could not swim a stroke.

After getting aboard, the *David* and righting the engine, (the trouble was caused by a piece of the iron ballast being thrown between parts of the machinery), I hauled Cannon aboard, started up fires, and, when ready, started the engine ahead, made the turn up stream between the *Ironsides* and a monitor just east of her, and as we turned came almost near enough to the monitor's quarter to touch her. As we headed toward the harbor and through the fleet and guard boats, they all fired wild, for they were about as badly rattled as we were. We passed right between the two guard boats, but for some reason neither fired a shot at us.

I reported the results of the expedition, as far as I could, to Flag Officer Tucker at Charleston, and he told me to come aboard the *Charleston*, but I said it was as much as I could do to keep the *David* afloat, and besides all my clothes were left down the harbor, so he gave me orders to beach the *David* in Eason's slip. The Flag Officer was considerate of those under his orders, and when he saw my condition gave the Quartermaster the orders to take his coat to me, but I declined it.

The next day, after making an examination of the *David* I found she was in fairly good condition, except for a number of holes in her upper works made by the rapid fire of small arms from the *Ironsides*.

In reporting the loss of Lieutenant Glassell and Fireman Sullivan, I expressed the belief that they might be prisoners aboard the Yankee ships, for they were good swimmers. As to Cannon, who could not swim, it was remarkable how cool and brave he was, and I doubt if I could have gotten back without him. The *Ironsides* was not apparently injured for she was at anchor in the same spot, but they had listed her some to port. I could not see what they were doing, but felt satisfied that had the torpedo been in the position we had first placed it, 8-1/2 feet, it would have done much better execution.

> [After the war, in 1877, Lieutenant Glassell submitted an article to the *Southern Historical Society Papers* entitled " Reminiscences of Torpedo Service in Charleston Harbor," which included details about the attack on the *New Ironsides* by the *David*. That section of his article is presented here and the paper has been reproduced in its entirety in Appendix C:
>
> "Mr. Theodore Stoney informed me that the little cigar boat built at his expense had been brought down by railroad, and that if I could do anything with her he would place her at my disposal. On examination I determined to make a trial. She was yet in an unfinished state. Assistant-Engineer J. H. Tomb volunteered his service, and all the necessary machinery was soon fitted and got in working order, while Major Francis D. Lee gave me his zealous aid in fitting on a torpedo. James Stuart (alias Sullivan) volunteered to go as fireman, and afterwards the service of J. W. Cannon as pilot were secured. The boat was ballasted

so as to float deeply in the water, and all above painted the most invisible color (bluish). The torpedo was made of copper, containing about 100 pounds of rifle powder, and provided with four sensitive tubes of lead, containing explosive mixture; and this was carried by means of a hollow iron shaft projecting about fourteen feet ahead of the boat, and six or seven feet below the surface. I had also an armament on deck of four double-barrel shotguns, and as many navy revolvers; also, four cork life-preservers had been thrown on board, and made us feel safe.

"Having tried the speed of my boat, and found it satisfactory (six or seven knots an hour), I got a necessary order from Commodore Tucker to attack the enemy at discretion, and also one from General Beauregard. And now came an order from Richmond, that I should proceed immediately back to rejoin the *North Carolina*, at Wilmington. [Glassell was on loan from the ironclad based at Wilmington, North Carolina.] This was too much! I never obeyed that order, but left Commodore Tucker to make my excuses to the Navy Department.

"The 5th of October, 1863, a little after dark, we left Charleston wharf, and proceeded with the ebb-tide down the harbor. A light north wind was blowing, and the night was slightly hazy, but starlight, and the water was smooth. I desired to make the attack about the turn of the tide, and this ought to have been just after nine o'clock, but the north wind made it run out a little longer.

"We passed Fort Sumter and beyond the line of picket-boats without being discovered. Silently steaming along just inside the bar, I had a good opportunity to reconnoiter the whole fleet of the enemy at anchor between me and the camp-fires on Morris' Island.

"Perhaps I was mistaken, but it did occur to me that if we had then, instead of only one, just ten or twelve torpedoes [boats], to make a simultaneous attack on all the ironclads, and this quickly followed by the egress of our rams, not only might this grand fleet have been destroyed, but the 20,000 troops on Morris' Island been left at our mercy. Quietly maneuvering and observing the enemy, I was half an hour more waiting on time and tide. The music of drum and fife had just ceased, and the nine o'clock gun had been fired from the admiral's ship as a signal for all unnecessary lights to be extinguished and for the men not on watch to retire for sleep. I thought the proper time for attack had arrived.

"The admiral's ship, *New Ironsides* (the most powerful vessel in the world), lay in the midst of the fleet, her starboard side presented to my view. I determined to pay her the highest compliment. I had been informed, through prisoners lately captured from the fleet, that they were expecting an attack from torpedo boats, and were prepared for it. I could, therefore, hardly expect to accomplish my object without encountering some danger from riflemen, and perhaps a discharge of grape or canister from the howitzers. My guns were loaded with buckshot. I knew that if the officer of the deck could be disabled to begin with, it would cause them some confusion and increase our chance for escape, so I determined that if the occasion offered, I would commence by firing the first shot. Accordingly, having on a full head of steam, I took charge of the helm, it being so arranged that I could sit on deck and work the wheel with my feet. Then directing the engineer and fireman to keep below and give me all the speed possible, I gave a double-barrel gun to the pilot, with instructions not to fire until I should do so, and steered directly for the monitor. I intended to strike her just under the gang-way, but the tide still running out, carried us to a point nearer the quarter. Thus we rapidly approached the enemy. When within about 300 yards of her a sentinel hailed us: Boat ahoy! boat ahoy! repeating the hail several times very rapidly. We were coming towards them with all speed, and I made no answer, but cocked both barrels of my gun. The officer of the deck next made his appearance, and loudly demanded, "What boat is that?" Being now within 40 yards of the ship, and plenty of headway to carry us on, I thought it about time the fight should commence, and fired my gun. The officer of the deck fell back mortally wounded (poor fellow), and I ordered the engine stopped. The next moment the torpedo struck the vessel and exploded. What amount of directed damage the enemy received I will not attempt to say. My little boat plunged violently, and a large body of water which had been thrown up descended upon her deck, and down the smoke-stack and hatchway.

"I immediately gave orders to reverse the engine and back off. Mr. Tomb informed me then that the fires were put out, and something had become jammed in the machinery so that it would not move. What could be done in this situation? In the mean time, the enemy recovering from the shock, beat to quarters, and general alarm spread through the fleet. I told my men I thought our only

The *David* is depicted approaching the USS *New Ironsides* (courtesy of Dan Dowdey).

The *David* explodes its torpedo against the side of the *New Ironsides* (Naval Historical Center).

chance to escape was by swimming, and I think I told Mr. Tomb to cut the water-pipes, and let the boat sink. Then taking one of the cork floats, I got into the water and swam off as fast as I could.

"The enemy, in no amiable mood, poured down upon the bubbling water a hailstorm of rifle and pistol shots from the deck of the *Ironsides*, and from the nearest monitor. Sometimes they struck very close to my head, but swimming for life, I soon disappeared from their sight, and found myself all alone in the water. I hoped that, with the assistance of flood-tide, I might be able to reach Fort Sumter, but a north wind was against me, and after I had been in the water more than an hour, I became numb with cold, and was nearly exhausted. Just then the boat of a transport schooner picked me up, and found, to their surprise, that they had captured a rebel.

"The captain of this schooner made me as comfortable as possible that night with whiskey and blankets, for which I sincerely thanked him. I was handed over next morning to the mercy of Admiral Dahlgren. He ordered me to be transferred to the guard-ship *Ottowa*, lying outside the rest of the fleet. Upon reaching the quarter-deck of this vessel, I was met and recognized by her commander, William D. Whiting. He was an honorable gentleman and high-toned officer. I was informed that his orders were to have me put in irons, and if obstreperous, in double irons. I smiled, and told him his duty was to obey orders, and mine to adapt myself to circumstances æ I could see no occasion to be obstreperous.

"I think Captain Whiting, felt mortified at being obliged thus to treat an old brother officer, whom he knew could only have been actuated by a sense of patriotic duty in making the attack which caused him to fall into his power as a prisoner of war. At any rate, he proceeded immediately to see the admiral, and upon his return I was released, on giving my parole not to attempt an escape from the vessel. His kindness, and the gentlemanly courtesy with which I was treated by other officers of the old navy, I shall ever remember most gratefully. I learned that my fireman had been found hanging on to the rudder-chains of the *Ironsides* and taken on board. I had every reason to believe that the other two, Mr. Tomb and Mr. Cannon, had been shot or drowned, until I heard of their safe arrival in Charleston.

"I was retained as a prisoner in Fort La Fayette and Fort Warren for more than a year, and learned while there that I had been promoted for what was called 'gallant and meritorious service.'

"What all the consequences of this torpedo attack upon the enemy were is not for me to say. It certainly awakened them to a sense of the dangers to which they had been exposed, and caused them to apprehend far greater difficulties and dangers than really existed should they attempt to enter the harbor with their fleet. It may have prevented Admiral Dahlgren from carrying out the intention he is said to have had of going in with 12 ironclads on the arrival of his double-turreted monitor to destroy the city by a cross-fire from the two rivers. It certainly caused them to take many precautionary measures for protecting their vessels which had never before been thought of. Possibly it shook the nerve of a brave admiral and deprived him of the glory of laying low the city of Charleston. It was said by officers of the navy that the ironclad vessels of that fleet were immediately enveloped like women in hoop-skirt petticoats of netting, to lay in idle admiration of themselves for many months. The *Ironsides* went into dry-dock for repairs."[7]— Editor]

6

The CSS *Juno*

About this time, a very fast side wheel steamer, called the *Juno*, ran into Charleston, and the Navy Department bought her, making use of her as a torpedo boat. Lieutenant Phil Porcher was put in command, with Master Charles D. Tucker and Pilot William Burkee as assistants. I was sent aboard to take charge of the engineering department, with Mr. [John H.] Dent as assistant. The crew consisted of thirty-five men.

> [The CSS *Juno*, was a fast, iron-framed paddle-wheel steamer. Built on the Clyde in Scotland in 1860 by the Tod and McGregor Company, she had been operated as a mail carrier between London and Glasgow. She sailed as a British blockade runner in the spring of 1863. Successfully evading the Federal blockaders, she ran into Charleston on July 8, where she was purchased by the Navy Department. She served as a dispatch, picket, flag-of-truce, and torpedo boat. (This *Juno* should not be confused with the steamer of the same name that was captured while coming out of Wilmington by the USS *Connecticut*.)[1]
>
> Lieutenant Porcher was from South Carolina and had resigned as a lieutenant from the U.S. Navy on February 2, 1861. He was appointed first lieutenant in Confederate service on March 26, 1861. He was assigned first to the Charleston station and later to the Savannah Squadron during 1861–1862. There he served on the CSS *Sampson*, which on November 7, 1861, participated in battle of Port Royal, S.C. Afterward he returned to Charleston and was was assigned to the *Chicora*. When the *Juno* was purchased by the Navy, he was given her command.
>
> Master Tucker was the son of Flag Officer John R. Tucker, commander of the Charleston Squadron, and Pilot William Burkee was one of the *Chicora*'s pilots. Dent had served with Tomb on the *McRae*.[2] — Editor]

A spar holding a torpedo, projected thirty feet from the bow and held about ninety pounds of powder. Strapped to the bow, just above the surface of the water, was a cotton bale, as a fender in case of striking a ship.

6. The CSS *Juno*

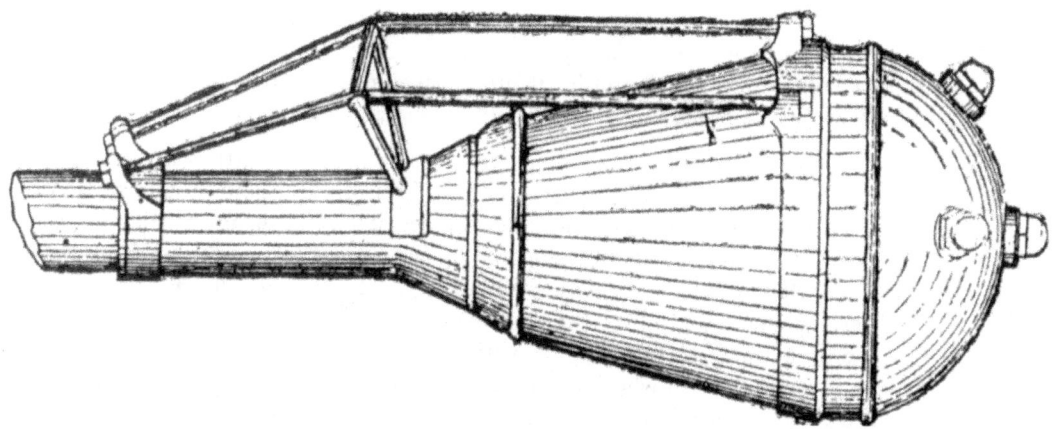

Drawing of a spar torpedo. The *Juno*'s torpedo may have been similar to this example (*Official Records Navy*).

The *Juno* was sent down on picket duty below Sumter after dark. While lying under low steam on the night of August 5, 1863, we were hailed by a large launch and ordered to surrender as a shot from a 12 pound howitzer passed over our bow.

The *Juno* was headed directly for the launch, and, not having much pressure on the boilers, we rammed the launch amidships. She struck against the cotton bale, and then swinging around against the port guard forward of the wheel, fired into us and at the same time boarded. We returned the fire with the few fire arms we had. As the officer in charge of the launch came over the rail, he had his sword in one hand and a boot in the other. One of my men from the fire room took possession of the boot, but I made him return it. Then he [the Federal] said, "We surrender."

The officer and his men were taken aft and put below. At this time I called the attention of Lieutenant Porcher to some men floating in the water on our quarter. He wanted to stop the ship and pick then up, but Pilot Burkee said the ship would be in a bad position if the engines were stopped, as she had little steerage way with the heavy launch against the port wheel, and there were some of the monitors coming up. Lieutenant Porcher very reluctantly gave orders to return to the harbor.

There were about twenty-four officers and men in the launch, and she mounted one 12-pound howitzer in the bow. Lieutenant Porcher was just as anxious to pick her men up as if they had been our own, but, had he done so the Yanks would have taken us, or we would have drifted ashore.

The next morning when the launch and prisoners were taken over to the flagship, the coxswain, a fine looking fellow who seemed to feel his position very much, remarked loud enough to be heard, "This comes from having an officer who gets you into trouble and can't get you out." The officer was Acting Master Haines. All the men were fine looking, and with a better officer, could no doubt have taken the *Juno*.

[Some of the Federal sailors reported that they were fired upon while they struggled in the water as the *Juno* passed by. Rear-Admiral John A. Dahlgren, Federal commander of the South Atlantic Blockading Squadron, wrote to General Beauregard complaining about the alleged violation of the rules of war:

FLAG-STEAMER DINSMORE,
of Morris Island, August 6, 1863.

SIR: Last night one of your steamers succeeded in running down a boat of this squadron, and it is stated by several of our men that they were fired at in the water after the steamer had passed over the boat. Of course it was obvious to everyone that under the circumstances our men were entirely helpless.

Such a practice is entirely in violation of every rule of civilized war, and call upon you to punish whoever can be convicted of having perpetrated such an act, otherwise it will be impossible for me to prevent retaliation by our men whenever the opportunity may occur.

I am, very respectfully, your obedient servant,

JOHN A. DAHLGREN,
Rear-Admiral, Comdg. South Atlantic Blockading Squadron.

GENERAL G. T. BEAUREGARD,
Commanding Confederate Forces, Charleston, S.C.

Beauregard forwarded Dahlgren's letter to Tucker who responded to the allegations:

FLAGSHIP *CHICORA*,
Charleston Harbor, August 10, 1863.

SIR: Your communication of the 6th instant to General Beauregard, C.S. Army, complaining that after the capture of the launch belonging to your squadron, that the men were "fired at in the water," has been referred to me.

I am happy to be able to state, from information received from the Confederate States naval officer in command at that time, that the men were not fired at in the water.

I highly appreciate your desire to conduct the war upon civilized principles, and it affords me great pleasure to join you in so laudable a desire.

Very respectfully, your obedient servant,

JOHN R. TUCKER,
Flag-Officer, Comdg. C.S. Naval Forces, Charleston, Harbor.

REAR-ADMIRAL JOHN A. DAHLGREN, U.S. NAVY,
Commanding U.S. Naval Forces off Charleston.

Acting Master Edward L. Haines, USN, commanded the Federal boats that night. He and 12 of his men were taken prisoner. Haines was exchanged over a year later on October 18, 1864, and ten days later filed his report of the incident from Philadelphia, part of which reads as follows:

"Before taking my station, I reported to Rear-Admiral J. A. Dahlgren. He ordered me to report to the officer commanding the U.S. monitor *Catskill*, she being the guard ship for that night. The admiral informed me that two or tree of the enemy's steamers were in the habit of coming down to Cumming's Point every night, and if they came within range, to fire upon and sink them if possible, and that Ensign B. H. Porter would be out in a small boat, and to be careful not to fire at him.

"In reporting to commander of U.S.S. *Catskill* (monitor) he ordered me to pull a short distance above her, toward Fort Sumter, and anchor the launches under my command in line, and in sight of each other, and signalize by firing and displaying lights any danger that might occur. I took the lead of the line toward the fort as my station. About 11 P.M., Ensign Porter came alongside and reported that a steamer had come down to Cumming's Point and was now lying close in, and that he thought she was a blockade runner. Leaving me he pulled for the *Catskill*. I immediately got my anchor and let my launch drop up toward Cumming's Point, in order to get a view of the reported steamer. Soon after getting underway I made out a steamer standing down the channel close to Morris Island. I immediately opened fire on her from my howitzer, and made signals as agreed upon to the fleet, at the same time pulled my boat toward shoal water, to avoid colliding with her. Finding I could not escape, I determined to board and try to take her, at the same time expecting answers from the other launches, or *Catskill*, they being in sight. I succeeded in boarding, her under a heavy fire of musketry. After a short resistance we were compelled by the superior numbers of the enemy to surrender. She proved to be the C.S.S. *Juno*, manned by a crew of 50 men, and protected outside and in by cotton bales. She also had a torpedo projecting from her bow for the purpose of blowing up any vessel she might strike. She immediately returned to Charleston Harbor, with my launch in tow, much injured from the collision, and transferred us to C.S. ironclad *Chicora*, Captain Tucker, commanding. On the following afternoon we were sent to Charleston jail, where found two of my boat's crew who were knocked overboard from the *Juno*, and swam to Sullivan's Island, where they were taken prisoners."[3]—Editor]

General Pierre G. T. Beauregard, overall Confederate commander at Charleston (Library of Congress).

Sometime later it was decided to load the *Juno* with cotton, account of the Navy Department, and I was ordered by the flag Officer to have her engines and boilers in condition to leave Charleston on a certain date and go out as her engineer officer. I reported my Department ready and was waiting to load the cotton, when I was sent on an expedition to North Edisto in command of the torpedo boat *David*, and while away on that duty was unable to get back in time to take

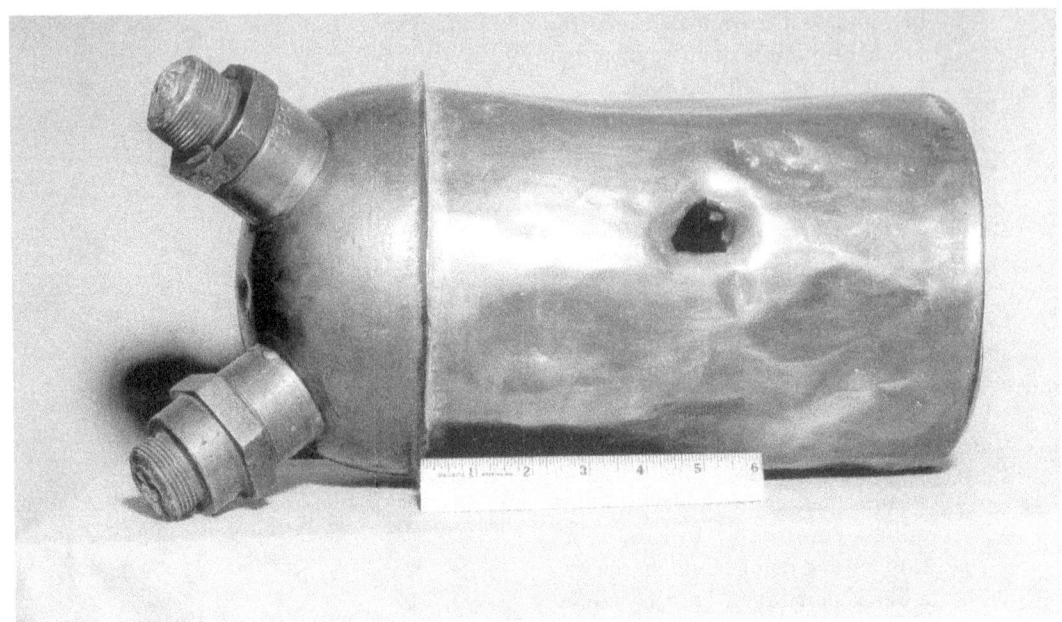

Two Confederate spar torpedoes recovered after the war (West Point Museum).

6. The CSS *Juno*

her out, and H. [Hugh] Clarke, of the *Chicora* was placed in charge, the *Juno* leaving Charleston the night after my return.

Flag Officer Tucker informed me of H. Clarke's being in charge of the engines, but said that if I wished, he would change the orders.

H. Clarke was a good engineer and had his family to care for on the salary of First Assistant Engineer. I had turned over to him my right as a commissioned officer for commutation on the Commissary, and was to take the ship, if I so desired, when she returned. One not acquainted with the condition of things at Charleston, as well as in the whole South, might imagine I was lacking in patriotism, but the truth was we had got to the condition of turning one suit inside out when we wished a change, and I was anxious to replenish my wardrobe. While on this subject, will say the last pair of boots bought by me before the surrender cost $250.00, and a new suit was not thought of.

H. Clarke put his family in my care until his return.

> [Hugh Clarke was appointed a first assistant engineer in the Confederate Navy on July 1, 1861. He had served on the CSS *Patrick Henry* and at Drewry's Bluff before coming to Charleston.[4] — Editor]

The *Juno* went to sea before midnight, and some time afterwards news came of the picking up at sea of Engineer H. Dent and Pilot William Burke, who had clung to a section of the bridge of the *Juno*, when she parted amidships in the Gulf stream, the same night or morning, and went to the bottom, Dent and Burke being the only ones who were saved. They were picked up by a small schooner about twenty-four hours after the loss of the *Juno*. Lieutenant Porcher was an excellent officer and a careful one. Undoubtedly the *Juno* was overloaded fore and aft, as her weakest part was amidships. The Flag Officer lost his son on the ship, also.

I was on special duty away from the city at times, and as there was yellow fever at Wilmington, Flag Officer Tucker permitted me to start a subscription in the fleet for Clarke's family. When Theodore Stoney and the merchants of Charleston heard of it, they most generously raised and turned over to me for the family about $4,500.00 while we got $500.00 from the Navy. Dr. Ravenel also obtained transportation to their home in Virginia, — another illustration of the generosity of the people of Charleston.

> [The *Juno* had been renamed *Helen*, and on the stormy night of March 9, 1864, she slipped out of Charleston with 220 bales of navy cotton on board. She was under the command of Lieutenant Porcher and had a crew of 30 including the son of Commander Tucker. Once she cleared the coast, heavy seas were encountered. At daylight a serious leak was discovered and Porcher decided to lighten the load by dumping 60 bales of the precious cotton overboard. The pumps were started, but soon the wind reached gale force and the little *Helen* was in desperate straits. By early afternoon the pumps could no longer keep pace with the rising water and soon the furnace was flooded and the fires put out.
>
> The crew attempted to set some sails in the howling wind, but with little suc-

cess. Now dead in the pitching sea, the strain on the water-logged hull was too much and she broke in two. The bow section disappeared almost immediately beneath the waves, but the stern section stayed afloat long enough for Porcher and some of his crew to launch a lifeboat. Tragically, it capsized, spilling the men into the turbulent sea.

The next day another blockade runner, the *Petrel*, which had left Charleston the night after the *Helen*, was drawn to the area by the sight of cotton bales floating on the water. Miraculously, they found Engineer Dent and Pilot Burke clinging to some wreckage from the pilot house. The two exhausted men were taken aboard and carried safely to Nassau, but the remainder of *Helen's* crew, including Porcher and Commander Tucker's son, had perished in the angry sea.[5] — Editor]

7

More Torpedo Attacks

Being in command of the *David*, with orders to make any changes I thought best, I had an attachment made that would permit the lowering of the torpedo to any depth, just before striking. Then we had ½ inch steel placed over the hull above the water line, also an adjustable cap over the stack to prevent the water from passing down, as it had done when attacking the *New Ironsides*.

[Tomb does not relate this operation in his memoirs, but during this time another type of torpedo boat was operating out of Charleston Harbor — the submarine *H. L. Hunley*, commanded by army lieutenant George E. Dixon. The *Hunley* was hand powered and Dixon found that by the time his men had propelled the submarine out to sea they were totally exhausted, so much so that there was a very real danger that they would not be able to return before daylight. As a consequence, Dixon requested to be towed to beyond Fort Sumter where his crew would then take over.—

In response to this request, Commander Tucker ordered Tomb to assist the *Hunley* with the *David*, and soon towing operations began. Tomb would tow the submarine, weather permitting, one to two miles out to sea where the tow line would be cast off, and the *David* would proceed on her own sortie or return to the harbor.

After several of these nightly forays, it was learned that the Federals had deployed an elaborate system of chain booms around their ironclads, which, in addition to being very dangerous for the submarine and the *David*, most surely would explode the torpedoes prematurely. In spite of this, Tomb continued his nightly missions into early January 1864, towing the *Hunley* well out past Fort Sumter on dark nights when the sea was relatively calm.

On one of these nocturnal sorties, both the *Hunley* and the *David* came quite near meeting disaster. At some point in the tow, Tomb ordered the *David* stopped for an unexplained reason. As the two vessels sat gently rocking with the swells, the *Hunley's* torpedo, which was being towed on a rope, came drifting up along-

The submarine boat *H.L. Hunley* on a dock in 1863 (Naval Historical Center).

side. The towline became entangled in the torpedo boat's rudder assembly, and Tomb and Dixon watched in horror as the glistening black explosive canister, its sides bristling with Captain Lee's fuses, drifted closer and closer. The torpedo scraped against the side of the *David*'s wooden hull and everyone held their breath. A crewman from the torpedo boat dived into the icy water, untangled the line, and pushed the torpedo away. It was a near miracle that both boats were not blown to pieces.

This would be the *David*'s last tow of the *Hunley*. Tomb later recounted that after submitting his report, Commander Tucker refused to allow the torpedo boat to be put at further risk and canceled the towing operations.[1]—Editor]

When ready for duty, I was ordered to North Edisto [River] to attack the U.S.S. *Memphis*, at anchor at that point. At this time I was also attached to the *Juno*, getting her ready to run the blockade, with a load of cotton for the Navy Department.

The *David* left Charleston on the 3rd of March, 1864, Chief Engineer J. H. Tomb, in command, Pilot J. W. Cannon, A. Coste, and Fireman James Lawless.

Captain Stoney was to have a section of artillery go down to the island to support us and assist us in getting away after we struck her.

Leaving Church Flats on the 4th of March, 1864, we proceeded on our way to North Edisto. When within plain sight of the *Memphis*, about midnight of the fourth, the pump gave out, and we had to return up the river to repair it.

Top: The *David* prepares to tow the submarine *H.L. Hunley*. *Bottom:* The submarine *H.L. Hunley* about to cast off after being towed out to sea by the *David*. (Courtesy of Dan Dowdey.)

The next night at about the same place and hour the pump failed again. I decided to make fast to the marsh, let the steam go down, and make repairs.

At 12:30 P.M. the 6th, we proceeded in the direction of the *Memphis*, whose lights were plainly in sight from our position up the river. When close aboard they hailed us, and since we paid no attention to their hail, they began a rapid fire with

The USS *Memphis* (*Official Records Navy*).

their small arms. As we were so near, they could not make use of their big guns or howitzer. The hail of shot struck the steel covering of the *David*, and did us no harm as every shot glanced. The next moment the *David* struck the *Memphis* under the port counter some 8 feet below the surface, and it was a splendid blow but did not explode the torpedo.

We then turned to port and came at her on the starboard quarter, but as the *Memphis* was working her engine and going ahead pretty fast our blow was but a glancing one. We passed under the counter and carried away a portion of our stack, but did not explode the torpedo. Realizing that we could do nothing more under the circumstances as the *Memphis* was well on her way, we turned up stream. The *Memphis* then opened fire with her heavy guns, but all her shells passed well beyond us.

[The official report of Acting Master R. O. Patterson, commander of the *Memphis*, adds additional insight into Tomb's attack:

U.S.S. MEMPHIS,
North Edisto River, South Carolina, March 6, 1864.

SIR: I have the honor to report that an attempt has been made by the rebels to blow up this ship, but am happy to state did not succeed. At 1 A.M. a torpedo boat was discovered about 50 yards distant, approaching us rapidly on the port quarter, from up river. We immediately beat to quarters and slipped the chain; in an instant the torpedo was under our port quarter, and we could not bring a gun to bear on her. The watch being armed at the time, we were enabled to concentrate a rapid fire with muskets, revolvers, and pistols down upon her, and into what looked like a hatchway, nearly in the center; the rapid firing seemed to stop her progress, and, dropping about 12 feet astern, in an instant she darted ahead again and at the same time we rang to go ahead, and our propeller, I think, must have caught and broken some of her gear, as she appeared to be disabled and drifted up river. In a few moments they showed a light, at which we fired a 12-pounder rifle shot; she then disappeared and an armed boat was immediately dispatched to search for and capture her if possible, but returned without success. This torpedo boat was about 25 feet long, painted lead color, and in appearance was like a ship's boat in the water, bottom up.

I am, sir, very respectfully, your obedient servant,

R. O. PATTERSON,
Acting Master, Commanding.

COMMODORE S. C. ROWAN,
Commanding, South Atlantic Blockading Squadron.[2]—Editor]

Arriving at Church flats, and making an examination of the torpedo we found that the first blow was a good one as the tube was smashed perfectly flat, and glass tube containing acid was broken, but being a defective tube, [it] did not explode. The second blow was not a good one, as the tube was but slightly bent, and glass tube not broken.

> [Upon learning of the attack and the failure of the torpedo to explode, Captain Francis Lee was incensed and fired off an angry letter to General Beauregard, which read:
>
> "General: It is reported that on Saturday night, March 5, 1864, Engineer Tomb, C.S. Navy, in charge of the cigar torpedo boat *David*, struck an armed vessel of the enemy in the North Edisto, but failed to destroy her in consequence of the torpedo not exploding. As this occurrence may disturb the confidence heretofore felt in the torpedoes prepared by me, I deem it due to myself to state that about 10 days since I saw Engineer Tomb, and in the presence of Mr. Theodore Stoney, I distinctly told him that the torpedo then on the *David* could not be relied upon, it having been exposed for the last six months to every vicissitude of weather and climate. I further told him that I would furnish to the vessel a new torpedo, thoroughly tested, and that could be relied upon. Notwithstanding this advice, Mr. Tomb went on the expedition above reported without the slightest knowledge on my part, and carrying the old torpedo. Under these circumstances it is scarcely necessary to ask why the expedition proved fruitless.... With the facts as above stated it may readily be determined whether the disaster may be most fairly attributed to a failure of the torpedo prepared by me, or to a willful disobedience to commonsense instructions on the part of Engineer Tomb."[3]—Editor]

After waiting some time for orders and not getting them, we returned to Charleston, and I reported to Flag Officer Tucker, and was told that the *Juno* would sail that night with Engineer Clarke in charge, as nothing had been heard of the *David* since she left Charleston, and the *Juno* had to sail that night. This was a great disappointment to me, but as stated in previous account of the *Juno*, it was a narrow escape.

The *David* enters one of the numerous rivers near Charleston (courtesy of Dan Dowdey).

The *David* was kept ready for service, and we would occasionally go down the harbor on picket duty, but outside of an unsuccessful attempt to reach the *Wabash* on the night of April 18th, we did not strike another ship.

My orders from the Flag Officer were to watch out for the monitors. If they should run into [the harbor] keep out of the line of fire as much as I could, and do all the execution possible with the *David*.

A combination torpedo expedition was gotten up by the army. The officers in command of three torpedo boats, (built by a company) were army officers, and I joined the expedition in command of the *David*.

It was a decided failure due to lack of organization, and on reaching Mosquito Island, the point we were to start from on our attack, all but the *David* were out of commission. Two had returned to Charleston disabled, and the third went to the bottom in 20ft of water while at anchor at Mosquito Island, through neglect on the part of the commander, who, after fixing the torpedo, anchored the boat so near the shore that she grounded. When the tide went out she slid into deep water and went to the bottom, leaving the *David* to finish the business.

[Since March 14, when a reconnaissance party visited the mouth of the Ashepoo River and reported two enemy warships anchored there as blockaders, General Beauregard had hoped to mount an attack utilizing several torpedo boats. The larger of the two ships was the USS *Wabash*, a 4,650-ton screw frigate mounting 45 heavy guns. Beauregard now had his opportunity. In mid–April of 1864, three torpedo boats, including the *David*, left Charleston and threaded their way through various streams and tributaries finally reaching the Ashepoo River on April 18. Two of the boats were army and were commanded by Captains Augustus Duqucron and E. R. Mackay. (Tomb, in his memoirs, indicates that there

The USS *Wabash* (above). Tomb attempted several attacks on her but without success. A "David"-type torpedo boat (below) abandoned when Charleston was evacuated. (Naval Historical Center.)

were three army boats.) The third boat was the original *David*. Unfortunately, two army boats suffered engine problems (and if there was a third, it evidently sank) and had to turn back, but the determined Tomb continued on alone. Later that night he headed for the *Wabash*.

At 150 yards he was spotted by one of the frigate's lookouts. Ensign Craven, officer of the deck, opened fire with musketry, beat the gong for general quarters, rang four bells for the engine room to start the engines, and ordered the starboard battery to open fire as soon as they were ready. The chain was slipped and Federal tars rushed to their stations as the giant warship, black smoke pouring from her funnel, began to move. The *David* was now only 40 yards distant when one of the starboard guns roared, sending a round shot splashing very near the torpedo boat. A second gun fired and the Union gunners believed they had scored a direct hit, for the dreaded torpedo boat had disappeared into the darkness.[4]

Although Tomb and the *David* were not hit as the Federal gunners supposed, he, nevertheless, had his share of problems. The sea was rough and the *David* took on water faster than could be bailed. Even moderate swells swamped the cuddyhole, and water in the bottom of the boat was creeping up toward the boiler. Tomb decided it was too much and broke off the attack. Twice more, according to Tomb, he headed for the *Wabash*, but the heavy sea prevented his completing the attack.[5]—Editor]

We proceeded down to the bay next night, but saw nothing of the enemy, and while Cannon was willing to go farther and hunt them up, I thought it best after such a failure, to return. The enemy had evidently heard of our intended attack, and I was afraid they might capture the *David*. It was a great satisfaction, however, to feel that the little *David* was not on the list of the missing. It is impossible to do much on an expedition of this kind, unless there is some one officer in charge of the boats.

8

The CSS *Leesburg*

When the *Atlanta* passed out of Savannah to attack the monitors in Warsaw Sound, she was captured by the Yankees after she had run aground, being unable to train her guns on the enemy. It was then that Flag Officer Tucker gave me the following orders:

Sir:
Proceed to Savannah by special train, or otherwise, and report to Flag Officer Brent for instructions to carry out the orders given you, etc.———.

My verbal orders were to see Flag Officer [Thomas W.] Brent and make an attempt to blow up the *Atlanta* before she was floated or out of the Sound. I went to the Isle of Hope and, after making an examination, found that the *Atlanta* was afloat and on her way to Port Royal.

The loss of the *Atlanta* was severely felt by Flag Officer Tucker. She was to be an addition to the fleet at Charleston, and I was in hopes of destroying her before she was floated, as they would be less apt to stop my boat here than off Morris Island.

[CSS *Atlanta*, one of the finest ironclads built in the Confederacy, was 204 feet in length and mounted two 7-inch and two 6.4-inch Brooke rifles. She was originally the English blockade runner *Fingal*, built at Glasgow, Scotland, in 1861. The *Fingal* was procured by the Confederate government in 1862 and converted into an ironclad ram at Savannah by Messrs. N. and A. F. Tift. This ironclad, with Commander William McBlair in command, was active at the Savannah station, usually flying the flag of Commodore Tattnall, who lived ashore in Savannah. On June 17, 1863, she ran aground in Wassaw Sound, Georgia, and was captured at dawn by the monitors USS *Weehawken* and USS *Nahant*. Pulled from the sandbar by the Federals, she was undamaged and later incorporated into the U.S. Navy as the USS *Atlanta*.—Editor]

Top: The CSS *Atlanta*. *Bottom:* After having run aground, the *Atlanta* was forced to surrender on June 17, 1863. (Naval Historical Center.)

When I reported to the Flag Officer, I was made a member of a board to test a number of torpedo boats built by the merchants of Charleston, about the same style as the *David*.

[Unfortunately, the exact number of David-type torpedo boats built by the Confederacy is unknown. Most, if not all, detailed records concerning their con-

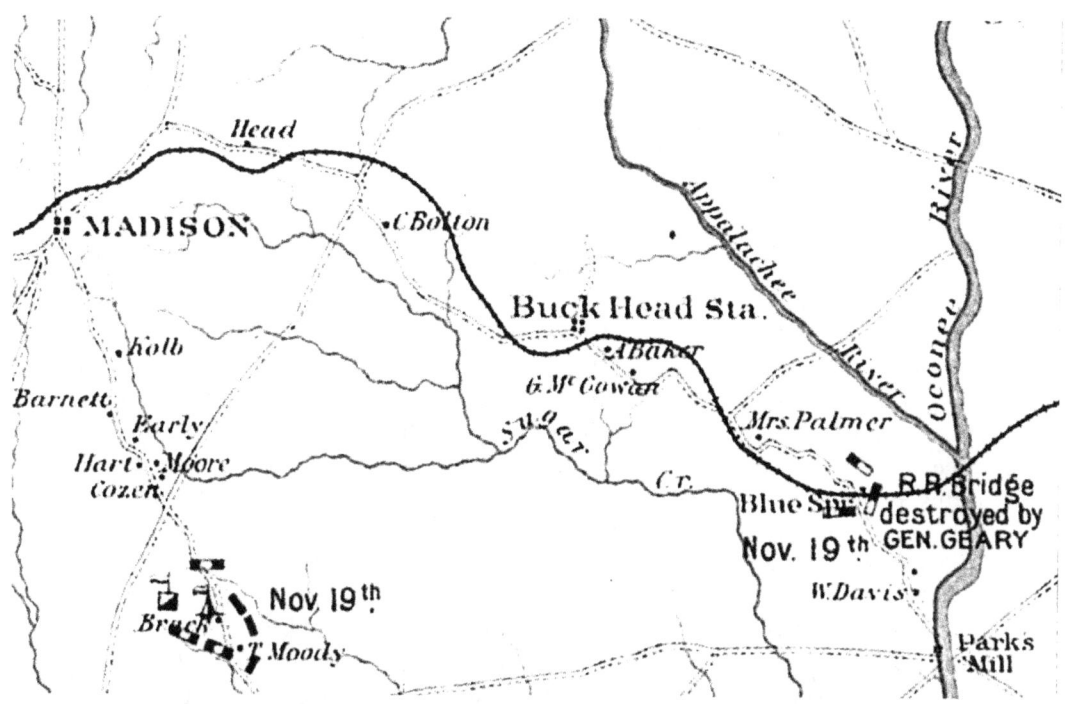

Wartime map of the area where the Georgia Central Railroad crossed the Oconee River (*Official Records*).

struction and operations were destroyed at the end of the war to prevent any possible Federal reprisals against those who employed "an engine of destruction not recognized by the rules of war." From documentation contained in both the Navy and Army Official Records, along with private correspondence, it is known that additional Davids were built at Charleston and at Stoney Landing on the Cooper River, which was the construction site of the original *David*.

Even before Tomb's attack on the *New Ironsides*, David Ebaugh had begun construction of another David at his landing on the Cooper River. With the partial success of the attack, other Davids were laid down at various locations in and around the city. It would take time, however, for these to reach operational status given the shortage of materials and skilled labor that always plagued ship construction in the South during the war.[1] — Editor]

While preparing for this, I was ordered to report to Major General Jones for special service in Georgia, viz: to blow up the Oconree bridge at the time Sherman would reach it.

I reported to General [Braxton] Bragg, and after some delay, got what I wanted in the way of powder etc., and also a large wagon and guard to protect the ammunition etc., that I had along. Unfortunately due to the delay caused by those in charge at Augusta, we did not arrive at the bridge in time. While waiting to hear from a guard I had sent ahead to a station which I think was called Mayfield, we got news that General [Judson] Kilpatrick and his troops had passed over, and were heading for Augusta. This was most disagreeable news to me and to Major Brown who was with me.

> [Tomb is probably referring to the Georgia Central Railroad bridge over the Oconee River near Griswoldville. After a brief skirmish, Kilpatrick's cavalry crossed there on November 23, 1864.[2]—Editor.]

In crossing a branch, our mules got stalled, and there was every chance of being captured by the Yanks. I sent Sergeant Davis up to the station for a couple of mules to assist us in pulling the wagon out, but he returned and reported that the old fellow was as hot as ----, and would not let us have a mule if he had one.

At this Brown and I went up and, while the old rascal did not express himself along that line, his wife was a terror, and said we were worse than Yankees as we and all of Wheeler's Cavalry, were nothing but butter milk cavalry, and that we stole all the fodder besides, and that Joe Brown the Governor would make it hot for us. At this [Major] Brown and I also got hot, but as we could do nothing to her, I picked out a bright looking darkey and taking him to one side, told him that he had mighty little time to bring out two mules, we knew that there were some on the plantation.

Sergeant Davis went off with him, and they soon came back with two good mules, and we pulled the wagon out, but held on to the mules and the darkey up to nightfall when we went into camp. The boy wanted to remain with us, but I gave him orders to return the mules to his master, though I did not much care whether he did so or not.

Before we got back to Augusta, we had to make a turn out of the line on which the Yankees were supposed to be heading, and not having either a commissary or a guard, had to forage on the "good people" along the road, and they were not all good by any means. There seemed to be a feeling that Joe Brown was more than the Confederate States so in one or two cases we had to take what we wanted, but as Major Brown had an order from General Bragg to seize all horses and mules along the road, he gave them an order on the C.S. Treasury.

While in the woods we came to a little cottage of three rooms. An old darkey saw that we were Confederates and opened the door. At least a dozen or more women came out all anxious to learn if the Yankees were near. We said no, but in truth we did not know ourselves, being in hopes that they were not, for it would have been bad for us if they were.

The next day was Sunday. As we were approaching Augusta, we came to a plantation; the house was some distance from the road, and being quite hungry, we asked the boy if we could get anything to eat there. He thought that we were Yankees, as I had on a dark blue overcoat, and both the Major and the Sergeant had on the Yankee blue that had been doing duty on both sides of Mason and Dixon's Line. He said his mistress did not sell meals.

We rode up to the house, and as we reached the porch, a very nice looking woman came out, while we could see two young ladies watching us through the window curtains. Brown did the talking and needed no better help than his stomach gave him, for we all had a good appetite. She evidently thought that we were

Yankees, who had left the main body, and were foraging. She said that she would have a meal prepared for us by the servants, but that she was not selling meals and requested that neither our men nor ourselves would cause any trouble to her or to those who were on the plantation.

When she found out from Brown, however, that we were just hungry Rebs, and not Yanks, it was like a ray of sunshine after a storm. She and her daughters had a fine layout of fried chicken, and other luxuries, on the dining room table, that made Sergeant Davis smack his lips. He was able to see it but was not included in the party.

The mother had become very much interested in some item of news from Augusta that the Major was telling and forgot that he was hungry, so I took my seat and requested permission of the young ladies for Davis to take a seat also, which was granted. While I was busy with a chicken leg, one of the young ladies started to pour some whiskey from a jug into my glass, but I told her that I did not drink, so she gave it to Davis. He took it so swiftly that I did my best to keep the young ladies from giving him any more.

A little darkey who was watching us and holding the jug, thinking from my looks, perhaps, that I was afraid Davis would drink it all, came to my chair, and said quite loud, "Dar is lots mo' in de holler, Mars. Cap'n."

The young ladies explained that their father had a small still in the hollow, but for domestic use only, and expressed the hope that it would not cause them any trouble. I told them that as far as I was concerned their father might have a dozen stills. It seems there was a very severe law about making whiskey from corn, etc.

This was certainly a fine family. The woman were of a type to make a man fight, if he had the least disposition to run away—as we had been doing the last few days. Major Brown said that she did not mention Governor Brown once, but was Confederate all the way through,—such a contrast to the woman at Mayfield. Major Brown told her of his orders to collect all horses, mules, etc., along the line Sherman was thought to be marching, but we did not for a moment consider taking hers.

After a fine meal we proceeded in the direction of Augusta, with not a sign of our guard but Sergeant Davis, and the wagon containing our munitions, etc.

The next place we struck, before reaching Augusta and turning our stuff over to the quartermaster, was a little two-room cabin in the woods, with not a sign of a chicken. There was a hall between the two rooms, and in it three or four red-headed children from 2 to 7 years of age. The building was made of logs. The woman who came out was not at all pleasing in her reception but said she would fry some bacon and nothing more.

Brown called up one of the boys, who was working on long stalks of sugar cane, and remarked to me, quite loud enough for the mother to hear him, "I say Tomb, that is a bright boy and you can see there is something in him, etc."

The boy had red hair, and was no doubt full of cane juice, so Brown told the truth about him. Just then his mother came out and said, "If the gentlemen will wait, I will fry some chicken and make some corn bread." The "gentlemen" waited, and she gave us some sweet potatoes and coffee with long sweetening.

General Braxton Bragg (National Archives).

Major General William J. Hardee (*Photographic History of the Civil War*).

I was very much disappointed at the result of the expedition, for I felt sure the bridge could have been blown up as the artillery passed over it. General Bragg was no doubt a brave officer, but things were moving badly about Augusta.

I reported to Flag Officer Tucker, and was sent on to Savannah to report to Major General [William J.] Hardee for special service outside of that city.[3] When the place was evacuated by us, [December 21, 1864] and Sherman took possession, I returned to Charleston by land, walking part of the way, and reported to Major General Jones, by whom I was ordered to proceed to Augasta and take charge of the obstruction of the Savannah River, between Augusta and Savannah.

Arriving in Augusta, I reported to General [Birkett D.] Fry, and he was certainly a fine officer to take orders from. Major Tilton, Q.M. at Augusta, furnished me with a good horse, and I proceeded down the river road to meet the expedition under [Acting Master's Mate Samuel A.] Brockington at Shell Bluff.

[The Shell Bluff Battery was located approximately 40 miles south of Augusta on the Savannah River. On January 31, 1865, Captain William W. Hunter, com-

8. The CSS *Leesburg*

mander of the Savannah Squadron, issued the following order from Augusta, Georgia, to Second Lieutenant William W. Carnes, commander of the gunboat CSS *Sampson*:

"The commanding officer of the CSS *Sampson* will direct S. A. Brockington, master's mate, Provisional Navy C.S., to proceed with a boat and boat's crew down the Savannah River till he finds either the steamer *Amazon* or *Leesburg*. Proceed with one of these, with a torpedo boat and two of the torpedo corps with the steamer alluded to, and lay down the torpedoes at the position designated by the torpedo corps, and return with the steamer, boat, and boats crew and torpedo corps to this place. Have the officer and boat's crew provided with one week's rations."[4]—Editor]

Brigadier General Birkett D. Fry (National Archives).

I was not the best horseman in the world to begin with, and while riding out Broad Street to the river road, I ran into a lot of Rebs who had just returned from Hood's Army in Tennessee. They had been badly used up out there, and did not feel in the best of humor, so when I passed them one fellow remarked to another, "The Navy is falling back." I was not at all sure that I could keep my seat if a gun should go off, and felt satisfied that if it did I would go off myself. I had a couple of plugs of tobacco in my sack, and calling to the man who struck me as being the leader, I handed him the tobacco, and asked the news from Hood's Army. In that way I got out of trouble.

The poor fellows were looking badly used up and would make a remark about anyone that came along just to cause a laugh, and anyone who fell back on his position as an officer, was apt to lose what dignity he had left.

About sundown, feeling rather hungry, I rode up to the fence in front of a cottage, thinking that I would ask for a little fodder for my horse, and in that way perhaps get some for myself. As I reached the gate, two young ladies came out, and dismounting, I asked if I could get fodder for the horse. I found out afterwards that the blue overcoat was the cause of much trouble, always causing me to be taken for a Yankee officer.

I had some trouble in making them understand that I was a Confederate naval officer, but after doing so, was informed that Wheeler's Cavalry had cleaned out all the fodder belonging to the family and there was no butter milk either.

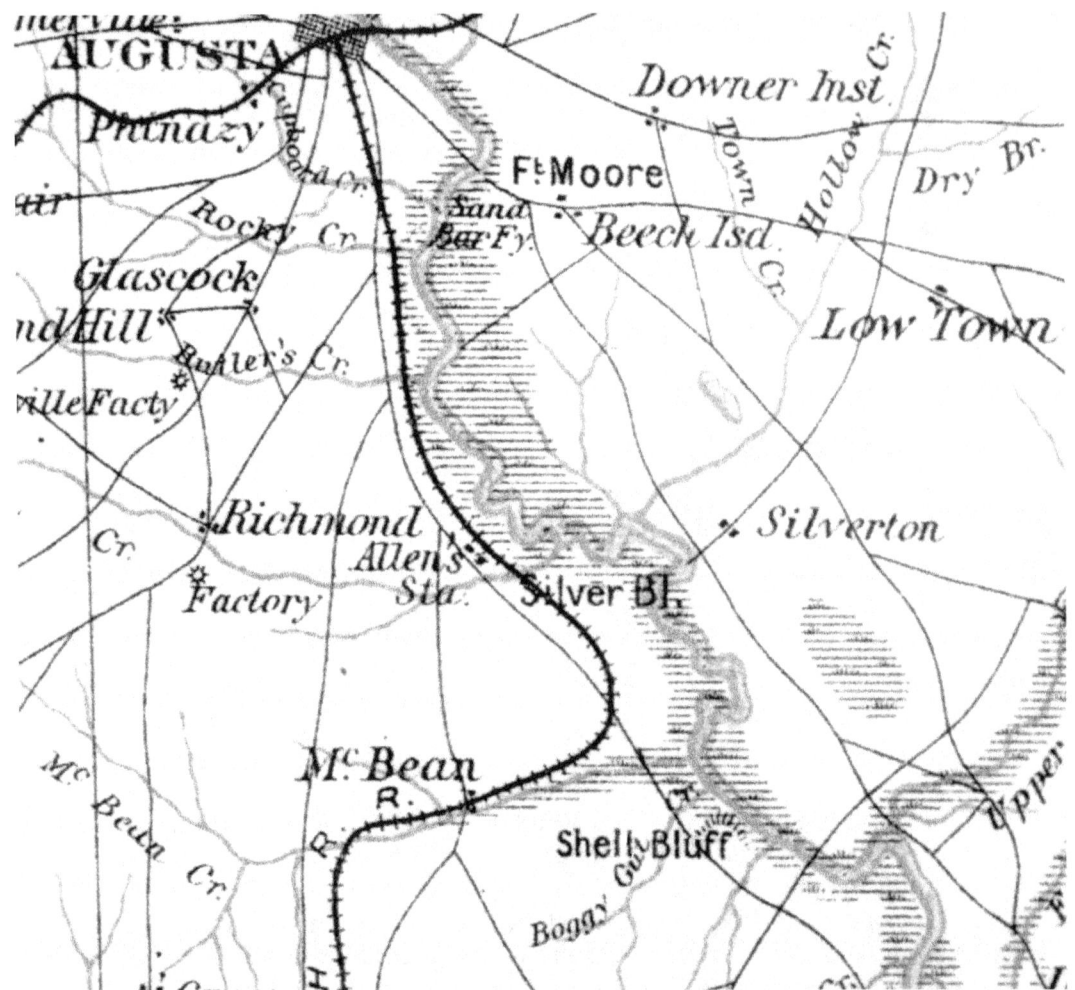

Wartime map of the Savannah River between Augusta and Shell Bluff (*Official Records*).

They said to come with them a short distance down the road and they would take care of the horse, but said nothing about me. This was soon cleared up however, as they had a boy take care of my horse, and then invited me into the house for supper.

At 9 P.M. I left, after a splendid meal, and a most pleasant visit, the family being more than kind. I gave them to understand that if any Yankees were coming up that way, I would do my best to let them know in time. They were related to General [David E.] Twiggs, and were from New Orleans, I think.

After some hours travel in the direction of Shell Bluff, I lost my bearings and taking off the saddle, made camp for the night, first looking out for the horse, who seemed to feel about as I did, tired out. I fell asleep and did not wake up before daylight the next corning, then proceeded in the direction of Shell Bluff, and there took command of the expedition blockading the river.

8. The CSS *Leesburg*

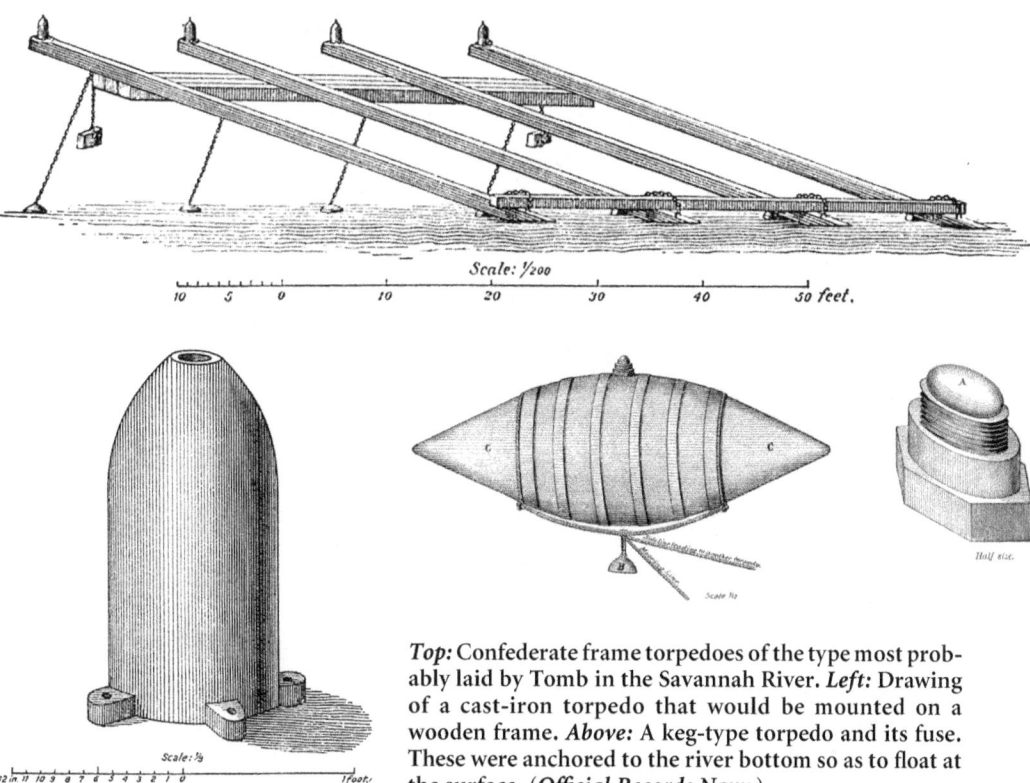

Top: Confederate frame torpedoes of the type most probably laid by Tomb in the Savannah River. *Left:* Drawing of a cast-iron torpedo that would be mounted on a wooden frame. *Above:* A keg-type torpedo and its fuse. These were anchored to the river bottom so as to float at the surface. (*Official Records Navy.*)

The steamer *Leesburg*, Captain Phillpot, was placed under my orders, and taking on a supply of torpedoes at Augusta, we proceeded down the Savannah River. Leaving the *Leesburg* at Shell Bluff, we got down a line at Catfish Cut, placing torpedoes some ten feet apart and three feet below the surface, as the river was gradually rising.

> [CSS *Leesburg* was a steamer employed in the Savannah River as a transport from 1862 through the end of the war. While Tomb mentions that "Captain Phillpot" was placed under his command, this was most likely the pilot, T. N. Philpot. The *Leesburg* was under the temporary command of First Lieutenant Joel S. Kennard.—Editor]

Returning to Johnson's landing, we found about 600 bags of corn, and 200 bales of cotton, C.S. property, gathered as tithe from planters. I reported this to General Fry, for as Sherman was likely to pass through S.C., he would take or burn it. General Fry said he had no authority to remove it, so when I took another load of torpedoes down, I took aboard about 300 bags of corn and enough cotton to make a breastwork on the *Leesburg*.

When I reached Augusta I turned it over to Major Worrison of the Quartermasters Department, but on my next trip brought up 250 bags. This I gave to Captain Howell, C.S.N., giving some part of it to a few families along the river who had nothing of the kind to plant. When passing around a bend in the river below Shell Bluff about daylight one morning on the *Leesburg*, we saw a canoe tied to the bank and a campfire. Sending Brockington in a boat with a guard, he found two Confederates in camp, sound asleep, with their heads resting on their saddles. When Brockington woke them up, they saw his blue overcoat, and the blue suits of the men who had taken them from the *Water Witch* captured below Savannah,[5] and they concluded the *Leesburg* was a Yankee gunboat, as she was painted black. They said that they belonged to Wheeler's Cavalry, and being sick of the war and good Union men, had gotten two days leave and then deserted. When brought aboard ship, they recognized Captain Phillpot, and saw they were in for it. I put then below, and when we got back from our expedition, put them ashore at Shell Bluff, with a report explaining who they were.

9

Badly Used Up

The next trip was delayed by lack of torpedoes, and while at Shell Bluff the steamer *Amazon*, Captain David Dillon, [civilian steamboat captain] came along side. Not wishing that he should in any way find out the position of the torpedoes, I put a guard at the gangway and prevented his coming aboard.

I reported to General Fry and while plotting the position of the torpedoes on the map, Captain Dillon entered the office. I turned up the map until he left. I then told General Fry my opinion of Captain Dillon. General Fry said that Dillon was a loyal Confederate, as he had brought his steamer in loaded with munitions of war etc., from Savannah, and could be depended upon in every way. I said Captain Phillpot was to be trusted as he was a good man, but Dillon was not, and there should be a guard placed on the boat.

I was granted leave for ten days while awaiting a supply of torpedoes from Charleston, and when I reported for duty, General Fry informed me that the *Amazon* along with a lot of cotton taken up along the river, also some corn, had been run into Savannah by Captain Dillon. He had put a corporal and three men aboard as a guard after I left, and they had reported that Captain Dillon and all but one guard had gone ashore at a lake, intending to get some corn whiskey at an old still. Captain Dillon returned for another jug and told the guard to take it to the camp, then he cut his lines and started down the river for Savannah. There were no other white men aboard and he made a run for Savannah. The river had risen since the last torpedoes had been put down, and the *Amazon* being of light draught, passed over them.

General Fry gave orders for me to take charge of a party, proceed down the river, and if she had not reached Savannah, to capture or burn her. We went below Hudson ferry and heard she was in Savannah, Dillon, cotton, and corn.

Captain Dillon was no doubt able to make a good thing out of his boat, as well as the cotton, and no doubt said he was a good Union man from the first. As we could not return to the *Leesburg* in the boats, we knocked out the bottoms and came up by land.

[U.S.S. *PONTIAC*,
Savannah River, Georgia, March 2, 1865.

ADMIRAL: I have the honor to inform you that the rebel steamer *Amazon*, lately employed by the rebel Government, steamed down the river this morning and gave herself up. She is in charge of David R. Dillon, who claims to be her owner; she has on board 75 or 80 bales of cotton, also claimed by him. Mr. Dillon assumes to be a citizen of Savannah and a Union man, and has embraced this the first opportunity to escape to the Union lines. I have taken possession of the *Amazon* and placed an officer and prize crew on board, and will await your further orders.

Very respectfully, your obedient servant,

S. B. LUCE,
Lieutenant-Commander.

ADMIRAL JOHN A. DAHLGREN,
Commanding South Atlantic Blockading Squadron.[1] — Editor]

Quite early one morning while we were on our tramp along the banks of the river, we saw two objects in the river, coming down in mid-stream. We found out that they were two canoes, each having one man aboard. White, who was from South Carolina, and whose people had lost everything through the destruction by Sherman, was anxious to shoot first, and then order them to surrender afterwards, but I would not permit it, so the two canoes came to the bank, a Yank in each with his gun. No doubt they thought from the way my few men laid along the bank, that we had a large party.

When I took them back from the bank to examine them, I found $17.00 in greenbacks, but no papers of any sort. One belonged to a Wisconsin regiment, and the other to a Michigan regiment. They were fine looking men. Both wore overcoats. We were a long way from Brier Creek, and there was not a man of our troop between that point and Savannah, except for our party of sailors, so there was every chance for them to escape. To keep guard over them was a little more than I cared for with the few men I had, so I decided to parole them.

These fellows were also opposed to the war and did not want to fight any more, just as our two Rebs had said they were. Brockington remarked it was wonderful how these fellows who were so tired of fighting would yet keep at it.

They offered me the $17.00, and their overcoats, but I told them to keep both. While I had no right to parole them without the consent of my superior officer up the river, I said I would swear [them] not to take up arms against the Confederacy, until legally exchanged. They felt so relieved at the idea that they were ready to swear anything.

No doubt they had information to take to the Commanding Officer at Savannah, as we could see from the fire and smoke, that General Sherman was destroying everything along his line of march through South Carolina. If it had been Sherman instead of the two privates, I would have been pleased to have White tumble him overboard. I saw what he had done in Georgia, when there was nothing in shape of an opposing Army to check him, but it looked worse for South Carolina. I sent two of the men to the river, and told them to sink one of the canoes, but let the Yanks have the other one and the two paddles. The last I saw of the Yanks, they were going like a streak down the river, and when my two men got back, each had on a Yankee overcoat, and said the Yanks were so glad to get away, that they gave them their overcoats. They said nothing about the $17.00. I thought that they would imagine that there was a large force of Rebs below Brier Creek, as they took us for a scouting party, and it would prevent them from coming very far out from Savannah, and so be a protection to our people, who were trying to put up their fences and homes.

No doubt Joe Brown felt satisfied with his work of changing Hood for Johnston. The people blamed Davis for all the trouble that we had in Georgia, but Joe Brown was the man who deserved most of the blame for our misfortune.

We did not see a sign of a Yankee gunboat at any time, showing that they gave us credit for being better prepared than we were, — just one 8-inch gun at Shell Bluff, and three lines of torpedoes put down after Savannah fell.

We went into camp on short rations, and the next day, as we were passing through a thick wood into an open space, we ran upon two old fellows splitting rails. At the time we struck them they were eating their noon lunch. I came up behind them, and when they caught sight of Brockington's and my blue overcoats, it must have given them a chill. Neither for a time said a word. After they got their wind, I asked the nearest one what chance there was for something to eat. By this time the men came up, and as they also had on "blue," it was clear to the two that we were Yanks, on our way up the river from Savannah. The oldest one said: "Colonel, I hope you will not take the little that was left us when your troop passed through to Savannah, there is little that is left us by them. I am too old to take an active part in this war, but I am a Georgian." About this time there was something about him that struck me as being familiar, and then I asked if his name were not Jefferson Roberts. This question almost knocked him off the log, as he thought he was to be arrested.

When I told him my name, however, and he saw that I was an old playmate of his daughter Georgia, he was delighted and soon had my whole party at his home a short distance away. It was such a pleasant visit, that I am sorry to say I forgot my orders to get back without delay, and was there two days before it struck me I was not laying torpedoes, and proceeded on my way to Augusta.

Mr. Roberts had lost everything of value, and was then trying to put in cultivation a portion of his ground. Georgia was as fine a woman as she had been a girl, and even with all the suffering and loss that had come to them, was yet hopeful of our success. As for myself, I hardly took time to think of our not being successful.

It was wonderful what the women of the South could suffer, and yet feel that success would come to us in the end. Brockington said if the men were as good as the women in the South, the result would not be in doubt at all.

The day I was leaving, I passed a man who was plowing in a field, and waiting for him to come near me, raised up and called to him. He looked in my direction and nearly had a fit, as it was one of those Rebs I had captured below Shell Bluff, and sent ashore with my report and a guard. His name was Davis and I asked him how it was that he was plowing, when he should have been shot as a deserter. He then told me that the officer at the fort had sent him along with others under guard to Augusta, but the guard being all "Home Guards" deserted in a body and went home, he also did the same, and had been at work ever since putting in a crop for his wife and four children, after that he intended to report for service.

I told him to come along with me, and if Miss Roberts would vouch for what he said, I might let him go for two weeks. Miss Roberts informed me that Davis was a good man in every way, and that hearing how badly off his family was, had deserted while on a two days leave, but said that he would return just as soon as he had his fence up and his crop planted.

I made out a paper that Davis had reported to me, and, as he could not join his regiment, was to report to the Commanding Officer at Wainsborro, Georgia, in twelve days, for duty. I gave him to understand he was liable to be shot for desertion, but while I had no right to give him these papers, it would help him out of any serious trouble. Davis was very much relieved at my doing this, but I told him that he might thank Miss Roberts for it and not me.

I was unable to see the family again for I was ordered to another duty after arriving at Augusta, but to this day the memory of that estimable family is with me. Mr. Roberts had not said he was opposed to the war when he thought I was a Yankee Colonel, but let me feel that he was a true Southerner, and not like some I struck who could be anything that suited.

Just before reaching Brier Creek we struck a large dwelling, and Brockington and I walked up and spoke to a fine looking fellow on the porch, requesting that we might be served with a meal, saying that we would pay for it; but he looked at us and said, "I can serve you but cannot take pay for it. I realize you can make me serve it, yet hope you will not disturb my people."

I saw we were up against it again, as he evidently took us for Yankees. I went so far as to show him my orders from General Fry, but he would not look at them, as he felt a Yankee could assume any orders or uniform to get a good meal. We got him to furnish us a large six-mule wagon and driver to get over the low ground below the creek.

The old man was Colonel Williamson and a gentlemen in every way, not a word about being forced into the war, etc. I had my doubts about his believing me, when I said his mules, wagon, and darkey would be back by sundown, but they were, I think, for I sent them back after reaching Brier Creek.

There was another old timer who was just the opposite to Messrs. Roberts and Williamson. As we came up to his front gate, my men being in the wagon, I met the old fellow and he was as sweet as sugar. When I requested some potatoes and bacon for the men, and some food cooked for Brockington and me, he told us to walk in. Passing the parlor, he called Brockington's attention to a life sized portrait of his departed brother, who, he said, judging from the short time he had seen us, looked so much like me, etc. Brockington could not see the least resemblance, all he could see was the bacon.

At the table the old fellow told me he had always been a Union man, and opposed to the war, and while he had a son in the Confederate service, he had not gone to the front, but was a recruiting officer at Wainsborro, Georgia.

It was my pleasure, when a boy in Savannah, to sample sugar from a number of hogsheads he had put out on the sidewalks, and frequently, while draining sweetness from the hogshead, would also feel a stinging blow on my anatomy that was unprotected and could not be watched.

I said nothing to ease his mind relative to my not being a Yankee colonel, but let him do all the talking. Had it not been for his wife, who was a nice old lady, and about half out of her head at the thought of our being Yankees, I would have given him a good send off; but the old lady let fall quite a number of dishes and I had not the heart to do it. I did make a note of the recruiting business, and when I got to Augusta reported it to General Fry, but do not know whether he went to the front or not, as we were being badly mixed up. Brockington said, "That old fellow will have a Yankee nightmare for the month."

The next experience was quite the reverse of this. About supper time we struck what we afterwards found out was Parson Wade, whom we soon made cheerful by telling who we were, and, after a most strenuous prayer, he gave us a splendid supper. Brockington said it was a good prayer because it was followed by such a fine supper, and my, how we did eat that chicken.

The Parson informed us that the news from below, was that the Yankees had been seen below Hudson Ferry, coming this way, and there were a number of sailors in the party. I made up my mind that the next time we went down, all the blue would be off. I was pleased to find that Mr. Wade was an old friend of my uncle, "Colonel Hamilton, of Dalton, Georgia," was the way he put it.

Striking the *Leesburg* we proceeded up the river in better condition than by marching. I gave Captain Phillpot orders to put ashore all the cotton we had for protection and to look after it himself, as he was the best man to have it, the way things were looking. Captain Phillpot was a fine fellow.

Upon my arrival at Augusta, I reported to Brigadier General Fry, and was referred by him to Major General [Pierce M. B.] Young, who had taken command of the Department. Much to my surprise, I was given orders by General Young to return and remove all the torpedoes I had taken so much trouble and risk to place in position in the river.

At first I could not believe that I understood his order, but he was most emphatic in having it done without delay, as General Sherman had ordered all the families of Confederate officers to leave the city, and they would come up the Savannah river by steamer. I told General Young, that except for our 8-inch gun at Shell Bluff, there was nothing to prevent the Yankee gunboats from reaching Augusta, and it would be best to bring them on land from Hudson Ferry to a point above the torpedoes, and then bring them up from that point on a steamer to Augusta. General Young would not do this, however, and told me to get my men ready, and see that the torpedoes were removed.

[On April 4, 1865, Commander Hunter had ordered Lieutenant Kennard to report to General Fry at Augusta and assume temporary command of the *Lees-*

Captain Sidney Smith Lee, director of the Bureau of Orders and Detail (Library of Congress).

burg for the purpose of transporting the families of Confederate officers that had been ordered out of Savannah by the Federal authorities. Kennard arrived on April 12. The families were to be picked up at Sister's Ferry above Savannah and transported up the river to Augusta. To do this safely, the torpedoes that Tomb had planted would have to be removed.[2] — Editor]

I saw General Fry and Flag Officer Hunter, both agreeing that it was ill advised to take them up. Then I went home to H. M. Carr, after sending a telegram to Captain S. S. Lee, C.S.N., requesting orders to proceed to the Gulf and assist in bringing in ordnance for General Gorgas, as I had accomplished the duty assigned me here in obstructing the river.

A David-type torpedo boat at the U.S. Naval Academy at Annapolis after the war (Naval Historical Center).

[Tomb wrote to Captain Sidney Smith Lee, chief of the Bureau of Orders and Detail. Lee was the older brother of General Robert E. Lee. Brigadier General Josiah Gorgas was chief of the Ordnance Department of the Confederate Army.—Editor]

I sent for a doctor, who, after a most careful examination and feeling my pulse, decided it was a severe case of malarial fever, and every indication of typhoid. With such a serious case as this on my hands, I felt that General Young could not send me on such a duty. He was fool enough not to see what the Yankees wanted in the way of a clear channel to Augusta, and it was not going to be my duty to take them up. There is danger enough in laying them, without the extra risk attending the fishing for them.

Lieutenant Kennard, C.S.N., was sent around to see how I was, and when I could start down the river, etc. As I was on the sick list and typhoid in sight, he saw it was a hopeless case. The doctor left positive orders that I was not to be disturbed nor eat anything for twenty-four hours, and the medicine to be taken every two hours. With all this serious trouble before me, I ate a good supper, put the prescription in the waste basket and went to sleep.

The next morning I received orders to report to Flag Officer Hunter, who gave me orders to proceed to the point designated, and furnished me transportation. When Captain Hunter gave me my orders, he also expressed his opinion about the wisdom of General Young's action in opening up the river. I paid my respects to Brigadier General Fry, who had more horse sense in an hour than his superior officer had in a lifetime, and yet General Young was a graduate of West Point.

I have no idea what was done with the torpedoes, but left $20 for the doctor. When he called to see his typhoid patient the next morning, no doubt he felt I was out of my mind as well as out of General Young's service.

That day I left for Florida, as all the ships at Charleston had been blown up and the city evacuated, and my little *David* also sent to the bottom.

10

The Cause Is Lost

There was a general feeling of depression, and it looked as if we were not to succeed in the struggle after so much loss of life and property.

There was more confidence at this time among the women than the men, as they would not believe that after all they had lost and suffered that the cause was lost.

The duty assigned me was to assist Captain Louis M. Coxetter to bring in ordnance and munitions for General Gorgas in charge of that department.

> [Coxetter had captained the privateer *Jeff Davis* at the beginning of the war and had later become famous as a captain of blockade runners. The intent was probably for Tomb to assume the position of chief engineer on one of Coxetter's runners. Considering the chaotic nature of events within the Confederacy at this time, it is amazing that Tomb's request had been approved by Secretary Mallory.
>
> Augusta, Ga., April 12, 1865.
>
> By order of the honorable Navy Department you will proceed to assist Captain L. M. Coxetter, in accordance with your request, and for that purpose you will proceed to the position necessary so to do. Respectfully,
>
> WM. W. HUNTER,
Flag-Officer, Commanding.
>
> CHIEF ENGINEER JAMES H. TOMB, Provisional Navy C.S.[1]—Editor]

Charleston being lost to us, I could not return there and report to Flag Officer Tucker. I never saw Flag Officer Tucker again. To one like me, who had been under [his] treatment, (even at times when I should have been reprimanded) it seemed a personal loss, besides there was the feeling of sadness that came to us all at the fall of Charleston, after one of the most gallant defenses ever made by a city, in this or any other country.[2]

I made up my mind that should the enemy enter Charleston while I was in command of the *David*, I would strike the first ship that made for the Flagship. I remember at one time having reported a hole in the boiler of the *Chicora* to Captain [James H.] Rochelle, when the signal was sent up from the flagship for the *Chicora* to take the place of the flagship *Charleston*, on duty below Sumter that night, and before I could correct it, they had sent that to the flagship, and we got orders to make repairs without delay, and report to the flagship. There was nothing for me to do but put on the man-hole plate, and, after doing so, start fires and report my department ready. When it came to Captain Rochelle, and through him to Flag Officer Tucker, I was quietly informed that it would be better for me to be a little more explicit in the future, but as Captain Rochelle had an engagement of some kind on shore that night, imagine that he did all he could for me.

Brigadier General Josiah Gorgas, Chief of Ordnance of the Confederate Army (Library of Congress).

[First lieutenant James H. Rochelle was normally the commander of the *Palmetto State*, but may have been temporarily in command of the *Chicora* at this point in Tomb's narrative. The ironclad CSS *Charleston* was built at Charleston, S.C., where she had been laid down in December 1862. She was launched and commissioned nine months later. She was not ready for service, however, until early in 1864 when she became the flagship of the Charleston Squadron with Commander Isaac N. Brown in command. The *Charleston* was set on fire and abandoned in Charleston Harbor when the city was evacuated by the Confederates on February 18, 1865.—Editor]

Another time when in command of the *David*, my orders were to report to the

First Lieutenant James H. Rochelle, commander of the ironclad CSS *Palmetto State* (Scarf, *History of the Confederate States Navy*).

Painting of Charleston Harbor by Confederate artist Conrad Wise Chapman. On the left is the ironclad *Chicora*, and to the right the *Charleston* (Naval Historical Center).

office of the Flag Officer at 9 A.M. I did this regularly, and at last concluded that I was of so little importance my not reporting would not be noticed. As I was working on the torpedo spar one morning, thinking best to fix it before reporting, the Coxswain came up and said the Flag Officer wanted to see me. I went up to the office, and, after waiting until some older officers got through, reported.

The Flag Officer waited until all the others were out of his office, and then turning to me said, "Mr. Tomb, have you not had orders to report here every morning at 9 A.M.?" I said, "Yes sir," but continuing said, "I thought it was not necessary to do so as there was nothing doing, and the torpedo spar was in need of repairs, etc."

"Suppose after this, Mr. Tomb, you let us do the thinking and you obey your orders. That's all Mr. Tomb."

Now it was considerate of him not to say this before the other officers, as he knew it was not from lack of respect, but of experience. After this happening I did more thinking than ever, and it was not lost by any means.

Once I reported a Commanding Officer as lacking in ability to fight his ship, and, while stating that there was no question of his courage, I said that he seemed to lose his head at times. I made this report while on special duty with the Army as it was correct, but evidently it was out of line in Naval Regulations, and Flag

Officer Tucker sent me on special service before anything was done about it. I afterwards realized my mistake, but not from any reprimand from him.

Small things like these show what goes to make a good officer, and when possessed by one in command, bring with it a feeling of affection that is stronger than respect and obedience.

Leaving Augusta, I passed through Atlanta on my way to Florida, and found that Sherman had certainly left a monument to mark his occupation of the city. At many points between Augusta and Atlanta, we passed old freight cars side tracked and occupied by women and children who had made their homes in them while refugees. I saw in one or two box cars a piano and a cow, I am sure that the cow was the more valuable to the refugees.

As we passed a small town called Forsyth, there were a number of men standing near the cars on the platform who had half-way decent hats, and as our train passed the soldiers reached out and captured the best part of the head gear. Once among the soldiers, a hat would change ownership two or three times before morning.

At Columbus I came near being captured by General Wilson, who was near there. When at Americus, on my way to Albany, I was so badly used up from walking and loss of sleep that I fell asleep on a lounge after a slight repast from a kind old lady, and before day, feeling the lounge in motion, woke up and found there were two old darkeys putting things into a wagon to take them back into the country, as they were under the impression that the Yankees would be there at any time, and that they would burn things up. I advised the old lady to stay right there as she was better protected than she would have been out in the woods.

Things were certainly looking bad for us all over the South.

At Albany I met Colonel Cooper Gibbs, who was assistant at Andersonville, and who was making arrangements to bring the prisoners to Jacksonville, Fla., for exchange, or to get them out of the state. Colonel Gibbs was a good man and officer, and I am sure, so far as he was able, gave the Yankee prisoners all the rations we had ourselves, as I had for each meal while in the trenches at Savannah, a piece of corn bread and a small sample of bacon. We could not take care of them, and it was the fault of the Yankee Government that they lacked food and clothing. It was certainly not ours.

When I arrived at Tallahassee, Fla., and reported to Major General [Samuel] Jones, I found there was little to do but wait for the end, as General Lee had surrendered in Virginia, and General Johnston was surrounded by Generals Grant and Sherman in North and South Carolina, but we could not tell just what was up, as there was so much conflicting news. The end came with the surrender of Johnston, and the entrance of Brigadier General Wilson, with Yankee troops, into Tallahassee.[3]

I was sent out to a Yankee Gunboat, off St. Marks, to inform the officers of the presence of General Wilson, and he could take all he could find of our navy, but up to this time I had not seen the first sign of a boat that could be called a gunboat. I remained aboard all night and was well treated, but felt so badly was glad to get ashore.

At this time while awaiting the approach of General Wilson, Major General Jones, issued an order to all officers and soldiers under his command to draw 60 days rations from the commissary. While at first not knowing what to do with it, I soon found a fellow who had a grocery store, which outside of a counter and some shelves, had not a sign of anything to sell but some tobacco, — so we made an exchange. He took my order for 60 days rations and I took his tobacco. This I turned over to the proprietor of the Leon Hotel to sell for me, and it brought me the magnificent sum of $7.50 in Yankee greenbacks.

Colonel Portlock, who was with me, would not bother with the rations.

We had nothing but Confederate paper to pay our hotel bill with, but, as the proprietor was a good fellow, and, like ourselves "in the soup," he took it as a souvenir.

Major General Samuel Jones, Confederate commander of the District of Florida at the end of the war (Library of Congress).

We had orders to report to General Wilson to be paroled, General Jones's Staff. Portlock, Dr. Minor and others were sent in by the way of Jacksonville, Florida.

Colonel Portlock was sent down here to report on the conduct of Wheeler's Cavalry, but up to the time the Yanks came and took us all in, we had not seen a member of Wheeler's Cavalry. The truth was that any renegade, who had a horse and a gun, would pass himself off as one of Wheeler's men, and as his command was badly scattered, it was easy to do this, and most of the butter-milk and fodder was taken by this class.

The parole was made out on May 16, 1865, and we started for Jacksonville partly by rail and the rest of the distance by wagon. When we reached Jacksonville, there was a dark cloud of Negroes over the city, as most all the soldiers were Negroes with white officers, and there was as much difference between them and the regulars as one could wish to see, and it gave them much pleasure to order us to move along and keep moving.

I called on a family named Samnis, and while for certain reasons knew that they did not feel perfectly at home, they were exceedingly kind, and gave me all the information possible about my family. As my brass buttons were not just the thing to go north with, I got a Mrs. Oakcus to cover them with black material of some kind, you might say they were "in mourning."

Jacksonville impressed me as a good town for a Reb to get out of, as the population there were mostly Yanks and nine-tenths of the rest were darkies.

10. The Cause Is Lost

We took passage on the old *St. Marys* for Port Royal, and arriving there had permission either to take up quarters at a small hotel, or draw our rations and cook them ourselves. We all went to the hotel, but captain Bryan, Dr. Minor, Brockington, and I decided we could not stop at the hotel in the condition of our finance, so we drew lots to see who would draw the rations, and, as luck would have, it came to me to be commissary.

So I went to a little restaurant in that beautiful city of sand hills and made a dicker with the proprietor. He agreed to furnish us with three meals a day, at fifty cents for the two, and he was to take the rations for the rest. I bagged my pride and shouldered my bag, and falling in with a long line of Yanks, and contrabands, received my rations and toted them to the restaurant and get my first good meal; for, considering one circumstance, the age of the beef, it was very good.

The next thing was quarters for the night, and we decided the hotel porch was just the thing. Dr. Minor, being the oldest, was given the most even surface and outside.

The next morning Portlock borrowed $1.00 to pay his hotel bill, and wanted to join our mess, but he was told it was full, so he got up another mess, and the restaurant man charged them .75 cts., in place of .50, and the best part of it was, Portlock had to tote the bag.

We left Port Royal on the transport *Argo*, and here we had another illustration of the character of soldiers who served through the war, but never fought. This class served out the rations or meal, and the percentage of darkies was fifty. We bought some coffee from the cook, at .50 cts. per four cups. We got badly left at the serving out of rations.

Standing one day near the galley, a Yankee soldier, who had evidently seen hard service, requested a chew of tobacco, and having a plug of "nigger head" left, handed it to him. He wanted to buy it, but I said I could not sell it, that he could have it as I did not use it.

This made us good friends at once, and he wanted to know if he could do anything for us, as he evidently saw how we had come out on rations, and his cheerfulness in using his kit each time there were rations, was the best return a man ever got for such a small favor as a plug of "nigger head" tobacco.

He told me he had been in Andersonville as a prisoner, and no doubt had suffered from lack of many things. Yet he could do a generous act for a Reb, while these fellows who had never been in battle, except as provost guard or commissary, had not the spirit to do it.

I understood he was from Boston, so I was made to confess that there could come something good from Massachusetts. Then too there was a uniform made for me by Simmons & Co., of Boston, Mass., that had Maryland buttons on it. It also did good service and when I turned it, it was just as good on the other side.

Arriving in New York, we received orders to line up on the saloon deck, and march to the P. M. [Provost Marshal] office. As I was anxious to reach Philadelphia, where I had friends, I requested Dr. Minor to answer to my name, while I took my coat off and went below, and assisted with baggage until I saw them pass out from the pier. Putting on my coat and side bag, I joined a Mrs. Gamble and daughter, who were on the steamer as passengers, and securing a hack, had the baggage placed in it and drove down to the ferry to take the train for Philadelphia.

When we arrived at the ferry landing, and asked the amount of fare, we were held up for two dollars. After paying, I looked up the bay and saw the *Argo* not over three slips from the ferry, while the rascal had taken over half an hour to reach it.

At this time I was in a hole. All I had was three dollars just before paying the bill, leaving a balance of only one dollar in my pocket. When Mrs. Gamble handed me five dollars to purchase tickets for herself and daughter, I went up to the ticket office and handed the agent five dollars. "Six dollars please, three each," he said. I told Mrs. Gamble that it was three dollars. She said it was $2.50 before the war, and very considerately requested that I tell her how much I paid for the cab. She then handed me the amount to buy the ticket and also the amount paid for the cab, for she said I did not need it, and it was for them. This just gave me the amount to buy my ticket, and not one cent left in my pocket.

When we arrived at Philadelphia it was quite dark, and after seeing them to the Continental Hotel coach, with baggage checks, I started up town to look for my friends. Mrs. Gamble wanted me to go to the same hotel, but I pleaded business, and said I would call on them and see if the baggage was all right. Turning up to Third and Walnut, I got a city directory, and found that the number was but 2200 or 2300 Locust St.

Taking my seat in the Walnut St. car, I took a good look at the conductor to see if I could stand him off for my 5 cts., but he struck me as being a "cash or no ride" conductor, so I handed him a slim 5 cent piece that I had on my watch guard. As he put it in a side pocket he remarked: "We have resumed specie payment again." I would not have parted with it for five dollars, as it was a souvenir of New Orleans, but I did not think that my uniform was the best to work the credit system on just then, with such a face as that conductor had.

I was fortunate in finding my friends at home, and the next day bought a suit of civilian's clothes, that made me look like a good citizen of Phila.

A few days afterward, I heard there would be a lot of Rebs at 18th & Market Sts., on their way south, and cleaning out all there was left of my tobacco and what little change I could muster, I passed it to them as they come along. The poor fellows were looking badly, and with a lost cause and desolate homes to receive them, what was there to cheer them up? The expression of gratitude from them for so small s favor, would have been more strongly expressed, had they known that I was a poor devil of a Reb like themselves.

Dr. Minor, who came with me on the *Argo*, had the magnificent sum of $100 in gold, and the way he got it was a little strange. He had sold one of his colored boys for that amount a short time before, and intended buying medicine and starting a drug store in Virginia.

Various Official Documents— Part A

Navy Department, Washington, D.C.
Official Reports from U.S.N. and C.S.N., from 1861 to 1865

Capture of *Wabash* launch, August 8, 1863.

C.S.S. *JUNO*,
Charleston, S.C., August 8, 1863.

The *Juno* had a large spar, with a 65-pound torpedo attached, and was sent down on picket duty below Fort Sumter at night. We had a cotton bale strapped to the stem, a few feet above the water line, to act as a fender if we had a chance to strike one of the enemy's ships. Lieutenant Philip Porcher was in command; master, C. Tucker; pilot, William Burk; engineer in charge, James H. Tomb; assistant engineer, C. Johnson. We laid below Fort Sumter, waiting, and had just started the engines ahead when a large launch came toward us and hailed us, ordering us to surrender, and the next moment fired into us from a 12-pounder howitzer in the bow. We immediately headed for her, striking her about amidships; but not having much headway on the *Juno*, the launch swung around to port, just forward of the wheel, and then boarded us. The *Juno* had no guns outside of a few small arms. All the engineer division with the balance of the crew fired upon them as they came over the rail. The officer in charge of the launch surrendered. As he came over the rail he had his sword in one hand and one of his boots in the other. One of my firemen got hold of the boot and I ordered him to return it. We marched them all aft below as prisoners. At this time there were three or four floating on the port side swimming. Lieutenant Porcher wished to pick them up, but the position of the ship was such we were afraid to stop the engines and had to continue into the harbor.

The next morning, when taking the launch over to the flag-officer to make our report, the officer, an acting master in the United States Navy, had little to say; but the coxswain, who was seated near me, remarked loud enough for his officers to hear him: "This comes from placing an officer in charge of a boat who gets you into trouble, but can't get you out." The officer said nothing.

JAMES H. TOMB,
First Assistant Engineer, C.S. Navy.[1]

Official report of the attack on the USS *Ironsides* by the torpedo boat *David*.

Charleston, S.C., October 6, 1863.

General: I have the honor to enclose copy of the report of Acting First Assistant Engineer J. H. Tomb, C.S. Navy, who accompanied Lieutenant Glassell in his expedition against the *Ironsides*. The report of Mr. Tomb is strictly correct and reliable.

Very respectfully, your obedient servant,

J. R. TUCKER,
Flag Officer, Commanding.

GENERAL G. T. BEAUREGARD,
   Commanding, etc., Charleston, S.C.

Report of Acting First Assistant Engineer Tomb, C.S. Navy.

Charleston, S.C., October 6, 1863.

SIR: I have the honor to report that on Monday evening, 5th instant, Lieutenant W. T. Glassell, Confederate Navy, in charge of the propeller *David* (a small submerged steamer), with the following crew, viz, James H. Tomb, acting first assistant engineer; Walker Cannon, pilot; James Sullivan, second fireman, started from the city and proceeded down the main Ship Channel, passing through the entire fleet of the enemy's vessels and barges until we arrived abreast of the U.S. frigate *Ironsides* at 8:30 p. m. We then stood off and on for thirty minutes waiting for the flood tide to make.

At 9 p. m., everything being favorable, and every one in favor of the attack, we headed for the *Ironsides*. When within 50 yards of her we were hailed, which was answered by a shot from a double-barreled gun in the hands of Lieutenant Glassell. In two minutes we struck the ship (we were going at full speed) under the starboard quarter, about 16 feet from her sternpost, exploding our torpedo about 6½ feet under her bottom. The enemy fired rapidly with small arms, riddling the vessel, but doing us no harm. The column of water thrown up was so great that it recoiled upon our frail bark in such force as to put the fires out and lead us to suppose that the little vessel would sink. The engine was reversed for backing, but the shock occasioned by the jar had been so great as to throw the iron ballast among the machinery, which prevented its working.

During this delay the vessel, owing to the tide and wind, hung under the quarter of the *Ironsides*, the fire upon us being kept up the whole time. Finding ourselves in this critical position and believing our vessel to be in a sinking condition, we concluded that the only means of saving our lives was to jump overboard, trusting that we would be picked up by the boats of the enemy. Lieutenant Glassell and the fireman (James Sullivan) swam off in the direction of the enemy's vessels, each being provided with a life preserver, and were not seen afterwards. The pilot stuck to the vessel, and I being overboard at the time and finding that no quarter would be shown, as we had called out that we surrendered, I concluded it was best to make one more effort to save the vessel. Accordingly, I returned to her and rebuilt my fires; after some little delay got up steam enough to move the machinery. The pilot then took the wheel and we steamed up channel, passing once more through the fleet and within 3 feet of a monitor, being subjected the whole time to one continuous fire of small arms, the *Ironsides* firing two XI-inch shot at us.

The pilot (Mr. Cannon) has won for himself a reputation that time can not efface, and deserves well of his country, as without his valuable aid I could not have reached the city.

The conduct of Lieutenant Glassell was as cool and collected as if he had been on an excursion of pleasure, and the hope of all is that he may yet be in safety.

The fireman (James Sullivan) acted in a manner that reflected credit upon himself, having remained at his post until relieved by me.

Very respectfully, your obedient servant,
J. H. TOMB,
Acting First Assistant Engineer, C.S. Navy.

FLAG-OFFICER J. R. TUCKER,
Commanding — Naval Forces Afloat, Charleston, S.C.[2]

Extract: Note book records; U.S.N., and C.S.N., Records.
Washington, D.C.

The *David* was repaired, a new spar attachment was placed on her so as to permit of the lowering of the torpedo to any depth from the interior of the boat. We also placed one-quarter steel over her above the water line and attached a cap over the stack to keep the water out after an explosion.

When the *David* reported to the flag-officer for duty his orders were to watch for the enemy in case they made an attempt to run into the harbor, and use the *David* to the best advantage, keeping out of the line of fire as much as I could, and watch for a chance to use the torpedo.

On the 6th of March, 1864, the *David* made an attack upon the USS *Memphis* in North Edisto. Captain Theodore Stoney had a section of artillery to go down to the island by land to assist us.

The night of the 4th we got near enough to the *Memphis* to see her lights, but our pumps failed to work and we returned up the river.

The next night about the same hour and spot the pumps again failed to work. We made fast to the marsh, and after making repairs, again proceeded in the direction of the *Memphis*.

At about 12:30 a.m. [March 6], as we came within hailing distance, they hailed us, but we paid no attention to their hail, and the next moment they opened on us with small arms, the shot striking the steel cover did no harm. The next moment the *David* struck her on the port quarter about 8 feet below the surface. The blow was a good one, but the torpedo failed to explode. We then made a turn to port and came back at her striking her on the starboard quarter. At this time the *Memphis* was going through the water at good speed and the blow was a glancing one, passing under her counter, taking a portion of our stack away, but the torpedo failed again to explode.

Realizing we could do nothing more, we headed the *David* up the river. The *Memphis* at this time was using her heavy guns upon us, but they did not come near the *David*, passing well overhead.

When we reached Church Flats and made an examination of the torpedo we found the first blow was a good one, as the tube or cap on that side was mashed perfectly flat, and the glass tube containing the acid was broken, but being a defective tube it failed to explode.

The second blow was not a good one, as the tube was slightly bent and the glass tube not broken. The expedition was a failure, caused by a defective tube. The torpedo held 95 pounds of rifle powder.

Chief Engineer James H. Tomb in command, and Pilots J. W. Cannon and A. Coste, and James Lawless, fireman.

We were detained at Church Flats two or three days waiting instructions from Flag Officer Tucker, but not receiving them returned to Charleston.

About April, 15, 1864 the *David* passed the bar in an effort to reach the frigate *Wabash*, but there was such a heavy swell that the *David* came near sinking. There was such a heavy swell that it rolled over her every time it headed for the frigate; so we had to return over the bar again, without accomplishing anything. There was very little buoyancy to the *David* on account of the ballast.

JAMES H. TOMB,
First Assistant Engineer, C.S. Navy.[3]

[Enclosure]

Charleston, S.C.
March 8, 1664.

GENERAL:

It is reported that on Saturday night, March 6, 1864, Engineer Tomb, C.S.N., in charge of the cigar torpedo boat *David* struck an armed vessel of the enemy in North Edisto, but the torpedo failed to destroy her in consequence of the torpedo not exploding.

As this occurrence may disturb the confidence heretofore felt in the torpedo prepared by me, I deem it due to myself to state that about ten days since, I saw Mr. Tomb, and in the presence of Theodore Stoney distinctly told him that the torpedo then on the *David* could not be relied upon, it having been exposed for the last six mouths to weather and climate.

I further told him that I would furnish the vessel a new torpedo thoroughly tested, and one that could be relied upon.

Notwithstanding this advice, Mr. Tomb went to the expedition above reported without the slightest knowledge on my part, and carrying the old torpedo.

Under these circumstances it is scarcely necessary to ask why the expedition proved fruitless. The most common precaution, indispensable to the proper use of all firearms not to rely on a charge of long standing has been neglected.

With these facts as above stated, it may readily be determined whether the disaster may be most attributed to a failure of the torpedo prepared by me, or to the willful disobedience of common sense instruction on the part of Engineer Tomb.

I have the honor to be, general, very respectfully, your obedient servant.

(Signed) FRANCIS D. LEE,
Chief of Engineers.

BRIG. GENERAL THOMAS JORDAN,
Chief of Staff, Charleston, S.C.[4]

My remarks to all of this were as follows:

Flag Office, Charleston, S.C.
March 8, 1864.

Respectfully referred to Chief Engineer, James H. Tomb C.S.N., for his information and comment.

Very Respectfully,
(Signed) JOHN R. TUCKER,
Flag Officer Command Afloat, C.S.N.

Charleston, S.C.
March 8, 1864.

Respectfully returned with the statement that no such conversation as reported by Captain F. D. Lee ever took place between us, and furthermore consider his communication altogether unwarranted and uncalled for.

Very Respectfully, Your Obd't Serv't.
(Signed) JAMES H. TOMB,
Chief Eng., C.S.N.

Captain F. D. Lee's communication was sent through Flag Officer Tucker, and it was returned through the same channel, and for that reason should have been on record with his; Captain Lee's Report.

It is hardly to be supposed that an officer going on such an expedition with the lives of his crew and the loss of his boat in view, would take a torpedo that had been reported defective and unfit for service.

The risk was ours and not Captain Lee's, and the only ground for his statement was, when in n general conversation a short time before this expedition, he suggested that I replace the torpedo in use with one containing a larger charge of powder, but nothing was said about the torpedo or tubes being defective. This had 95 pounds and he thought 120 pounds might be better, and that was the substance of the conversation.

Captain Lee evidently got my boat mixed with another boat using his torpedo.

(Signed) JAMES H. TOMB,
Chief Engineer, C.S.N.

P. S. Captain Lee afterwards personally acknowledged to me in the presence of Captain Theodore Stoney that he was in error, stating that it was the amount of charge and not the condition of tubes or torpedo, he had reference to. When going on an expedition the top plug was always taken out to see if the powder was dry, and in this ease it was found to be perfectly dry when we took out the tubes, and made an examination at Church flats, after the return of the *David* from her attack on the U.S.S. *Memphis*.

JAMES H. TOMB,
Chief Engineer, C.S.N.

Report of Rear Admiral John A. Dahlgren, U.S. Navy.
Regarding attack upon the U.S.S. *New Ironsides*, off Morris Island, S.C. by the Confederate Torpedo Boat David, Oct. 5, 1863.

FLAG-STEAMER *PHILADELPHIA*, October 7, 1863.

SIR: Another attempt to blow up the *Ironsides* has been frustrated.

About 10 o'clock on the night of October 5, some explosions, as if of small arms, were heard in the direction of the *Ironsides*; the duration was quite brief, and then all was still. As soon as I could reach the frigate, I learned that a torpedo had been exploded near the *Ironsides*, and that Acting Ensign Howard had been mortally wounded by a shot from the torpedo vessel.

In the morning it appeared that a man had been picked up, who admitted that he had been in the torpedo. His account was, that the vessel was shaped like a cigar, had a maximum diameter of more than 6 feet; length, he could not be sure of, but it was said to be about 50 feet. There were four persons in it. The torpedo contained 60 pounds of powder, was secured on a bar 10 feet long projecting from the bow, and immersed perhaps 6 feet.

The vessel left Charleston about dark on the evening of the 5th instant, passed down outside of us, and then, returning, made for the *Ironsides* and struck her fairly amidships. It was not quite 10 o'clock, and many officers were still on deck. The torpedo was seen approaching and hailed, when some shots were fired from her, one of which wounded the officer of the deck mortally; immediately the explosion followed, and the effect of the apparatus may be considered as complete, yet no impression is visible on the armor or exterior planking. The prisoner says that, fearing the explosion, he jumped overboard just as the torpedo was hailed.

After I had heard this prisoner, I learned that another had been taken, whom, however, I did not see, as the story of the first sufficiently explained the movements of the torpedo. About noon I learned from papers found on the last prisoner that he had been the commander of the torpedo, and was a lieutenant in the Confederate Navy. These papers (four in number) I transmit herewith, from which it seems that the vessel was called the "David," probably to point to the presumed success against the *Ironsides*, which was to enact the Goliath. The project, it appears, had also been regularly concocted, as one document is dated September 6. The report of Captain Rowan, the commander of the *Ironsides*, has not been received at this date.

How far the enemy may seem encouraged, I do not know, but I think it will be well to be prepared against a considerable issue of these small craft. It is certainly the best form of the torpedo which has come to my notice, and a large quantity of powder may as well be exploded as 60 pounds.

I was concerned for the monitors, and am now on the way to Port Royal for a day or two to see what can be done to arm those which are there against these machines. Captain Rowan is in command, and I gave personal instructions to the commanders of the monitors, which it is but just to them to say were almost needless. The vessels themselves should be protected by outriggers, and the harbor itself well strewn with a similar class of craft. Their three ironclads are so provided, and I do not doubt that when an attack is made by us there will be a number of these torpedoes at work on our vessels. The subject merits serious attention, for it will receive a greater development.

I wish that I could have transmitted the report of Captain Rowan, but it had not been received, and I desired to inform the Department as soon as possible.

The outside of the hull near the locality of the explosion was examined by the divers, and it is reported to me verbally that no impression of any consequence is to be seen, except, perhaps, the removal of some copper, which, by the way, has occurred in other places, from other causes, and so leave an opening to the worms.

I have the honor to be, very respectfully, your obedient servant,

JNO. A. DAHLGREN,
Rear-Admiral, Comdg. South Atlantic Blockading Squadron.

HON. GIDEON WELLES,
Secretary of the Navy, Washington, D.C.[5]

Special Orders,   Headquarters, Dep., South Carolina,
                                      Georgia, and Florida.
No. 186   Charleston, S.C., September 18, 1863.

VII. Lieutenant Glassell, C.S. Navy, having volunteered for the duty, will report to Brigadier General Ripley for special service against the fleet of the United States off this harbor. He will be assisted by Captain Theodore Stoney as first officer, James H. Tomb, engineer, and Charles Scemps and James Ables as assistants.

By command of General Beauregard.

JNO. M. OTEY,
Assistant Adjutant-General.

LIEUTENANT GLASSELL, C.S. Navy.

FLAGSHIP *CHARLESTON*,
Charleston, S.C., Sept. 22, 1863

SIR: You will assume command of the torpedo steamer *David* and when ready will proceed to operate against the enemy's fleet, off Charleston Harbor, with a view of destroying as many of the enemy's vessels as possible, reporting the results to me.

Very Respectfully, Your obedient servant,

JOHN R. TUCKER
Flag-Officer, Comdg. C.S. Naval forces, Charleston Harbor.

LIEUTENANT COMMANDING W. T. GLASSELL, C.S. Navy,
C.S. *David*, Charleston, S.C.[6]

Report of Captain Rowan, U.S. Navy,
commanding U.S.S. *New Ironsides*.

U.S.S. *NEW IRONSIDES*,
Off Morris Island, South Carolina, October 6, 1863.

SIR: I have the honor to report the circumstances attending the explosion of a torpedo against the side of this ship last night at a quarter past 9 o'clock.

About a minute before the explosion a small object was seen by the sentinels and hailed by them as a boat, and also by Mr. Howard, officer of the deck, from the gangway. Receiving no answer, he gave the order "fire into her." The sentinels delivered their fire, and immediately the ship received a very severe blow from the explosion, throwing a column of water upon the spar deck and into the engine room. The object fired at proved to be (as I subsequently learned from one of the prisoners) a torpedo steamer, shaped like a cigar, 50 feet long by 5 feet In diameter, and of great speed, and so submerged, that the only portion of her visible was the coamings of her hatch, which were only 2 feet above the water's edge and about 10 feet in length.

The torpedo boat was commanded by Lieutenant Commanding Glassell, formerly a lieutenant in our Navy and now our prisoner. He states that the explosion threw a column of water over the little craft, which put out the fires and left it without motive power, and it drifted past the ship.

Nothing could be seen from the gun deck, and to fire at random would endanger the fleet of transport and other vessels near us. The marine guard and musketeers on the spar deck saw a small object, at which a very severe fire was kept up, until it drifted out of sight, when two of the monitors, the *Weehawken* and *Catskill*, passed under our stern and were close to it, when it suddenly disappeared. Two of our cutters were dispatched in search of it, but returned without success.

I hope our fire destroyed the torpedo steamer, and infer the fact from the statement of Lieutenant Commanding Glassell, who acknowledges that he and Engineer Tomb and pilot, who constituted the crew at the time of the explosion, were compelled to abandon the vessel, and being provided with life-preservers, swam for their lives. Glassell hailed one of our coal schooners as he drifted past, and was rescued from a grave he designed for the crew of this ship.

Very respectfully, your obedient servant,

S. C. ROWAN,
Captain, Commanding.

REAR-ADMIRAL JNO. A. DAHLGREN,
Commanding, South Atlantic Blockading Squadron.[7]

Report of Admiral Dahlgren on effect of torpedo *David* on *Ironsides*.

(Confidential) U.S. FLAGSHIP *PHILADELPHIA*,
At sea, October 7, 1863

MY DEAR SIR:

I send you a lengthy official report of the new torpedo vessel *David* to which I will only odd a few lines.

Among the many inventions with which I have been familiar, I have seen none which acted so perfectly at first trial.

The secrecy, rapidity of movement, control of direction, and precise explosion indicate, I think, the introduction of the torpedo element as a means of certain warfare. It can be ignored no longer. If 60 pounds of powder, why not 600 pounds? I would advise therefore, that the subject be fully traversed on the basis developed by the enemy, and then improved on afterwards.

The *David* moved so rapidly that but a few moments intervened between getting sight of her and the blow.

By all means let us have a quantity of these torpedoes, and thus turn them against the enemy. We can make them faster than they can.

Very respectfully, your obedient servant,

JOHN A. DAHLGREN

ASSISTANT SECRETARY FOX[8]

Report of Rear-Admiral Dahlgren, U.S. Navy,
regarding Lieutenant Glassell, C.S. Navy.

No. 191. FLAG-STEAMER *PHILADELPHIA*,
Of Morris Island, October 12, 1863.

SIR: My regular mail, prepared for the *Araqo*, again failed, as that vessel steamed away from the boat of the *Wabash* carrying the mail, though less than 200 yards distant. I have therefore sent a tug with the letters to Fortress Monroe; also Lieutenant Glassell, of the rebel Navy, who commanded the torpedo vessel *David*, and was picked up after the attempt.

It is desirable that this officer should not be allowed to return here until some time has elapsed, as he could not fail to be of great service to the enemy in future operations of the same kind.

I have the honor to be, very respectfully, your obedient servant,

J. A. DAHLGREN,
Rear-Admiral, Cmndg. South Atlantic Blockading Squadron.

HON. GIDEON WELLES,
Secretary of the Navy, Washington, D. C.[9]

Report of Rear-Admiral Dahlgren, U.S. Navy,
regarding injuries sustained by the U.S.S. *New Ironsides*.

No. 258.–Confidential. U.S.S. *PHILADELPHIA*,
Off Charleston, November 19, 1863.

SIR: Captain Rowan informs me that upon removing coal in the bunkers of the *Ironsides*, it is discovered that the damage done by the torpedo was much more serious than first appeared.

I have not yet received a written report, as the examination is not yet concluded, but will inform the Department at the earliest date.

I need not urge the importance of keeping the facts from publicity. Everything will be done here to that end, though it is difficult to evade the researches of public correspondents.

I have the honor to be, very respectfully, your obedient servant,

JNO. A. DAHLGREN,
Rear-Admiral.

HON. G. WELLES.[10]

Report of Rear-Admiral Dahlgren, U.S. Navy, forwarding reports regarding injuries sustained by the U.S.S. *New Ironsides*.

No. 279.
FLAG-STEAMER *PHILADELPHIA*,
Off Morris Island, November 30, 1863.

SIR: I enclose, for the information of the Department, reports on the injuries to the *Ironsides* from the torpedo.

I am not informed, however, that the vessel leaks unusually, and so long as that is the case she ought to be retained here until at least the attack on Charleston has been effectual, which I hope is not far distant now.

I have the honor to be, very respectfully, your obedient servant,

JNO. A. DAHLGREN,
Rear-Admiral, Comdg., South, Atlantic Blockading Squadron.

HON. GIDEON WELLES,
Secretary of the Navy, Washington, D. C.[11]

[Enclosure.]

U.S.S. *NEW IRONSIDES*,
Off Morris Island, November 28, 1863.

ADMIRAL: I enclose herewith, in obedience to your order, the report of the carpenter, Mr. Bishop, giving a detailed account of the injuries this ship received by the explosion of the torpedo.

The ship is very seriously injured, and ought to be sent home for repairs as soon as it is possible to spare her services here.

I have the honor to be, very respectfully, your obedient servant,

S. C. ROWAN,
Captain.

REAR-ADMIRAL JNO. A. DAHLGREN,
Commanding South Atlantic Blockading Squadron.[12]

[Sub-enclosure.]

U.S.S. *NEW IRONSIDES*,
Off Morris Island, South Carolina, November 24, 1863.

SIR: In obedience to your order, I have examined the injuries discovered in the coal bunkers, resulting from the attack made on this ship by the rebel torpedo boat *David* on the night of the 5th ultimo, [and find them] to be as follows:

One hanging knee abreast the engine room started off 10 inches from the clamps and ceiling; two strake clamps and five strakes ceiling broken in two in a perpendicular line; the hanging knee is started entirely from the beam and the beam badly smashed; the fore-and-aft piece that forms the engine room is split for about a space of 4 feet and likewise started from the ends of the spur beams from 3 to 4 inches. Six of the lap knees are also started. The stanchions that support the fore-and-aft piece of the engine room and likewise from the coal bunkers are entirely gone at the head. The ceiling is started off from the frame of the ship for a space of 10 feet, both forward and aft of the hanging knee; forward of the knee, where the ceiling forms a butt, it has started 10 inches from the ship's frame, and the side of the ship is sprung in from 4 to 5 inches for a space of some 40 feet. When the ship was examined outside by the divers, they reported the planking abreast the engine room shattered for a space of 6 feet in depth, 10 to 12 feet in length, and about 1½ inches in the face of the planking. The oakum is also started in the seams. In examining the gun and berth decks I find the spirketing and waterway on berth deck started in 3 inches for a space of 20 feet. The bulkheads and shelving of three store rooms abreast the engine room were entirely knocked down. The stanchions that support the fore-and-aft piece that forms the engine room on gun deck were carried away at the heel, carrying the joiner work with them. The stanchions that support the spar deck around the engine room were jumped out of the iron sockets by the shock. The waterway on the gun deck abreast the engine room is started from the deck three-quarters of an inch for a space of 30 feet, causing the deck to leak badly. The above injuries were all caused by the explosion of the torpedo. In my opinion this ship ought to be docked as soon as she can possibly be spared from this harbor.

Very respectfully, your obedient servant,

T. H. BISHOP,
Carpenter, U.S. Navy.[13]

Abstract log of the U.S.S. *New Ironsides*,
Captain S. C. Bowan, U.S. Navy, commanding.

October 5, 1863, — Off Morris Island. From 8 to midnight: At 9 p.m. discovered a very peculiar looking steamer which at first appeared like a boat standing toward our starboard beam from seaward; hailed her rapidly four times, and she making no reply, fired into her with musketry; she returned fire, dangerously wounding Ensign C. W. Howard in charge of the deck. Almost at the same time the steamer struck us near No. 6 port, starboard side: exploding a large torpedo, shaking the vessel and throwing up an immense column of water, part of which fell on our decks. The steamer then dropped astern; continued firing at her with musketry as long as she was in sight; also fired two guns from starboard broadside. Dispatched second and third cutters in pursuit. The explosion of the torpedo knocked down armory bulkhead and store rooms in wake of the explosion. William L. Knox, ordinary seaman, leg broken; Thomas Little, master at arms, several severe contusions from the shock of the explosion.[14]

Extract from the Diary of Rear-Admiral Dahlgren, U.S. Navy.

October 5, 1863.—Had an event tonight. It was not quite 10 p.m. when the signal officer announced that General Terry had informed General Gillmore by telegraph that there was trouble among the vessels-heavy musketry firing. The tide was too low to get out of the creek, so I had to get information as I could, but there was no signal, no further firing, nor could anyone tell. Got out into the channel during the night and steamed to the *Ironsides*, where I learned that a torpedo had been exploded under her.

Tuesday, October 6.—Quite early a frightened wretch was brought to me as taken out of the water after escaping from the torpedo. He gave a full statement. The vessel was about 50 feet long, made like a cigar, 5 to 6 feet in diameter, with an engine which would drive her 8 to 10 knots. At the bow was a bar 10 feet long, with a torpedo at the end holding 60 pounds of powder, with four nipples to act by percussion. There were 4 persons in the boat, and they stood on the bottom with their heads out of the hatch, which was made in the part out of water. They left Charleston at dusk, passed our vessels in the dark, then returned and attacked the *Ironsides*. He could not tell whether the captain or the pilot fired at and wounded the officer of the deck. The immense jet of water that came down put out the fires of the *David*.

It seems to me that nothing could have been more successful as a first effort, and it will place the torpedo among certain offensive means. The captain was also picked up. His name is Glassell, and he was formerly a lieutenant in our Navy; now in that of the Confederates. I did not see him, as I could get nothing from him. What became of the other two and the boat no one could say. They may have perished or not.

October 7.—I concluded to visit Port Royal to see the fleet engineer and superintendent of monitors, in order to have some fixture for keeping off torpedoes from the monitors, as they might be fatal.

October 10.—Returning found things as I left them. * * * About sunset poor Howard died of the one little buckshot which struck him from the torpedo. I had made him a master the next day, but a Higher Power has given him a better promotion. (It savors to me of murder.)

November 18.—Captain Rowan came on board to report that in removing coal in bunkers of *Ironsides* it was discovered that the injury from torpedo was very serious, and extended down toward the keel.[15]

Extract from report of the Secretary of the Navy of the Confederate States, November 30, 1863.

On the evening of the 5th of October, Lieutenant W. T. Glassell, in charge of the torpedo boat *David*, with Assistant Engineer J. H. Tomb, Pilot Walker Cannon, and Seaman James Sullivan, left Charleston to attempt the destruction of the enemy's ship *New Ironsides*.

Passing undiscovered through the enemy's fleet, he was hailed by the watch as he approached the ship, and answering the hail with a shot from a musket, he dashed his boat against her and exploded the torpedo under her bilge. The fires were extinguished and the boat was nearly swamped by the concussion and the descending water, and Lieutenant Glassell and Sullivan, supposing her to be lost, swam off and were picked up by the enemy. Engineer Tomb and Pilot Cannon succeeded in reaching Charleston with the boat.

Although Lieutenant Glassell failed to accomplish his chief object, it is believed that he inflicted serious injury upon the *Ironsides*, while his unsurpassed daring must be productive of an important moral influence, as well upon the enemy as upon our own naval force. The annals of naval warfare record few enterprises which exhibit more strikingly than this of Lieutenant Glassell the highest qualities of a sea officer. Lieutenant Glassell and Assistant Engineer Tomb are respectfully recommended for promotion.[16]

Report of General Beauregard, C.S. Army.

Charleston, [S.C.], October 6, 1863 — 7:12 P.M.

Last night Lieutenant Glassell, C.S. Navy, gallantly attempted to blow up the *Ironsides* with the small cigar torpedo boat *David*. Explosion occurred at roper time, but either charge was too small or torpedo too near surface water. Damage thus far not apparent. Lieutenant Glassell and 1 man were captured; other 2 returned safely with boat. Commotion on board the *Ironsides* reported very great.

G. T. BEAUREGARD

GENERAL S. COOPER.[17]

12

Various Official Documents— Part B

Navy Department, Washington, D.C.
Official Reports from U.S.N. and C.S.N., from 1861 to 1865

> Notes from papers of First Assistant Engineer Tomb, C.S. Navy, regarding the submarine torpedo boat.

Charleston, S.C., January, 1864[5].

There was a submarine torpedo boat, not under the orders of the Navy, and I was ordered to tow her down the harbor three or four times by Flag-Officer Tucker, who also gave me orders to report as to her efficiency as well as safety. In my report to him I stated, "The only way to use a torpedo was on the same plan as the *David*—that is, a spar torpedo—and to strike with his boat on the surface, the torpedo being lowered to 8 feet. Should she attempt to use a torpedo as Lieutenant Dixon intended, by submerging the boat and striking from below, the level of the torpedo would be above his own boat, and as she had little buoyancy and no power, the chances were the suction caused by the water passing into the sinking ship would prevent her rising to the surface, besides the possibility of his own boat being disabled." Lieutenant Dixon was a very brave and cool-headed man, and had every confidence in his boat, but had great trouble when under the water from lack of air and light. At the time she made the attempt to dive under the receiving ship in Charleston Harbor, Lieutenant Dixon, James A. Eason, and myself stood on the wharf as she passed out and saw her dive, but she did not rise again, and after a week's effort she was brought to the surface and the crew of 7 men were found in a bunch near the manhole. Lieutenant Dixon said they had failed to close the after valve.

The last night the *David* towed him down the harbor his torpedo got foul of us and came near blowing up both boats before we got it clear of the bottom, where it had drifted. I let him go after passing Fort Sumter, and on my making report of this, Flag-Officer Tucker refused to have the *David* tow him again. The power for driving this boat came from 7 or 8 men turning cranks attached to the propeller shaft, and when working at their best would make about 3 knots. She was very slow in turning, but would sink at a moment's notice and at times without it. The understanding was that from the time of her construction at Mobile up to the time when she struck *Housatonic* not less than 33 men had lost their lives in her. She was a veritable coffin to this brave officer and his men.

J. H. TOMB.[1]

Report of Lieutenant-Colonel Dantzler, C.S. Army.

Headquarters Battery Marshall,
Sullivan's Island, February 19, 1864.

LIEUTENANT: I have the honor to report that the torpedo boat stationed at this post went out on the night of the 17th instant (Wednesday) and has not yet returned. The signals agreed upon to be given in case the boat wished a light to be exposed at this post as a guide for its return were observed and answered. An earlier report would have been made of this matter, but the officer of the day for yesterday was under the impression that the boat had returned, and so informed me. As soon as I became apprised of the fact I sent a telegram to Captain Nance, assistant adjutant-general, notifying him of it.

Very respectfully,

O. M. DANTZLER,
Lieutenant-Colonel.

LIEUTENANT JOHN A. WILSON,
Acting Assistant Adjutant-General.[2]

Note: The *Hunley* went out on the night of the 17th inst., under the command of Lieutenant Dixon, and sunk the U.S.S. *Housatonic* with a crew of 300 men and mounting 12 guns. Most of the crew took to the rigging and were saved by their own ships.

J. H. T.

Order of Flag-Officer Hunter, C.S. Navy, to Chief Engineer Tomb, C.S. Navy, regarding special duty.

Augusta, GA., April 12, 1865.

By order of the honorable Navy Department you will proceed to assist Captain L. M. Coxetter, in accordance with your request, and for that purpose you will proceed to the position necessary so to do.

Respectfully,

WM. W. HUNTER,
Flag-Officer, Commanding.

CHIEF ENGINEER JAMES H. TOMB, Provisional Navy C.S.[3]

Order of Brigadier-General Fry, C.S. Army, to Chief Engineer Tomb, C.S. Navy, to proceed to Shell Bluff battery, and assume command of special expedition.

Headquarters Engineer's Department,
Augusta, Ga., April 12, 1865.

CAPTAIN: You will proceed without delay to Shell Bluff and there await the arrival of Master's Mate Brockington with navy and torpedo boats from this point. You will then take charge of the expedition under the general instructions given to Messrs. Brockington and White and proceed as therein ordered.

Respectfully, your obedient servant,

B. D. FRY,
Brigadier-General, Commanding Post.

JAS. H. TOMB,
Captain and Chief Engineer, Torpedo Corps.[4]

I would not take them up on orders of Major General Young, Commanding department, feeling it was the only protection Augusta had from the enemy's vessels, and Com. Hunter as well as General Fry, were of the same opinion.

There being no way for me to avoid the duty, as Gen. Young insisted on their being removed to permit of Sherman sending the families of Confederate officers to Augusta.

I was put on the sick list, and telegraphed Captain S. S. Lee, C.S.N., for special orders to the Gulf to avoid this duty, and in this way got out of a most unpleasant duty.

Following letter from Flag Officer Hunter,
in regard to Torpedoes in Savannah River

Augusta, Ga., April 12, 1865.

I have the honor to acknowledge the receipt of your note of this day requesting a detail of men of my command to report to Lieutenant Commanding J. S. Kennard, Provisional Navy C.S., temporarily commanding the Confederate steamer *Leesburg*. In compliance with your request I have directed Lieutenant Commanding J. S. Kennard to select the men alluded to. In transferring these to the *Leesburg* for temporary service, I would respectfully state that as the whole motive of removing the torpedoes in the Savannah River can properly only be known to you, there is, in my mind, very cogent reasons why the torpedoes should not be removed or their location known. The latter can not be kept from the enemy if any attempt shall be made to remove them, because of the notoriety the act will occasion.

I am, general, very respectfully,

WM. W. HUNTER,
Flag-Officer, Commanding.

BRIGADIER-GENERAL B. D. FRY, Provisional Army C.S.[5]

Special order of Major-General Jones, C.S. Army, to Chief Engineer Tomb, C.S. Navy, to proceed to Augusta, Ga., for duty in testing torpedo boats.

> Headquarters District Of South Carolina,
> Charleston, S.C., November 22, 1864.

J. H. Tomb, chief engineer, C.S.S. *Chicora*, having reported at these headquarters in obedience to instructions from Flag-Officer Tucker, will proceed without delay to Augusta, Ga., and carry into execution the special instructions given him by the major-general commanding.

By command of Major-General Sam Jones:

> Chas. S. Stringfellow,
> Assistant Adjutant-General.

CHIEF ENGINEER J. H. TOMB.[6]

Note: — This was to blow up the Oconee bridge before the advance of Sherman's Army, J.H.T.

Order of Flag-Officer Tucker, C.S. Navy, to Chief Engineer Tomb, C.S. Navy, to serve on a board for testing certain torpedo boats.

> Flagship *Charleston*,
> Charleston, S.C., November 18, 1864

Sir: Previous to your return, a board of officers was convened for the purpose of examining and testing certain torpedo boats.

As you are the senior chief engineer in this squadron, you will be pleased to report to Commander Hunter (who is the senior officer of the Board) for the purpose indicated.

Commander Glassell (who will be the active party of the Board), together with yourself and Chief Engineer Darcy, who is also one of the board, will examine and test these boats, and report jointly.

Very respectfully, your obedient servant,

> John R. Tucker,
> Flag Officer, Commanding Afloat

CHIEF ENGINEER JAS. H. TOMB, Provisional Navy C.S.[7]

Order of Flag-Officer Hunter, C.S. Navy, to Acting Master's Mate Brockington, C.S. Navy, to proceed to special duty with, Chief Engineer Tomb, C.S. Navy.

> Augusta, Ga., March 13, 1865.

You will proceed with Chief Engineer James H. Tomb, Provisional Navy C.S., with two men of the naval command at this place, and when the temporary duty for which you and they are hereby assigned shall be accomplished, you will return with all dispatch with the men alluded to and resume your duties on board the C.S.S. *Sampson*. Till you return, or the return of Lieutenant Commanding Carnes, Provisional Navy C.S., place Master's Mate A. W. Johnson, Provisional Navy C.S., in command of the *Sampson* and impart to him all orders and information neces-

sary to the proper execution of his duties, and enjoin him to be vigilant and careful of all the public property committed to his charge.
Respectfully,

W. W. Hunter,
Flag-Officer, Commanding.

MASTER'S MATE S. A. BROCKINGTON, Provisional Navy C.S.[8]

COPY

Forwarded with pleasure,
by Your Obedient Servant
J. H. Tucker,
Flag-Officer Comdg. Afloat.

Confederate States of America,
Navy Department,
Richmond, October 9, 1863.

Chief Engineer,
JAMES H. TOMB, C.S.S. STEAMER *CHICORA*, Charleston, S.C.
Sir:

You are hereby informed that the President has appointed you a Chief Engineer in the Provisional Navy of the Confederate States, "for gallant and meritorious conduct in the attempt to destroy, by torpedo, the U.S. ironclad frigate, *Ironsides*, in the harbor of Charleston on the 5th day of October 1863," under the command of Lieutenant Glassell.

You are requested to inform the Department of the receipt of this appointment.

I am very respectfully, your obedient servant,

(Signed) S. R. MALLORY,
Secretary of the Navy.

While in Charleston, about September 24, 1864, I was offered the command of a number of torpedo boats being built by private parties, and sent in my resignation to the Department, but was informed by the secretary of the Navy that "it could not be accepted, as my services were required in the position I was in, as Chief Engineer of the Fleet."

What pleased me more than anything in this, was the endorsement of Flag Officer Tucker, Viz:

"In forwarding the resignation of Chief Engineer Tomb, my only endorsement thereon was 'forwarded with regret.' I state this for the information of Mr. Tomb."

Your obedient servant,

(Signed) J. R. TUCKER,
Flag-Officer Commanding Afloat.

13

To South America

[The remainder of Tomb's memoirs relate his experiences in South America during the Paraguayan War. To more readily understand this portion of the memoirs, it will be helpful for the reader to have a brief outline of this major war in South America.

The Paraguayan War, also called the War of the Triple Alliance, was fought from 1864 to 1870. It was the bloodiest conflict in Latin American history and was fought between Paraguay and the allied countries of Argentina, Brazil, and Uruguay.

Paraguay had been involved in boundary and tariff disputes with its more powerful neighbors, Argentina and Brazil, for years. The Uruguayans had also struggled to achieve and maintain their independence from those same powers, especially from Argentina.

In 1864 Brazil helped the leader of Uruguay's Colorado Party to oust his Blanco Party opponent. The dictator of Paraguay, Francisco Solano López, found himself at war with Brazil in December 1864. Bartolomé Mitre, president of Argentina, then organized an alliance with Brazil and the Colorado Party–controlled section of Uruguay (the Triple Alliance). By demanding the right to place troops in the Argentine province of Corrientes, he violated Argentina's desire to remain neutral and provoked the alliance of Brazil, Argentina, and Uruguay against Paraguay on May 1, 1865.

López's action, following his buildup of a 50,000-man army, then the strongest in Latin America, was viewed by many as aggression for self- and national aggrandizement, but as the war wore on many Argentines and others saw the conflict as Mitre's war of conquest.

At the opening of the war in 1865, Paraguayan forces advanced northward into the Brazilian province of Mato Grosso and southward into the province of Rio Grande do Sul. Logistical problems and the buildup of the allied troop strength, which soon outnumbered Paraguay's by 10 to 1, then forced the Paraguayans to withdraw behind their frontiers. In June 1865, Brazilian naval forces defeated a Paraguayan flotilla on the Paraná River at Riachuelo, near the Argentine city of Corrientes; by January 1866 the allies had blockaded the rivers leading to Paraguay. It was about this time that Tomb arrived in the Argentine capitol of Buenos Aires.

In April, Mitre led an allied invading force into southwestern Paraguay but was prevented from advancing for two years. Fierce battles were fought; the most notable was won by the Paraguayans at Curupayty in September 1866. This inhibited any allied offensive for nearly a year. Both sides suffered heavy losses in the campaign.

In January 1868, Mitre was replaced as commander in chief by the Brazilian Marquês (later Duke) de Caxias. In February Brazilian armored vessels broke through Paraguayan defenses at the river fortress of Humaitá, near the confluence of the Paraná and Paraguay Rivers, and pressed on to bombard Asunción, the capital. Tomb acted as a scout and advisor to the Brazilian admiral on the position of Paraguayan torpedoes during this offensive. In the Campaign of Lomas Valentinas in December, the Paraguayan army was annihilated. López fled northward and carried on a guerrilla war until he was killed on March 1, 1870.

The Paraguayan people had been fanatically committed to López and the war effort, and as a result they fought to the point of dissolution. The war left Paraguay utterly prostrate; its prewar population of approximately 525,000 was reduced to about 221,000 in 1871, of which only about 28,000 were men. During the war the Paraguayans suffered not only from the enemy but also from malnutrition, disease, and the domination of López, who tortured and killed countless numbers of people. Argentina and Brazil annexed about 55,000 square miles of Paraguayan territory. Argentina took much of the Misiones region and part of the Chaco between the Bermejo and Pilcomayo rivers, while Brazil enlarged its Mato Grosso province from annexed territory. They both demanded a large indemnity (which was never paid) and occupied Paraguay until 1876. Meanwhile, the Colorados had gained control of Uruguay, and they retained that control until 1958.

Although López had successfully invaded the Brazilian province of Mato Grosso in late 1864, his invasion of Uruguay in 1865 was a disaster. The allies defeated him at Tuyutí in May 1866, captured the fortress of Humaitá in July 1867, and forced López to withdraw into northern Paraguay, where he was killed.[1]

Tomb's memoirs continue: — Editor]

When the Civil War ended in 1865, I like many other Confederates had nothing to start with and little prospects for the future in the South. I was fortunate through some friends in Philadelphia to secure a position with an oil company in Oil City, Pennsylvania, to sink wells on a farm that they paid $25,000 for and was said to have every prospect of oil.

I had a gang of some fifteen men all of them Union soldiers returning from the war. There were a major and a captain in the party working under me, but they did not know I was a Reb, and I took pains not to inform them of that fact. They were a fine lot of men and with the exception of one, not at all unfriendly to the South. This one was the "limit" and at night about the camps said the South was full of snakes or rebels and like snakes would come to life again and they

Paraguayan dictator Francisco Solano López.

would have to exterminate us. This man was one of the best workmen in the party, but one day he let a tool fall into the well so I gave him a note to the superintendent in Oil City requesting that he be given another position, for while he was a good workman he could not work under me and he never came back. This was a good lesson for me also not to express myself over freely.

There were quite a number of wells being put down all through this section and nothing more was needed to float the stock at .50 cents but the derrick and everyone had stock. The indications as to oil were always good, and if the pump brought up fresh water, salt water, or air, the report was always "good." After the well struck oil, it took five barrels to pay for working it. We put down three wells on the farm before I left, and not one drop of oil did we get. After I left for South American, the company went "broke" for $50,000.

I went to New York and got letters from the Argentine Minister, Sarmiente, to General Mitre, President of Argentina, and left New York on the bark, *Clareta*, Captain Race commanding, for Buenos Ayres. After seventy-seven days we arrived off the River La Platte and struck a pampero that came near smashing the *Clareta* as we passed out between La Isla de Lobos and Maldenali Light. At one time we were so near the coast that Captain Race felt the ship was lost.

[Bartolomé Mitre was born in Buenos Aires in 1821. He is remembered as a statesman, military leader, and historian. After being exiled in Chile, Bolivia, and Peru, he returned to Argentina in 1852 and participated in the Overthrow of Roses carried out by General José Urquiza. In 1853, Mitre was appointed Minister of War of the provincial government of Buenos Aires, and, through this position, tried to resist the plan of Urquiza to unite the province as the Republic of Argentina. In 1859, troops under the command of Mitre were defeated by those of Urquiza, and Buenos Aires joined with the confederation, but later backed out of the agreement. Mitre was declared Governor of the Province of Buenos Aires in 1860, and this time defeated Urquiza in the battle of Peacock in 1861. However, Mitre and Urquiza settled their differences and Buenos Aires was again brought into the confederation. The following year Mitre became the nation's first constitutionally elected president, serving the republic for a period of six years.[2] — Editor]

When we arrived at Montevideo, Captain Race had me up to the best hotel for a good dinner. As he had informed me he was good in Spanish, I gave him the bill of fare to order. Beefsteak was his limit, so we took two orders of beefsteak, as his Spanish was no better than mine. As time passed and I came to Montevideo again, I would often think of that dinner and Captain Race.

When we arrived at the outer anchorage at Buenos Ayres, it was some miles from the city, we were told it would cost $100.00, to take each person to the landing. As my reserve fund was about $10.00, it was a serious thing, but I found it did not amount to more than $4.00, as the paper money was about on a par with Confederate money. At that time all shipments to Buenos Ayres had to be put in small schooners or lighters, and then watching the tide, would be sent up on shore, and at low tide wagons would drive out to the lighters and take the freight to the landing or custom house. The mole for passengers extended quite a distance out and was

General Bartolomé Mitre, president of Argentina.

built of timber. I was fortunate in securing room and board at a Mrs. Bradley's at moderate rates, and found them very friendly, there being two daughters who were good looking and fond of music.

One of my letters of introduction was from Lieutenant Mitre in New York, who was a son of President Mitre, was addressed to the proprietor of a newspaper. I was not able to speak Spanish and when I presented the letter at the office, a very nice old gentleman behind the desk, who was not able to speak English, did his best to make me understand in pantomime that the president was out in Palermo. As I was about to leave, a man came in who could speak Spanish and English and made it clear to me. I had three letters but I never made use of them. I found out that you could be put off until tomorrow, mañana. After frequent calls, I found that General Mitre was up the river with the army, and I was furnished with first class passage on the *St. Espiqade* to go up the river. I found that Argentina had no navy to mention, and the officers got their pay any time between January and December. I was told to call on Admiral Tamandaré, who was in command of the Brazilian Navy. I found him to be a fine officer and gentleman. His mastery of English was better than my Portuguese. We got along very well and he gave me passage on the transport *Lily Bell* to Rio de Janeiro. Captain De Forrest was in command of the steamer and I had seen him in Charleston while he was running the blockade. Arriving in Rio de Janeiro, I presented my letter from the Admiral to Minister Lobo of Marine. I then called on Minister Savaria of Foreign Affairs, who gave me a letter of introduction to Emperor Dom Pedro, the Second, who was at his palace at San Christobal, some five miles out.

While at Mrs. Bradley's in Buenos Ayres, a little incident took place which was most displeasing to me. I was at supper and one of the guests, a captain of a ship made a remark that I took exception to and I made use of rather strong language to him, and then left the table and went to my room, feeling that Mrs. Bradley and her daughters would take exception to my remarks, also.

I was counting my funds, when a gentleman came to my room and introduced himself as Mr. Sullivan, a contractor. He informed me that Mrs. Bradley and daughters were quite in my favor as what I said was right. Then he informed me that it would please him to lend me some funds as I might be short. It was quite a time before I could say anything, and then when he handed me $50.00, I told him I would accept $30.00. Sullivan told me to let him know if I needed more at any time and he would let me have it. I paid him back six or eight months later. About a year later a friend told me that Sullivan was in Buenos Ayres without a cent as he had lost all he had in a contract to get a ship off a bank in the Parama River. I gave Watson a check on the bank in Buenos Ayres for $50.00 to give Sullivan and said that he could have more if he needed it. The amount was paid back to me a few months later as he secured a good contract. What he wanted was a good suit of clothes before he could do anything.

My Interview with Dom Pedro the Second

When I arrived at the Palace of San Christobal, a guard took my letter to the Emperor and conducted me to a reception room on the second floor with instructions to an officer to show me into the Emperor's presence. There were quite a number of naval officers in the waiting room. They were all decorated, in fact, they all looked like admirals. After a short time I was told that the Emperor was ready to receive me and [I] passed out of a door to a porch that overlooked a garden. Not seeing anyone I was heading toward the door on the right. There was no regular door, just a heavy curtain with the coat of arms of Brazil. I heard someone call me and turning saw a fine looking gentleman, who motioned for me to come that way and then put out his hand to me. Thinking it was meant for a handshake, I shook it and shook it hard, and it seemed to surprise him. Then he passed between the heavy curtains into a room and I was waiting to get another call when he came to the curtains and in broken English invited me to enter. When I got to the room there was no one there but the person who had put his hand out and after a good look at him I saw that it was the Emperor, himself. I hardly knew what to say. Evidently he saw that I did not lack respect but was ignorant. The time I was with him was only about thirty minutes. I never was so impressed with anyone as I was with him, as he put me at ease right away. No doubt it was a change for him also as I found out afterwards I should have kissed his hand. I had two other interviews with the Emperor which were similar, but I did not shake hands.

[Dom Pedro II de Alcântara (1825–1891) was emperor of Brazil from 1831 to 1889. At the age of five he succeeded under a regency when his father, Pedro, abdicated. Pedro II was declared of age in 1840. His long reign was characterized by great social change, material progress, and wars with neighboring nations. He was extremely popular, but the economic and social tendencies of his time betrayed him. In 1850 the slave trade was prohibited; in 1871 a law was passed providing for gradual emancipation; and in 1888, when Pedro was in Europe, a law abolishing slavery was signed by his daughter Isabel. Brazil's modernization led to widening divisions between the feudalistic countryside and the rapidly growing urban populations and newer export sectors. A coalition of the urban middle class, coffee planters, and the military increasingly disparaged the monarchy and its ties to the traditional landed class. They advocated the creation of a modern republic that would support the new coffee and industrial capitalism, finding additional allies in the church. Discontent became widespread, and the military, representing this diverse opposition, overturned the empire. The revolution was

Dom Pedro II, emperor of Brazil.

led by Manuel Deodoro da Fonseca. Pedro II was exiled and spent the remainder of his life in Europe.³— Editor]

At another time when I had returned from the seat of war, the commandant of the Arsenal, Broisneau, requested me to remain in his office while the Emperor went through the shops. The Emperor asked me about conditions at the seat of war and I told him, "The navy was ready but the army was waiting for mules, that when the mules came they had to wait for hay, and when the hay arrived the mules were about half dead and the army could not advance." I doubt if there were at that time another king or Emperor his equal, as his whole thoughts were for his people. The Emperor told me to call on Minister Savaria. The next day I did so and as he could speak good English, we got along splendidly. The secretary informed me that Lopes had no navy now but that if I could suggest something to remove the torpedoes in the Paraguay River they would like me to do so and bring the plan to him the next day.

> [Francisco Solano López was born in 1826 and was the first son of Carlos Antonio López, a member of a prestige family of Assuncíon. In 1844, his father became Paraguay's president and López was reared to inherit the government of his country. At the age of 18 he became Brigadier General of the Paraguayan Army. From this point his father made him responsible for the modernization of the Paraguayan forces.
>
> Observers noted that one of the most important experiences of his life was his stay in Paris in the year of 1853, during his trip to Europe to buy arms. There, Solano López observed the intrigues, trappings, and pretensions of Europe's countries' foreign policies. In particular he became very impressed by Napoleon III, emperor of France.
>
> When he returned to Paraguay he was not alone. Elisa Alicia Lynch, an Irish woman he met in Paris, was with him. After the consolidation of power and López's father's death in 1862, she became a person of enormous influence in Paraguay. She bore López five sons.
>
> Immediately after Solano López achieved power, relations with neighboring countries begin to deteriorate. The main problem was the disputed lands with Brazil and Argentina and the influence López felt these countries exerted over La Plata Region.
>
> It does not mean that Solano López was responsible for the war. Its causes were complex and have to do with the historical animosity between the new countries inherited from Portugal and Spain. The fact, however, is that at the end of his policy maneuvers, two traditional enemies joined together in order to put an end to his government.
>
> Still today, Solano López is a controversial person. For some, his foreign policy was a complete disaster. He undertook a war he could not win. His anxiety for recognition led to miscalculations and errors, which resulted in Paraguay's submersion as a free country for at least a decade.
>
> For others, he was a hero, a patriot who resisted Argentina and Brazil's aggressive plans of isolating Paraguay, and a man who mobilized the nation for five years of war against powerful enemies.

Despite these different opinions, one fact remains: he fought until the last breath. On March 1, 1870, he was killed in the last action of the war.

Elisa Lynch buried Solano López with her own hands.[4]—Editor]

Going back to the hotel I made a sketch of what I thought would answer the purpose and the next day presented myself. I found they were ready to accept anything I gave them. The minister also said that coming from North America I might be short of funds and gave me an order on the treasury for 400 mil reis, about $200.00, and sent a messenger to get it. Then he gave me a letter to the Commandant of the arsenal to give me any assistance and let me select the model of ironclad from which to make my drawings. I was in the drafting room all Sunday long, and selected the *Remandere* as the best suited for my design. When working on it, I was impressed with the good will and confidence shown in me by the officials. The minister asked me to submit my sketch to the Commandant of the Yard and if he approved it to return and make a contract. When I submitted the plan to Broisneau, he told me he had no experience with torpedoes and what he wished to know was, "Would I go up on the ship when the attachment was in place?" I told him I certainly would and he put his approval on it. Then the minister made out the order that gave me first-class passage to and from the seat of war and every courtesy was shown me while in the service. My contract specified that the government was to give me ten days' notice if they wished to cancel it and I was to give them only two days' notice if I wished to do so. It was all in my favor and it was Minister Savaria who did it. The impression made upon me by all the officials from the emperor down was always the best.

When the machine was ready, it was shipped on a transport and I went along. There was quite a list of officers on board, but I had good quarters and there was also a good table. There was one dish they had which is much like one we have in the South called "Hopping John." This was made of a mixture of beef, farina, tomatoes, peppers, and bacon, all boiled together, and as a rule I made a meal of it. One day I was up on the bridge and could look right down into the gallery and saw that the cook had no shirt on. The perspiration was a sight. I asked the officer of the deck what dish they were making as they would pull the beef to shreds before putting it into the boilers with the other ingredients, and then work it with a big spoon. I saw a good bit of perspiration go into the boilers as I watched him. At dinner I passed it up for good, as it was over rich for me. There was a Captain Rice, who was also very fond of this dish, but I never told him about the perspiration.

When we arrived at Pasa de Patre, I had my quarters in the Captain's cabin with Captain Barboso. He as well as the other officers were not over anxious to have the machine attached to the *Tamandaré*. There was a young German in the ship who could speak Portuguese very well, and I had the Admiral turn him over to me as interpreter, and he was a great success. After the machine was attached I would sleep below, but none of the other officers would do so. López would send down floating torpedoes at night and they were made by a man named Bell from North America. Those that came down the river on the surface were put in the

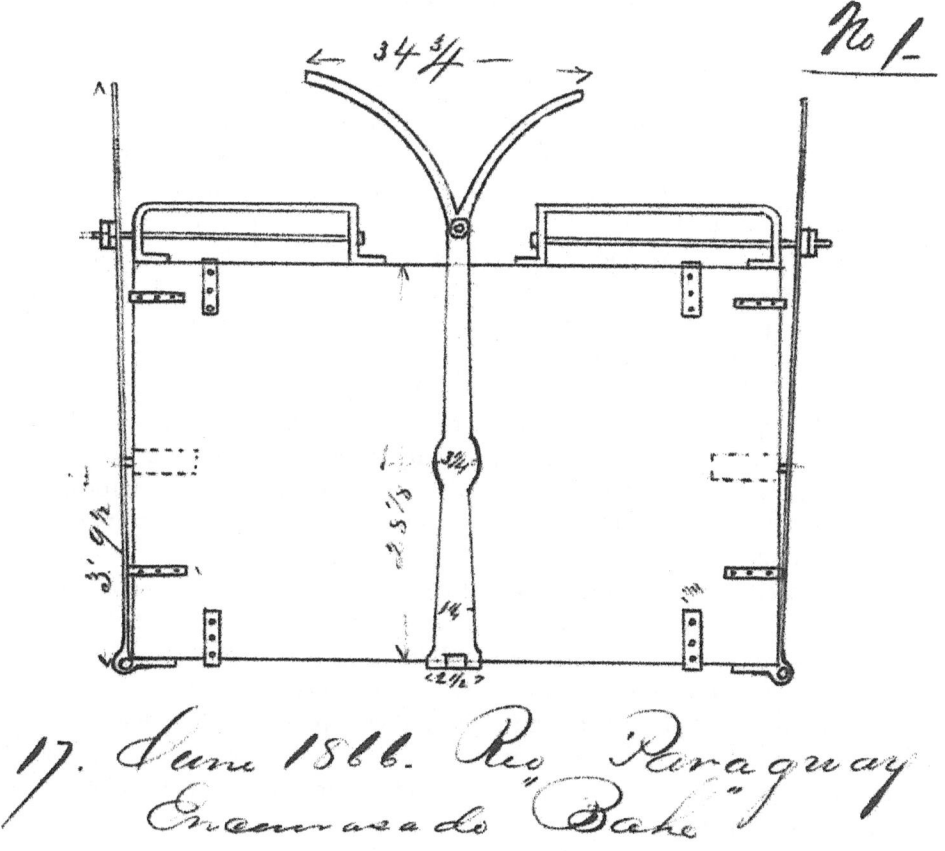

Sketch by Tomb of his machine to snare torpedoes. A note indicates it was attached to the ironclad *Bahia* (Tomb Family Papers).

bottom of a canoe and in the shape of a box, having from 200 to 500 pounds of powder in them. They would be exploded by a gun put through the front of the box with line leading to another canoe up the river. These never did any damage to us. There were others anchored in the channel by a line. These had a number of boxes, one inside of the other lined with tin, the third box contained the powder. There were two arms at each end connected to a piston that passed into a tube containing sulphuric acid, and this glass tube breaking, the fulminate caused it to explode. They were about three to five feet below the surface and contained 100 to 300 pounds of powder. Then there were others lying on the bottom of the river. A line passed from the torpedo to the chaco or woods, then up the river to a point that would give the guard watching for ships to pass up a good chance to blow them up, if the powder was dry. I passed up the chaco side of the river by orders from the Admiral and found one line leading up the bank to a tree, but the guard had left his post. I cut the line and made a buoy fast to it and we got the torpedo to the bank, finding some 700 pounds of powder in it, but two thirds of it was wet and in bad condition.

The greater part of the time I was in the Paraguay River I was attached to the ironclad *Tamandaré*, to which my machine was made fast and I was detailed to work it. I messed with Captain Barboso and the pilot. I also kept in touch with what our force was doing by the captain, who would take toothpicks and small portions of bread and place them on the table, each representing the allies and would show me how each division was advancing or falling back. While interesting at times, it was also rather monotonous, and the time hung heavy on our hands with nothing to do but watch.

Captain Kepper, who was in command of a transport, came up the river one day with coal for the fleet and had me aboard for supper. When it was time for me to return to my ship, Kepper told me all the boats had been run up for the night and I must remain all night and have a fine breakfast. As there was nothing else to do, I remained. The next morning before I was up, the ship was on its way down the river. I made Kepper understand that it was a serious position for me to be in, and then he said that he was going to report to the flagship for orders and that I could see the admiral and that I could also ask him to accept my resignation as I wanted to return to "Rio." I did so and the Admiral told me he would not accept my resignation as he was well satisfied with what I had accomplished. I told him I was doing nothing and drawing a good salary. The Admiral said, "How can you do anything if we are doing nothing. You return to the *Tamandaré* and Captain Barboso will send you to my ship, the *Arpa*, as you will like it better." When I returned to the ship and made my report, Captain Barboso did not know what to do about it, so sent over to the Chief of the Division who informed him I was under the Admiral's orders and to send me to the *Arpa*.

There was a young Lieutenant aboard the *Tamandaré* named Vitor de La Mar, he understood English well and we had become good friends with all the officers. Foster, my interpreter also went along with me and I got a large stateroom with Lieutenant Alfredit of the Swedish Navy so I was well fixed. There was nothing doing just then with the Fleet and my duty was light. The Admiral had a large

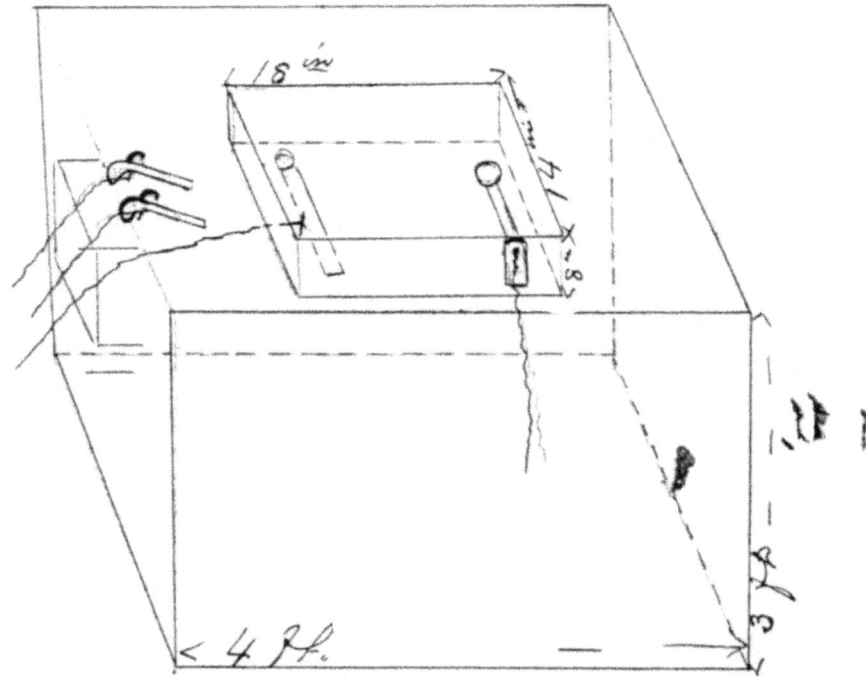

Sketch by Tomb of a Paraguayan torpedo that was carried in the bottom of a canoe (Tomb Family Papers).

salon and at times there were quite a number of guests at his table. The Admiral was quite a linguist. He would converse with a French officer on one side, a Spanish officer on the other, and address a few words to me in English on the opposite side of the table. At times I would not understand him and would have to guess the answer by watching his face to tell if the answer should be yes or no. He did this to show he was well up in English.

There was a remarkable engagement at Etapero between a "chata" or flat boat mounting one 68-pounder on a pivot manned by Paraguayans who came down abreast of our fleet or ironclads and opened fire at us at close range. The fire from the chata was good, dismounting one gun and wounding a number on the *Taman-*

daré, Lieutenant de La Mar being one of them. After some little time the chata was sunk, but the Paraguayans hauled the gun back at night and mounting it on another chata, came down again to the same position and the first shot struck the *Tamandaré*, but a shot from one of the ships struck the gun and smashed it and that was the end of the engagement.

When the Paraguayans evacuated the fort, the Admiral thinking it might be mined, sent me inside to make an examination, as all their mines had lines attached to them, but there were no mines or guns either. Some little time before they evacuated the fort, the Brazilians had taken a small island just in front of the fort and were mounting guns on it. López sent an expedition of some 900 troops one night to take it and did so, massacring all on the island, but before they could get back, the ship opened fire on them and not half of them got back safely. For days after this you could see red shirts floating on the river as they all wore red shirts. It was said the expedition was planned by a Madam Lynch who was with López all the time.

14

Loss of the *Rio de Janeiro*

[In the year prior to Tomb's arrival in South America, the Battle of Riachuelo had been fought on June 11, 1865, between the Paraguayan Navy and those of the Triple Alliance. On June 8, the Paraguayan fleet had gathered at the capital of Asunción for a morning departure down the Paraguay River toward the fortress of Humaitá. López himself was to go aboard the *Tacuarí*. As soon as he arrived at Humaitá on the morning of the following day, López began to prepare for the attack on the alliance squadron, which was stationed farther downriver at Corrientes. Here, in a wide section of the river called Riachuelo, the ships of the Brazilian Navy were lending their support to the land forces of the Triple Alliance who were attempting to expel the Paraguayans from Corrientes. López's intention was to strike the Brazilian ships at dawn on June 11. His squadron consisted of nine ships: the flagship *Tacuarí*; the newly arrived *Paraguarí*, which had been built in England; the captured Brazilian steamship *Marquês de Olinda*; and the *Ygureí, Ybera, Yporá, Jejuí, Salto Oriental* and the *Pirabebé*. Along with these ships, six low-lying flat bottomed barges, known as *chatas*, with one eight-inch cannon each, would be towed to meet the enemy. The squadron mounted 36 guns. Commodore Pedro Inácio Meza was chosen to command the assault. In addition, the Paraguayan ships would have the support of a battery of artillery under Colonel José Maria Bruguez that had been placed along the shoreline of the river.

Brazil's squadron, anchored near Corrientes, included the *Amazonas* (flagship) and the gunboats *Jequitinhonha, Belmonte, Parnaíba, Ipiranga, Mearin, Iguatemi, Araguarí* and the *Beberibé*. Total firepower of the squadron amounted to 59 guns with Admiral Francisco Manuel Barroso in command.

Meza's plan was to run down the Paraná River before daybreak of June 11 in order to reach the enemy by dawn. Surprise, he hoped, would compensate for the fact that the Paraguayan ships were outgunned. At 2:00 A.M. the fleet left Humaitá, and at 5:00 A.M. the *chatas* joined with them. Unfortunately, a problem with the engine of the *Iberá* delayed the departure and it was not until approximately 9:00 A.M., in broad daylight, that the ships reached Riachuelo. After placing the *chatas* near the shore, Meza ordered his ships to steer directly for the enemy in an attempt to separate the Imperial Squadron. Barroso ships were stationed near the confluence of the Paraná and two narrow channels. The attack, if not an entire surprise, caught Barroso's ships anchored inline with their heads toward the shore.

Meza's squadron passed by the enemy ships while sending a blistering fire into them. Each of his vessels chose one ship to engage. Soon the *Amazonas* was under intense fire from the *Tacuarí*, while the *Ipiranga* was exchanging fire with the *Salto*. In the fray the two squadrons changed position with Meza finding himself below the enemy squadron and cut off from his base at Humaitá. The Paraguayan commander attempted to lure the Brazilian ships into shallow water where they could not maneuver as well as his own shallow draft vessels. The *Jequitinhonha*, Barroso's largest ship after the *Amazonas*, ran aground on a sandbar and became an easy target for the merciless artillery of Bruguez. The *Belmonte* was hit several times by the fire of the *chatas*. The *Parnaíba* struck the shore and began to drift out of control. Soon she was surrounded by several Paraguayan ships. The crew of the *Marquês de Olinda* boarded the Brazilian ship, and a deadly fight took place on *Parnaíba's* deck. Repeatedly, the Paraguayans tried to take control of the ship, but with stiff resistance the *Parnaíba's* crew fought off the enemy. A desperate final assault was repelled and the ship slipped away from the Paraguayans.

At this point, things began to change. Despite the difficulties in maneuvering, the superior firepower of Barroso's ships began to take effect. The *Jejuí* was sunk by close-in fire, and the *Marquês de Olinda* had her boilers shot through and was put out of action. The *Paraguarí* was rammed by the *Amazonas* and laid helpless. Meza gave orders to retreat, and at 1:00 P.M., the fight was over. Of the eight Paraguayan vessels, only four were able to return to Humaitá. The others were sunk, captured, or lay helpless on sandbars (this included the *Paraguarí*, the *Jejuí*, the *Marquês de Olinda* and the *Salto Oriental*). Two *chatas* were sunk and the other four fell into Brazilian hands. Some days later, however, the Paraguayans were successful in taking the *Paraguarí* back, sending the ship to Assuncíon for repair.

The Paraguayan losses are not entirely known. The Brazilian estimate of 1,000 casualties was probably exaggerated. Meza died some days later in Humaitá from wounds that he had received during the battle. The Imperial Squadron lost one ship — the *Jequitinhonha*— and two others, the *Parnaíba* and the *Belmonte*, were severely damaged. The *Ipiranga* was slightly damaged. Barroso had 104 men killed, 123 wounded, and 20 missing. The Paraguayans had failed in their attempt to take command of the entire Paraná River from Assuncíon to Montevidéo. In addition, they could not replace the ships lost, while Brazil was fast adding new units to her fleet. More than a year later, it was the Brazilian Navy's turn to take the offensive.[1]— Editor]

While I was attached to the flagship *Arpa* of the Brazilian Navy under Admiral Tamandaré, I received orders to proceed up the river at night and see if there were any torpedoes in the channel along the chaco side of the river and between a

Top: Battle of Riachuelo by Victor Meireles (Brazilian Archives & Fine Arts Museum). *Bottom:* The Imperial Navy on the Paraná River (1866) (Brazil).

Top: The *Ipiranga* (right) and the *Salto Oriental* exchanging fire. *Bottom:* Exchange of fire between Marines aboard the *Amazonas* and a Paraguayan ship (probably the *Paraguarí*). (Brazilian Archives.)

line of piles with which López had closed the channel. Chief Pilot Echebani with a crew of twelve men went along with me. I made use of a sharp grapnel and cutter and found an open passage of some eighty feet between the piles and no torpedoes. Just outside of the line of piles I could see from the action of the water that there was, what I thought, three torpedoes between the end of the obstruction and a battery of two guns manned by the Paraguayans. As we returned down the river, we went alongside of the *Rio de Janeiro* and made a clear report of the opening and also of the torpedoes between the piles and the battery.

The commander of the *Rio de Janeiro*, Captain Silvado, could speak English well and was a fine officer. We then proceeded to the flagship and made the same report to the Admiral, about 1:30 a.m. At 9:30 a.m. the three ironclads, *Brazil*, *Bahia*, and *Rio de Janeiro*, passed up through the opening we gave them, the *Rio de Janeiro* being the last to pass up. While engaging the battery, Captain Silvado evidently forgot about the instructions he had received about the torpedoes in the channel, and worked his ship outside of the obstruction to get near the battery. As I looked the ship drifted broadside down the stream and the stern came over one of the torpedoes. There was an instantaneous explosion and a great column of water went up and in a few minutes the ship went down with most of the officers and crew. Captain Silvado got partly out of the after port but his foot got caught inside and he went down with his ship. Captain Silvado had better instruction as to the torpedoes than the other ships, but forgot it in working his guns on the battery. The Paraguayans would not surrender and stuck to their guns to the last.

Curapete was a few miles above the point and was held by the Paraguayans, who had one 8-inch gun mounted on a pivot at the highest point of the bluff and a light entrenchment toward the Brazilians. There was also a line of piles from the chaco out to midstream. The Admiral sent me up with a guard along the chaco side of the river to see if there were any torpedo lines leading into the woods. I left the guard and went up by myself and found one line leading from a point on the river up to a tree. I cut the rope and tied it to a buoy so as to mark the position of the torpedo.

When the torpedo was raised, it held upwards of 500 pounds of powder, but was in bad condition as two-thirds of the powder was wet. There were three boxes, one inside the other, and the center one held the powder. When they pulled the line a small lever forced a piston into a tube containing sulphuric acid in a glass tube and fulminate caused the explosion. The construction was very poor. No doubt if a ship had passed over it before the powder got wet she would have been lost. At the point where I found the line attached to the tree there was a mat of cowhide on the ground and a block of wood for the observer to sit on. I went on up until I got in front of Curapete end with my glasses could take in all of the bluff. Outside of the 8-inch gun there were no others on the bluff, as far as I could see.

I made my report to the Admiral who was very much pleased. When they decided to make the attack about three weeks later, López had mounted some thirty guns facing the allies. These were three weeks lost. Then the Admiral wanted to know if there was clear water between the piles and the chaco. I was

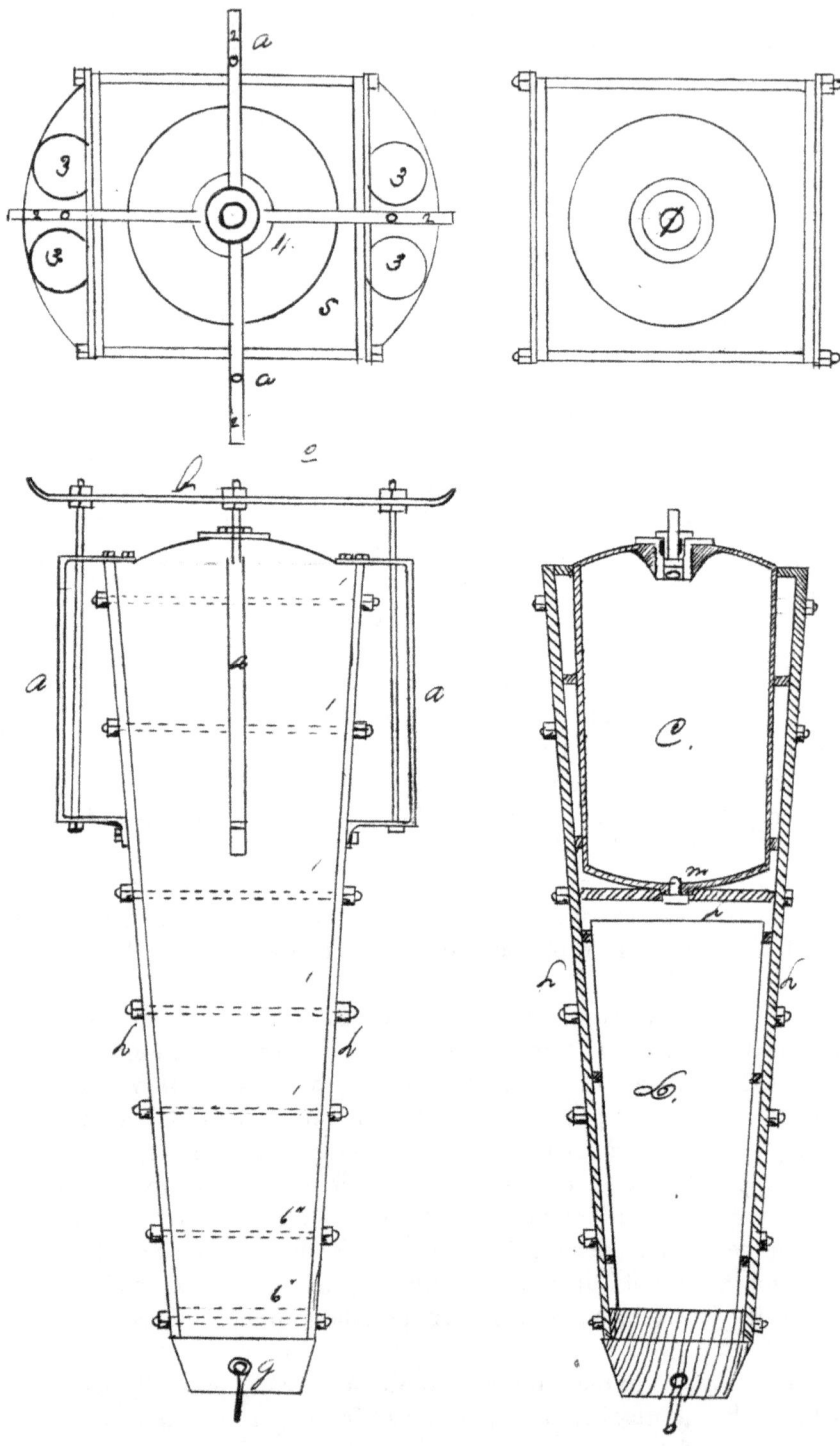

A sketch by Tomb of a floating Paraguayan torpedo (Tomb Family Papers).

sent up in a barge commanded by an ensign. When half way up the river, the ensign saw an object he took for a floating torpedo. The Paraguayans would place a box containing powder in a canoe with a gun in the end and a long line leading to another canoe with a crew. When the torpedo was near a ship, they would pull the line and explode it. I had my interpreter, Foster, tell the ensign to pull across the stream and I would cut the line with my grapnel, but the launch turned down stream, making fine time, and that was the end or Expedition No. 1. The object we ran away from was an empty canoe and it was one on me.

About ten days later we made another start. This time there were two canoes. One commanded by Lt. Victor de Lamar, who was a fine young officer. The other was in command of Chief Pilot Echebani. We had gone up quite a distance along the chaco side of the river, when the pilot informed us that he saw some canoes pass over from the Paraguay side. Victor asked me what I thought and I told him to push ahead. Just then a noise over head in the woods was heard and both canoes turned and made good speed going downstream. The end of Expedition No. 2.

This was a bad layout for me, but Victor said it was up to him and not me as he was in command. I went to Chief Barros and requested that he give me four Indians from the ship's crew and no officer as then I would be responsible if we turned back. The Chief was a little in doubt about it, but at last he decided to let me go up as I had requested. He let me have his night glass and revolver. We left the flagship about midnight. I was up in the bow and foster was steering. When abreast of the Paraguayan pickets, the men stropped their paddles. When I asked Foster what the trouble was, he told me the man were afraid I would take them over to López as I was not a Brazilian. I put down my glass and put the pistol near the man in the seat next to me and told Foster to tell them that if they did not paddle at once it was all up with them. They responded very quickly. We reached the piles and obstruction and found a good opening between the piles and chaco end no torpedoes. At the end of the piles between them and the bluff, there was every indication of two or three floating torpedoes just under the surface. In order to verify my report to the admiral, I made Foster take off his shirt and shinny up to the top of a pile and make it fast as there might be some doubt as to the truthfulness of my report. The next morning the white shirt was quite plain to us and Foster was short one shirt, but I gave him one of mine and he was much better off for the exchange. The Admiral was very much relieved at my report of the clear space along the chaco, and the white flag on the pile made my report a safe one. Chief Barros made me a present of his revolver and it came in use while at Asuncion. I gave a good report concerning the four Indians who composed my crew. After one little stoppage, they did splendidly and seemed to have every confidence in me. I also made my report to the Admiral and suggested that the Paraguayans, seeing the white flag on the pile, might place torpedoes in the channel on the chaco side and close the opening that I had found clear.

It was at least three weeks before we made the advance on the works and by that time the Paraguayans had a large number of field pieces behind the trenches, and also a barrier of trees and posts in front of the trenches. The *Brazil*, *Bahia*, and *Tamandaré*, all ironclads, passed up through the piles along the chaco side and then came to anchor in front of the bluff in midstream. There was just one 8-inch gun mounted on a pivot and quite low in the ground. It was well served as the whole side of our casemate of 4-inch iron was badly dented and bolts were started from the wood backing.[2] The *Brazil* right ahead of us had one gun dismounted and a number of the crew were wounded. The *Bahia* was a turret ship and was only struck a few times.

About 3:00 p.m. the Admiral sent up signals for us to return down the river as the army had failed to take the works. About two thirds of our shots went over the bluff or into the bank, and the last shot was from the 8-inch gun on the bluff. We were not in it at all as the Paraguayans had the best of us, both army and navy.

Admiral Joaquim Marques Lisboa, Baron of Tamandaré (Brazilian Archives).

As the *Tamandaré* made the turn down stream, her stern came within a few feet of a torpedo and Tomb got quite near the side port as she passed. It was a close call. Tamandaré was anxious to make the attack before López could strengthen the works, but it took the allies so long to decide as to the attack that López was ready for them when they came.

There was a good bit of criticism in the newspapers at this time about the Fleet not passing up the Paraguay River to Asuncion, but Admiral Tamandaré refused to go up until the army was ready to advance and hold the ground taken. He was right for had he dome so, the Paraguayans would have placed torpedoes in the river and boarded the ships also. No one could question the Admiral's courage or ability, and it is my opinion it was not a case of Farragut passing the batteries on the Mississippi River.

It was interesting to see how many councils of war there were on the flagship. Minister Octaviana, General Ozero, and General Palledora all had to be consulted and it took twenty-one days to decide although Tamandaré was ready on the first day. There seemed to be a desire on the part of the army to put off for tomorrow what should be done today.

While with the Admiral on the *Arpa*, I received a letter from Commodore Thomas J. Page of the Confederate States Navy, who was at Corrientes. I requested

The Allied Fleet in Curuzu near the Humaitá Fortress (Brazilian Archives).

permission from the Admiral to go down the river to see him. The Admiral called his aide and had him write a letter to Commodore Page inviting him to return with me to the *Arpa* as his guest. I took the letter to Commodore Page and he came back with me to the flagship and was a guest of Admiral Tamandaré for a couple of weeks. The Commodore appreciated it very much, but not more than I did myself, as I felt the Admiral was as hospitable as he was brave. You seldom find as many good qualities in one holding the position of Admiral Tamandaré.

> [Captain Thomas Jefferson Page had been a commander in the United States Navy when he resigned his commission upon the outbreak of war. He had served briefly in the Virginia Navy until that service's personnel were transferred to Confederate service. He was in command of the Gloucester Point battery on the York River until the army's evacuation of the Peninsula during McClellen's advance on Richmond in the spring of 1862. Later, he commanded the forces manning the guns on Chaffin's Bluff on the James River below Richmond. Sent to Europe in 1863, he was given command of the CSS *Stonewall*, the only European-built ironclad to eventually sail under the Confederate flag. On May 19, 1865, Page surrendered the *Stonewall* to Cuban authorities at Havana after learning that the American Civil War was over.[3] — Editor]

After the fall of Asuncion, the capital of Paraguay, the death of López, and capture of Madame Lynch who was with President López, the city was full of desperate characters who frequently waylaid people returning to their ships at night. One of the officers of the steamer *Guayara* going aboard one night in a shore boat owned by a Greek was hit on the head by the boatman, who proceeded to rob him. Just as he was struck, he gave a call and Captain Watson of the steamer and first

The armored ship *Brazil*, built in France in 1863–1864 and incorporated into the Imperial Navy in December 1864 (Brazilian Archives).

A model of the Brazilian warship *Tamandaré* (Brazilian Archives).

officer started for him in the ship's boat. The boatman seeing them coming made for the lending, and left his boat with the officer lying insensible in the bottom. I was a guest about the *Guayara* and Captain Watson brought the boat along with the officer back to the ship. The doctor took care of the injured officer and the boat belonging to the Greek was run up to the davit. When the *Guayara* got back to Buenos Aires, the boat was sold for $18.00 and it was given to the officer who had been assaulted, so it was not so bad after all.

There was a Doctor Newkirk, who had a drug store on the Market Square, and all the English speaking people in the city as well as officers of the ships made it a center for gathering news. I was up there one night and about 9:00 p.m. I was on my way back to the landing to take the boat for the ship. At that tine there were no sidewalks to amount to anything, and the streets were in bad condition. As I was walking along the sidewalk it struck me that the safest place was in the middle of the street, as all persons had been assaulted while they were passing the shacks, called houses. I was pretty well down toward the landing when one of two men, who were standing near the bank or sidewalk started toward me. I stopped and waited for him to get close to me. When he wanted to know, "What time it was," I told him I had no watch, but he said that I had a chain. I had the revolver that Chief Barros had given me and I gave him a good chance to see it, telling him at the same time that the street was wide enough for both of us and for him to go to the right, and he did so very quickly and I moved on towards the landing.

At another time our ship was lying at Paraná. The town was some distance back from the river. I was rather late in making my return to the ship. It was about 8:30 p.m. and I was in doubt as to the direction to take to reach the lending. Seeing a couple of natives seated near a fire roasting beef on a stick, I asked them the direction to the landing. They were very friendly, but hard-looking pair to face after dark in Paraná, as it had a bad reputation. The direction they gave me was correct, but the night was very dark and the distance at least a mile or more. I thanked them and made a start in the direction they gave me and when a short distance away from them, I made a turn and came back to the town and took up quarters at the hotel, returning to the ship the next morning. When I told Commander Bloem about it, he said it was well I did so as those fellows would have struck me before I had reached the landing as I had no pistol. A man's life about that time was worth about .75 cents after dark. I will say that Villa Paraná was a lively town as the fleas gave me no rest all night, but the landlord of the hotel was honest and it was a safe place to spend the night.

The Brazilians in particular were exceedingly humane in their treatment of the Paraguayans taken prisoners; whereas López took no prisoners and was the worst kind of a despot. López made it a rule to keep all the family of the soldiers back in the country, and in case any of his men deserted the members of the family would pay the penalty.

The Brazilian Admiral hearing that there was a large number of Paraguayans up at a village called San Pedro, suffering from lack of food and clothing, sent a steamer up the river and brought at least 500 old men, women, and children down to Asuncion and issued rations to them. I saw them when they landed and it was a sad sight as they were people who at one time had good homes in the city. There was one little girl about 14 years old — at that age in Paraguay they are considered women — who had little more then a fig leaf for a dress. She could speak Spanish well. Most of the natives spoke Guarena. She had auburn hair, eyes that were between blue and black and fine features. I told the steward to give her a sheet to make a dress for herself, which she did in about five minutes. She cut a hole in the center, put her head through the hole, and made use of a cord packing yarn for a waistband. She looked well-dressed alongside of the others on the boat. I asked her what she was going to do to make a living when she got home. She said she had no home in the city as she was from the country. Her father and mother were with her. She said she was going to sell things to her people in the market. I gave her $5.00 to make a start and forgot all about it.

They would sit on a rock or box in the market, an open lot or square, and display their merchandise, mostly thread, common muslin, calico, etc. Captain Muer told me he had bought some thread from a little Paraguayan girl and when he had paid her for it had asked what she would take for all her merchandise with herself thrown in. She gave him back his money and told him that neither he nor any other Gringo could buy her. Sometime after this when I was passing through the market, I was very much surprised to find that it was my little friend, Marguerite, from San Pedro. She had invested the $5.00 I had given her in merchandise and was doing well. When in Asuncion, I would always go to the market and buy a few things and leave them with her. She had her money in a small leather bag about her neck and would hand it to me to count to see how much she had made. She got her goods from the stores near the market. The stores would let her have the merchandise with the understanding that all she failed to sell she could return and get credit for. I asked her how she could sell at the same price as the

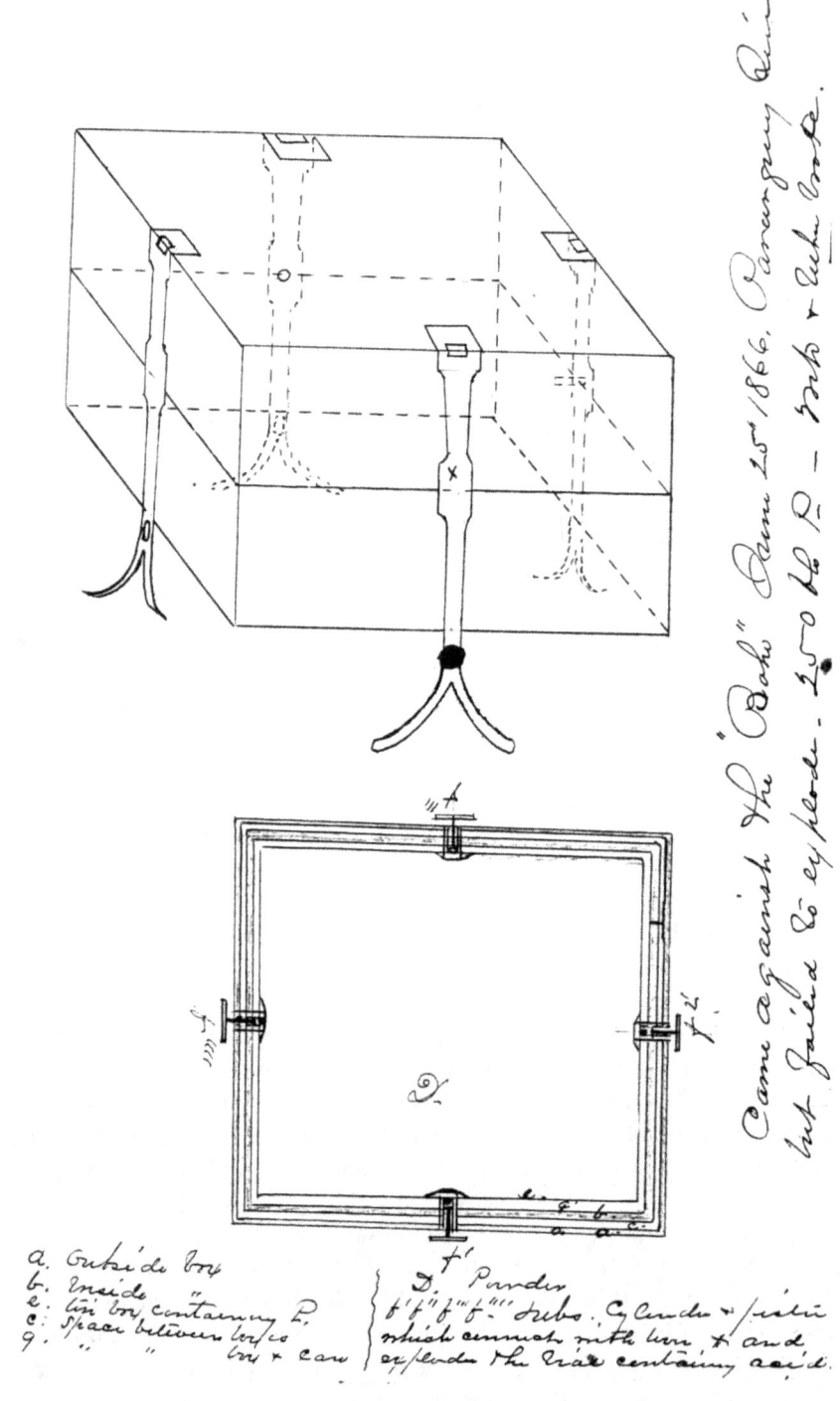

A sketch by Tomb of a Paraguayan torpedo that struck the *Bahia* but failed to explode (Tomb Family Papers).

stores and yet make anything on the sale. While I was there a Paraguayan woman bought some calico, and after she left she told me she had cut her yard stick off five inches and had made that much on the sale, yet she was honest in everything else outside of business. One day while talking to her she gave me the bag to hold and without thinking I walked away with it. She ran after me, put in a coin, took out some change, and gave the bag back to me and went back to her stand in the market.

One time while in Buenos Aires, I got a lady interested in her and she said she would take her into the family and then give her every chance. When I told Marguerita about it, she said she would not accept the invitation as the Argentineans were enemies of Paraguay. I found that all the women, high and low, had a great pride in and attachment for their country, but a fear of López. I think the women are the best patriots in all countries.

When our ship got orders for Rio, I went up to the market to say goodbye, and I asked her if she would go to North America with me. She looked up and asked me if I would take her father and mother, also. I said no. Then she said it was a long way from Paraguay but she would go with me. As I was not serious, her answer was a surprise to me, and I saw it was not doing the right thing and it made me feel badly. I could not say anything more but took her bag and put $10.00 in it and left for the last time.

While on my way up the Paraná River on the *St. Amecota*, I made good friends of the Padre Americus, who was attached to the ship. He held services in a small church at La Posadas where I had the pleasure of pulling the bell rope. The padre had done his best to convert me, but when I told him I was not a good subject he let up. I remember one time he was playing cards, (he was well up in the game) a call came for him to attend one of the crew who had died. He went out to do his duty, but did not leave the cards on the table. I do not know what he did with them, as he had them up his sleeve when he came back to finish the game. The padre failed to appear at meal time one day and was found lying on the deck of his stateroom dead. The doctor said it was caused by an overdose of some drug that he was in the habit of taking for his nerves.

The nights were close and the boy would always make up my bed or mats on the saloon table, my head being up against the mast. That night after the padre had been laid out his head rested against the back of the same mast, but I did not know it. When the boy asked about making my bed, I said to lay the mat at the same place as before. The boy said, "But the padre," and left. When I went into the saloon, there was my friend, the padre, lying with his head within a few inches of my pillow and it was not a very cheering sight. Then I knew what the boy meant. I took in the situation and felt that as the padre was one who would not injure me when alive, certainly, he would do me no harm if dead. I laid down on my mat as I knew all the officers who had been in the saloon that night would have the joke on me if I didn't. I was up early next morning and can't say it was a restful night. We put the padre ashore at Eumata as there was a large church there. He and I were good friends all the time and I was more than sorry at his death.

The padre was well educated and had given me a very clear account of what brought on the war with Paraguay. Brazil was in the right to my way of thinking, and as much as Dom Pedro wished to, he could not avoid it. López was not a president, he was a despot.

15

Adiós South America

After the Battle of Etapere and our failure to take the works, the press of Rio de Janeiro caused the Emperor to make a change in the command of both the troops and the navy [January, 1868]. The Admiral informed me that he would return to Rio de Janeiro and that I could serve with the admiral who took his place. I told him that I would prefer to return to Rio de Janeiro as I did not care to remain with the new admiral and would like to have him accept my resignation. The Admiral said he could not accept my resignation but would let me go to Rio de Janeiro and report to the Minister of Marine and that he was going on the corvette *Neteroy*. He told me I could go with him or on the *Presidente*, under command of Commander Bloem who would go to Rio Grande du Sul, Porto Alegre and Saint Catharina, and this would give me a chance to see the country as he would like to have me remain in Brazil.

I selected the *Presidente* and left the *Arpa* for Rio de Janeiro stopping at Corrientes, Parana, Rosario, Buenos Aires, and Montevideo and then to Rio Grande.

When leaving the *Arpa*, Lieutenant Victor de Lamar, gave me letters of introduction to his family in Rio Grande. He also gave me his uniform coat that had been torn by a portion of the shell that had wounded him in the engagement with the chata at Etapere, which I was to give to his mother.

On arriving at Rio Grande I requested Commander Bloem to go up to the house with me as I was a little afraid of my Portuguese. When we arrived at the house, Captain De la Mar, who was captain of the port, met us, was very friendly and showed us to the parlor. I might say that the customs of the country are rather different than ours as the men put their arms about each other. This always made me feel uncomfortable. After a short time Victor's mother and two sisters came in and I was wondering if I would have the pleasure of going through a like performance with them as they were beautiful girls. Mrs. De la Mar put her hands on my shoulders and told me how much she appreciated my friendship with her son, Victor. I was uncertain as to what I was to do, and as she was Victor's mother and

Above: Vice-Admiral Joaquim José Ignácio, who replaced Admiral Tamandaré as commander of the Allied fleet in January 1868 (Brazilian Archives). *Left:* The Marquis of Caxias, who replaced Commander in Chief Mitre in January 1868 (Brazilian Archives).

very fine looking, I decided it was up to me to kiss her and did so, but it evidently was not just the right thing for me to do as all three left the room in a hurry, and Captain De la Mar looked blank. Commander Bloem was smiling and told him that it was the custom in North America to kiss the mother of a boy sending a friend with a message from the seat of war. Then the mother and daughters came back, smiling, and I soon felt at home and in the few days of my stay in Rio Grande they made it very pleasant for me. I learned more Portuguese in that time than I had for a month. They did not make it uncomfortable for me, when I at times made blunders. They were fine girls and very much like their brother.

When we left Rio Grande we passed up to Porto Alegre, situated near the mouth of five small rivers, and at quite an elevation. The streets were the best I had seen in Brazil. There were quite a number of fine buildings and homes and it was a beautiful city. I found the city had a large number of Germans, who were leading in all kinds of business.

Leaving Porto Alegre, we proceeded to the Island of Saint Catharina. At this place there was an American consul who was a very good friend of mine as I had taken lunch with him two or three times. It appeared that two sailors from a whaling vessel, who were afflicted with scurvy, had been left in his care. One was about eighteen and the other thirty-five. He asked me if I could get the captain to take them to Rio de Janeiro so that they could go to the marine hospital. I asked Commander Bloem if he would take them, and he did so giving them every attention while on the ship, and on arriving at Rio de Janeiro sent them to the hospital. I was told by the consul later that he had received letters from the boys' mothers thanking him and stating that the boys were well. I never thought they would get well as they were in bad condition from lack of fresh provisions aboard their ship.

Arriving at Rio de Janeiro, I submitted my resignation to the Minister of Marine, but he said he would like to have me return to the fleet as the Admiral was well satisfied with my services. I suppose it was two weeks before he would accept my resignation. He gave me an order on the department for transportation to any point requested. I found that all countries are alike in one respect, and that is in having business with officials. The subordinate officials give you back talk, no consideration and tell you to come back tomorrow. It was so in my case and when I handed my papers to a subordinate, he looked at it, took his cigarette from behind his ear and took a good puff. I told him it was today with me and not tomorrow. He said the order did not state what class of passage. The chief of that department requested me to come to his desk and read the order to his subordinate, stating that he would give me first class passage to any point requested by me. He did so and handed me $300.00. I always found the high officials polite and considerate but the subordinates are the same all the world over.

When ready to sail for England, I had my reservation made on the R.M.S. *Duro*. The rate of passage was 30 to 60 pounds first class. I took a 30 pound stateroom with Captain Johnson of the Argentine Navy. While our room was quite comfortable in port, it was hot when steam was up and we were at sea. I found the steward to be a good fellow and he gave me a berth in a cooler room. Then a friend from Rio, who had a 60 pound room with a vacant berth in it, had me keep him company to Liverpool, while my friend, the captain, was in a stew all the way over.

I was surprised to find out when the ship was ready to sail that the Emperor Dom Pedro II and wife were to make passage in the ship to Lisbon. When the ship sailed, the Emperor was on deck the greater part of the time and was just as pleasant with the passengers and crew as he was when I had my interview with him at the palace and the navy yard.

I had instructed the bathroom boy to have my bath ready quite early in the morning and then call me. One morning I was a little late getting up and found the bathroom I had used was occupied. Seeing another room was open and the water running, I took possession and was having a good time in the tub, when there was a knock on the door and someone said the Emperor was ready to take his bath. Then I knew I was in for it but I did not answer but made a good bit of noise in the tub and he left. I got out on short notice and went to my room before the man got back. I found out from the boy that that bathroom was reserved for the Emperor and had I taken pains to look around the room would have seen it was private. I found, however, that the water was just the same as in my room. I never made another break like that.

When we arrived at Lisbon, there was a strict quarantine against Rio and all passengers would have to go to quarantine except the Emperor and family. The Emperor refused to permit this and said what was right for the passengers was also right for him and they would all go together. Dom Pedro II was an emperor by nature. He was a born one.

There was an amusing incident when the tender brought out the passengers going to England. There was a shortage of young women on the *Duro*. We all lined up at the rail to see how many would come from Lisbon. Bets of five and ten shillings were made that we would get at least three in the bunch coming aboard, and to be safe I bet on one and lost out for when she got over her seasickness, she had been all made up, and was about forty. There was not one who was passing fair and all but those who took up the shillings were in low spirits. When they all got to the table, Captain Johnson said in all his travels of sixty-five years he had never seen such a homely bunch of women. The vote was unanimous.

Captain Johnson gave me some information about the Argentine Navy that was in line with what I heard myself when in Buenos Aires. He said the Argentineans in Buenos Aires were fine people but the navy was a lot of cook shops and no one but the paymaster knew how many there were on a ship and he never told stories out of school. There was one thing you could depend upon, however, and that was that the paymaster would pay you sometime between January and December unless some broker would cash it at a discount. He had a good opinion of General Mitre and the people of the city. In that I agreed with him and also as to their looks. They dress and walk well and the Portanians — a cross between Europeans and natives — are fine looking and most of them speak English fluently, as I found out one day. I was walking with a friend along one of the streets. Two young ladies were walking in front of us. Thinking, like many others did, that they would not understand English, we began to say what we thought about them. I said the blonde was the better looking, but the brunette was good looking also. We must have gone four squares out of our way before we turned back to the mole. They did not show from their manner that they understood a word we said. Some time later I was invited to a party and most of those present were English. The lady of the house said that she wanted to introduce me to a young lady who spoke English and was also good looking. I was all upset when she introduced me to one of the young ladies we had seen on the street. She told me she had heard all we said and they also had gone out of their way just to hear what we would say. I was very much relieved, however, when I learned all my remarks were in her favor. After that I was very careful of my remarks as they understood English better than most of us did Spanish.

I was in Buenos Aires one time just about Christmas and a major in the army took me to one of the large churches for a special service. We got in the church it was beautiful with candles and flowers. There were no pews, just the marble floor. What struck me was that there were so few men and so many women. You could see a poor person in one spot and right alongside of her one in silks. All seemed deeply interested in the service. While we were standing in the aisle, the padre came up to us with some long candles and gave one to the major and one to me, and then lit them. After he left, I asked the major what we were to do with them as I intended to follow him as he was a good Catholic. The padre left us holding the candles and they began to run — just as I felt like doing. Then when the padre

15. Adiós South America

Left: Sarah Green (believed to be Tomb's wife). *Right:* A photograph of James H. Tomb taken in St. Louis in 1896. (Both courtesy of Harvey B. Arche.)

was clear of his last candle and was out of the way, the major blew his out and laid the candle behind a column. I did the same and then we left. I am sure the major was a good churchman as he always took his hat off while passing a church.

> [Tomb's memoirs end here. Unfortunately, his account of his service in the Brazilian Navy, where he signed his name with the rank of O Maquinista (Machinist), is not as complete as that of his Confederate service. Tomb never dated any of his memoirs or the various articles for numerous historical publications. This has made it very difficult to place his memoirs, especially the Brazilian writings, in proper chronological order. In spite of this, his account provides a unique and fascinating look at evolving naval technology set against the backdrop of turbulent events that shook the two continents of North and South America.
>
> Returning to the United States in 1872, after ten years of naval service and finding no viable means of employment in Florida, Tomb went to St. Louis where he became the proprietor of the Mono House, a hotel on North Sixth Street. One year later, on November 10, he married Sarah J. Green in Hempstead County, Arkansas. Sarah, who was born August 20, 1854, bore two sons and a daughter while the couple resided in St. Louis. Both sons, James Harvey (b. 1876) and William Victor (b. 1878), were graduated from the U.S. Naval Academy at Annapolis, attained the rank of captain, and served in World War

Left: James H. Tomb (center) and his two sons, James Harvey (left) and William Victor (right). ***Right:*** James H. Tomb holding a crab on the beach at Jacksonville. (Both courtesy of Harvey B. Arche.)

I. The senior Tomb was to experience his share of heartaches, however, for on December 4, 1880, Sarah passed away and less than two years later on October 10, 1882, his little daughter Isabella (b. 1879) also died.

No doubt grief stricken, Tomb remained in St. Louis where he then owned the prestigious Benton Hotel on Pine Street between 8th and 9th. The Benton was the talk of the town and advertised "Charges Moderate, for Gentlemen Only, and Built with Strict Regard for Safety from Fire."

On March 14, 1898, with national newspaper headlines screaming "Remember the Maine," Tomb, at age 59, wrote to the Secretary of the Navy, John D. Long, in Washington, DC:

> Dear Sir: In the event of war with Spain I would fully tender my services to the department only requesting that I be placed in command of a small torpedo boat with a spar torpedo attached. I fully understand that the Department has but few regular torpedo boats, and they must of necessity be placed under the command of regular naval officers, but as this would be but a small boat and outside of the regular service, feel that in a general engagement I could perhaps destroy one of the ships or boats of the enemy, and prevent the destruction of one of our ships. I would not want any pay, only the command of the boat. I would state for the information of the Department that I was

attached to the command of Flag Officer John R. Tucker, CSN, at Charleston, S.C., in 1863, and fully understand the responsibilities and risk attending a service of this kind, and would not be lacking in the performance of my duty.[1]

Secretary Long responded a few days later thanking Tomb for his "patriotic motives" and promising to place his application on file "to receive consideration should an emergency arise requiring your services." The need for his services never arose, however, and Tomb, unlike some other Confederate veterans, never had the opportunity to serve in the Spanish-American War.

All during this time Tomb had maintained close contact with his family in Jacksonville, and in 1905 he sold all of his interests in St. Louis and returned to his hometown in Florida. He built a house at 2705 Park Street where he lived for many years. A cousin of Tomb's operated a cotton mill in Dalton, Georgia, and he evidently spent several summers in Dalton helping to run the mill. During this time, Tomb continued to maintain a warm and frequent correspondence with a W. S. Wells of New Haven, Connecticut. Wells had been a second assistant engineer on the USS *New Ironsides* when Tomb and the *David* made their torpedo attack on the night of October 5, 1863. The two opposing veterans became close friends, even to the point of exchanging Christmas gifts every year. Their letters are not only filled with descriptions of everyday events in their own lives, but both men also wrote extensively about their deepening anguish over the events that were unfolding in Europe during World War I. Both men wrote at length expressing their concern over the depredations being committed in the Atlantic by submarines of the Imperial German Navy. Both marveled at the fact that they were each participants at the beginning of this age of underwater warfare.[2]

In 1915, Tomb had a monument constructed in Evergreen Cemetery in Jacksonville honoring the crew of the *David*. The inscription reads:

James H. Tomb (right) with his sister Mattie (left) and son William Victor (center). After the death of Tomb's wife Sarah, Mattie, who never married, lived with James and raised the two Tomb boys (courtesy Harvey B. Arche).

Top: James and his sister Mattie on the front porch of their home in Jacksonville. *Below:* James H. Tomb in his final years. (Both courtesy of Harvey B. Arche.)

15. Adiós South America

Top: The Tomb family plot in Evergreen Cemetery, Jacksonville, Florida. *Left:* The obelisk erected by Tomb in honor of the crew of the CSS *David*. *Above:* Grave of James H. Tomb, Evergreen Cemetery, Jacksonville, Florida. (All courtesy of Kevin Spargur.)

IN MEMORY OF MY
SHIPMATES OF THE
CONFEDERATE
TORPEDO BOAT DAVID
CHARLESTON S.C. OCT. 5, 1863
LIEUT. W. T. GLASSELL, C.S.N.
PILOT W. J. CANNON, C.S.N.
FIREMAN JAS. SULLIVAN, C.S.N.
CHIEF ENGINEER
JAMES HAMILTON TOMB, C.S.N.

A decade and a half later at age 91, after succumbing to pneumonia, Chief Engineer James Hamilton Tomb was laid to rest on May 25, 1929, beside the obelisk.

Tomb, along with thousands of others, had left his home and family to do battle against an invading enemy and to struggle for a better life in an independent southern nation. His courage and devotion were not unique, for many at this time displayed similar spirit. His courage and devotion, however, involved him in a new and controversial method of naval warfare, and that was unique. Attacks conducted on enemy vessels such as was carried out by the torpedo boat *David* and the submarine *H. L. Hunley* had never occurred before in the history of naval conflict. Tomb was an active participant in this momentous event, and interestingly, he was also closely involved with the *Hunley* through his friendship with Lieutenant Dixon, the submarine's commander. His service in the Brazilian Navy, where he reported directly to the Admiral of the Imperial Fleet during the Paraguayan War, further illustrates the esteem and high value placed upon his knowledge of torpedo warfare.

By 1929, Tomb had lived to see this underwater warfare develop to a state of perfection that he could have never imagined in 1863. Arguably, the German submarines that prowled the Atlantic Ocean during World War I and wrecked such havoc on Allied shipping efforts, could trace their heritage back to the CSS *David* and that cold, moonlit night in 1863. Tomb must have watched in amazement — or perhaps in horror — as to just what his efforts had wrought. — Editor]

Appendix A

Submarines and Torpedo Boats, C.S.N.

by James H. Tomb, Chief Engineer, CSN

(*Confederate Veteran* Magazine, April 1914)

The first torpedo boat to be called the "David" was built at Charleston, S.C., in 1863 by Capt. Tho. Stoney Ravennel and other merchants of that city, but was not a submarine boat in any way. At the time this boat was being constructed Lieut. W. T. Glassell, C. S. N., Maj. Francis D. Lee, Engineer Corps, C. S. A., and I, Chief Engineer C. S. N., had been experimenting with the first and second cutters of the *Chicora* with a torpedo attached to a spar projecting some ten feet from the bow and held in position seven feet below the surface by perpendicular rods at the bow and stern of the cutter. While the attachment was not just what we wanted, it did very well. The torpedo was made of copper and contained sixty-five pounds of rifle powder.

Lieutenant Glassell made three attempts with the first cutter to reach the monitors at anchor off Morris Island, and I made two in the second cutter; but in each case we had the same trouble and made the same report to Flag Officer Tucker—viz: "We could not depend upon the crew pulling with any force when within sight of the enemy, and as each trip was made on the last of the ebb tide, so as to strike on the first of flood, we made no headway when we struck it, and so we had to return without accomplishing anything."

At this time the *David* was not quite ready. Captain Stoney and others made application to Flag Officer Tucker for Lieutenant Glassell and myself to take charge of the boat and after attaching the torpedo make an attack on the United States steamship *New Ironsides*, the most powerful ship of the enemy lying off Charleston. Captain Stoney named her the *David* from the great disparity between her and the duty she had to perform in the effort to destroy the *Ironsides*.

The David was built of wood in the shape of a cigar, fifty feet long by six feet beam amidships. The boiler was forward and the engine aft. Between them was a cuddyhole for the officers and what other crew the boat might carry, which was entered by a hatchway. The hull was about half above water.

The torpedo was attached to a spar made of a three-inch boiler tube and was fixed in position before leaving the dock in Charleston, and it could be neither raised nor lowered after starting on the expedition. A two-bladed propeller drove the *David* about seven knots. The torpedo was of copper, having three tubes which contained a glass tube filled with sulphuric acid and fulminate, etc., between; the outside tube was of lead.

When ready for action the boat was so well submerged that nothing was visible except her smokestack, the hatch coamings, and frame holding the torpedo spar. Lieut. W. T. Glassell was in command. Under him were Engineer James H. Tomb, Fireman J. Sullivan, and Pilot W. Canners.

The Confederates desired very much to destroy the frigate *New Ironsides*. The night selected was October 5, 1863, about one year previous to the destruction of the *Albemarle* by Lieutenant Cushing of the United States navy. There was a mist over the harbor when the *David* started. Running down guard boats, reaching the *Ironsides* shortly before 9 P.M. As the flood tide had not yet set in, we laid off and on till 9 P.M., when it was thought best to run for the *Ironsides* before we were discovered. When within a short distance of her, and steaming about seven knots, they hailed us; but the only reply was a shot from a double-barreled gun in the hands of Lieutenant Glassell. The next moment we struck her some fifteen feet forward of the counter. The torpedo exploded, and the big frigate was shaken from stem to stern, but the explosion produced a bad effect on the *David*. The volume of water thrown up, passing down the smokestack, put out the fires and filled the body of the boat, as well as disabled the engine. Lieutenant Glassell then gave orders for each man to look out for himself, and we all went overboard. Lieutenant Glassell was picked up by a transport schooner, Sullivan by the *Ironsides*, and Canners, who could not swim, stuck to the *David*. I swam some distance down the harbor; but finding that my clothing was impeding my progress, and looking back and seeing that the *David* was still afloat, I concluded to return and try to save her. After getting aboard I adjusted the machinery, started tip the fires once more, and, helping the pilot aboard, proceeded up the harbor, turning between the *Ironsides* and a monitor to prevent them from using their heavy guns on us in passing. The *Ironsides* fired three shots from her heavy gains, which passed over us.

All this time there was a heavy fire directed on the *David* from small arms from the deck of the *Ironsides*, riddling every part of the *David* above water. As we returned up the harbor we passed through the fleet and by the guard boats without further damage to us; and rounding under the stern of the flagship, I made my report to Flag Officer Tucker with nothing on but my undershirt.

The damage to the *Ironsides* was not as serious as it would have been had the torpedo been eight feet below the surface in place of six and a half, as was intended; but finding a flaw in the tube we had for a spar, it was necessary to bring it up that much. There was some serious damage done to her hull, however, as she did not fire another shot on Charleston and was sent North later for repairs.

I was put in command of the *David* and had one-quarter inch of steel placed over the hull above the water line, a cap put over the stack to prevent water from passing down, and arranged the spar so that we could lower it to any depth from the inside or keep the torpedo above the surface.

When the *David* was ready for service, I was sent to the North Edisto to make an attack on the United States steamship *Memphis*, Engineer Tomb in charge, with Pilots Canners, and Acosta, and Fireman Lawless. A section of artillery under Captain Stoney was sent ahead to assist the *David*.

On the night of March 4, 1864, we reached a point just above the anchorage of the Memphis, whose light was plainly seen; but the feed pipe gave out, and we decided to return up the river. The next night about 11:30 P.M., when in about the position, the pump again gave out; but making fast to the marsh, we repaired the pump and proceeded on down in the direction of the *Memphis*. About 12:30 A.M. of the 6th we came within hailing distance, but paid no attention to the hail, and they began firing upon us with small arms; but the shot, striking the steel shield, passed off without doing any injury to the boat or crew. The next moment the *David* struck her on the port quarter under the counter, the engine of the *David* backing at the time. The blow was a fine one, but the torpedo failed to explode. We then made a turn to port and came back at her on the starboard side; but as the *Memphis* had been working ahead, we passed under her counter, carrying away a portion of the *David's* stack, made glancing blow, and again failed to explode the torpedo. Failing in our last attack, we decided to return to Church Flats and examine the torpedo, etc. As we steamed back up the river the *Memphis* made use of her heavy guns, but all the shot passed well over us and did no damage.

Reaching Church Flats and making an examination of the torpedo, we found that the first blow was a good one, as the tube containing the acid was mashed flat, but, being defective, had failed to explode. The other one was not a good blow, as the lead tube on the outside was bent the least bit, but the tube containing the acid was not broken. The torpedo contained five pounds of rifle powder, thirteen pounds more than we used on the *Ironsides*; and had the tube been perfect, we would have blown the whole stern from the *Memphis*.

The *David* returned to Charleston, and while on duty, passing out beyond Fort Sumter at night, did not make another attack on the blockading ships, except on one night in April, when we ran out of Charleston, intending to strike the United States steamship *Wabash*; but there was such a heavy swell that in heading for the *Wabash* the sea would roll on board the *David*, and she came so near sinking that we were compelled to return to Charleston. We headed for the *Wabash* three times.

The *David* had orders to tow the submarine torpedo boat commanded by Lieutenant Dixon past Fort Sumter whenever he wished to run out to make an attack on the blockaders, and in towing him out we came near being blown up by his torpedo getting adrift, (At this stage the CSS *H. L. Hunley* was towing its torpedo on a long line) I advised Lieutenant Dixon to use the torpedo just as it was used by the *David*, as I did not think his boat had sufficient power to back out if it was submerged, and the suction from the sinking ship would be apt to keep him under the water. Lieutenant Dixon gave me to understand that he would remain on the surface. I requested Flag Officer Tucker to relieve the *David* from the duty of towing his boat on account of the danger. That same month Lieutenant Dixon ran out of Charleston and striking the United States steamship *Housatonic*, sank her, and he was lost with all on board the torpedo boat, as she went to the bottom with the *Housatonic*.

When we think of the number of brave men who lost their lives on this ill-fated craft, it brings out the fine qualities of Lieutenant Dixon who in all this never lost confidence either in the boat or himself. There were in all thirty-three lost in her from her first appearance at Mobile to the sinking of the *Housatonic*. The army or the navy had no more gallant officer than Lieutenant Dixon, of the C.S.A.

Appendix B

Manuscript of James H. Tomb

[In addition to his memoirs and various articles, such as that written for the April 1914 edition of *Confederate Veteran*, Tomb also wrote — evidently for his family — an additional account of his experiences with the torpedo boat *David* and the submarine *H. L. Hunley*. A copy of this original manuscript was recently made available to this author through the graciousness of his great-great-nephew, Harvey B. Arche of Liberal, Missouri. Tomb's manuscript had been preserved by Mr. Arche's father, O. Harris Ball, who could always remember "feisty Uncle Jimmy." Much of this account is similar to his other writings, but contains slightly more detail concerning certain events. Tomb's handwriting was not the best, and some portions are barely legible. Where doubt exists as to a word, a [?] has been inserted. Otherwise a conscious and deliberate effort has been made to reproduce Tomb's words just as he wrote them. Here, then, is Tomb's own account of the *David* and the *Hunley*.— Editor]

    The first experiment made with a torpedo attached to a small boat was made by Capt. Francis M. [D.] Lee, Engineering Officer, CSA, at Charleston, SC, in 1862. When attaching a 15 lb. copper torpedo to a spar projecting from the bow of the boat and some five feet below the surface, the boat was drawn up to a pontoon [barge] by a line and when in contact, exploded the torpedo and destroyed the pontoon without injury to the boat. After this Capt. Lee, Lieut. W. T. Glassell, CSN, and myself, experimented with the 1st and 2nd cutter of the CSS *Chicora* in 1862 & 1863, not having a steam launch to make use of at the time.

    Lieut. W. T. Glassell took the 1st cutter and I the 2nd and attaching a spar to which was made fast a 40 lb. copper torpedo having four caps that would explode from contact with the ship. The cutters had a crew of six men and officers. Lieut. Glassell as well as myself passed down below Fort Sumter three times in a vain attempt to reach the monitors laying at anchor off Morris Island. We wished to strike the monitors on the first of the flood tide as they would be moving up stream, and [it] would also give our crew some chance of saving themselves in case of the cutter being destroyed from the explosion or fire of [the] enemy.

We passed Fort Sumter making very good headway each time, but when within sight of the monitors and making the first of the flood tide, neither of the boats could make the least headway, the crew apparently pulling for all they were worth. After three expeditions of this kind with like results, Lieut. Glassell, as well as myself, realized we could do nothing except with a propelling power that one man could control with steam, and we made report to Flag Officer John R. Tucker, CSN, for as so stated as being the cause of our failure to reach the enemy.

At this time the merchants of Charleston, Capt. Theo. Stoney, Ravenel, & others, had in course of construction a small cigar shaped boat 50 ft. by 6 ft., and to be propelled by steam. They made application to Flag Officer Tucker that Lieut. Glassell be placed in charge of her, and Eng. Tomb to assist him for the purpose of fitting her out as a torpedo boat. We received orders to take charge of her for that purpose. She was circular built of wood, 6 ft. amidships and 50 ft. long arriving to a sharp point at each end. The boiler was forward and engine aft having a double engine [gear?] geared to a shaft and driving a two bladed propeller. She would make about 7 kts. when loaded down to her limits. The hull was some eighteen inches above the surface forward and a few inches aft.

We made use of a piece of a 4½ inch oak, grooved with a clamp over the top to hold the spar in position that was attached to the torpedo. The spar was a 3-inch boiler tube 12 ft. long, at the end having a wooden socket holding the torpedo in position. When first arranged the torpedo was 8 ft. below the surface, but discovering a flaw in the tube, we had to bring it up, it was not over 6½ ft. below the surface. The torpedo was made of copper and contained 65 lbs. [of] rifle powder. There were four tubes on the head of the torpedo containing fulminate, the glass tube containing sulphuric acid being covered by a thin leaden tube and requiring but slight pressure to break it.

Lieut. Glassell was not satisfied with the depth of the torpedo, but we decided to make the attack without further delay.

The USS *New Ironsides* had taken her position off Morris Island and did more damage than all the monitors to our coasts, and we decided to make her the object of our attack. The disparity in size of the *Ironsides* and the torpedo boat was such that Capt. Stoney named the torpedo boat "The David" and from this came the application of David for all torpedo boats used in the CSN.

Lieut. Glassell reported the *David* ready for service and Flag Officer Tucker instructed him to make the attack on the *Ironsides* when the weather and the tide suited him. Lieut. W. T. Glassell was the commander, and under him was his Ast. Eng. James H. Tomb, Pilot J. Cannon, and James Sullivan, fireman.

The night selected for the attack was Oct. 5, 1863. We attached the torpedo at the wharf in Charleston and at 7:30 we started down the bay on the last of the ebb tide, the intention being to strike the *Ironsides* on the first of the flood when she would be swinging off the harbor and for us a better position to strike under her quarter, and a chance for us to get back to the harbor on the turn of the tide. There was quite a haze over the harbor when we started, and after passing Fort

Sumter we worked out to eastward from the *Ironsides* running abreast of her about 8:30 P.M., passing through the fleet and guard boats without being seen. At this time the *Ironsides* was swinging down stream on the last of the ebb. After waiting until near 9:00 P.M., we decided it was best to run for the *Ironsides* as they might see us at any moment as the haze was lifting. The steam was permitted to rise in the boiler, and the *David* headed for the frigate making about 7 kts. When within hailing distance they hailed us, but Lieut. Glassell answered by firing a double-barreled shotgun, and then threw it overboard, when they opened on us with small arms from the ship. The next moment the *David* struck the ship some fifteen feet forward of the stern under the counter, the engine of the *David* being reversed at the time. The point struck was the starboard quarter.

The explosion of the torpedo was terrific and the volume of water thrown up passed down the stack and also into the body of the *David* putting out the fires and flooding the boat. The engine would not work from this cause and I so reported to Lieut. Glassell who gave us orders to save ourselves as the *David* was sinking. We all went overboard. Lieut. Glassell and Sullivan had life preservers, but I did not as they had been washed away. I swam in the direction of Morris Island, but my clothing [?] could not make any headway. Looking back and seeing the *David* was still afloat, I decided to swim back and see if we could not save her from the enemy. When I reached the boat I found the pilot hanging to the life lines as he could not swim a stroke. I got aboard after taking all my clothes off, and adjusting the engine and starting up the fires in the boiler, pulled the pilot aboard and made ready to steam back up the harbor. The *David* was laying between the *Ironsides* and a monitor just to the east, in turning the *David* up stream, had to turn between them to prevent their making use of their heavy guns on us. All the time they were pouring a steady fire into all parts of the *David* that was above the water line and she was riddled, but we did not get a shot. In passing up we came close under the counter of the monitor, but they did not fire on us, and the next minute we were going past her on the port side. The *Ironsides* fired three shots from her heavy guns, but if intended for us, did not come near the *David*.

We passed through the fleet and guard boats, and reaching the harbor, reported to Flag Officer Tucker the results of the attack as far as I could know, and the loss of Lieut. Glassell and Sullivan. Having no clothing, the Flag Officer tendered me his own coat, and as the *David* was in a sinking condition, gave me orders to beach her between the docks in Charleston.

The *David* was placed under my command with orders to repair and make such alterations to her torpedo arrangement as I thought best. I had ¼ steel placed over the upper portion of the *David* running three inches below the water line, a cap placed over the stack to prevent the water passing down it into the boiler and furnace and adjusted by a line from the body of the boat. The torpedo attachment was arranged so it could be held above the surface of the water or lowered to any depth desired from the inside when about to make the attack upon a ship.

The *New Ironsides* did not sink, and at first, Union authorities believed that the damage was only slight, but as coal was removed from a bunker it became evident that she was seriously injured. Towed north to the Philadelphia Navy Yard for repairs, the *New Ironsides* was out of action for more than a year and never hurled her huge shells at Charleston again. The exact damage was kept secret throughout the remainder of the war for fear that the Confederates would learn just how close they had come to sinking the most powerful warship in the Union Navy.

With Lieutenant Glassell a prisoner (He had been rescued by a passing Union boat), Tomb was promoted, and as he stated in his manuscript, given command of the *David*. It was during the latter months of 1863, that Tomb and the *David* would cross paths with another even more innovative vessel operating out of the besieged city of Charleston.

The *David* did picket duty beyond Fort Sumter, except running out one night in an effort to strike the frigate *Wabash* laying outside of the harbor, we came near another ship. We could have sunk the *Wabash* had the swell not rolled over and into the *David* and nearly filling her with water. We made three efforts to reach her but had to give it up and return to Charleston.

The *David* was ordered by the Flag Officer to tow the submarine *Hunley*, in charge of Lieut. G. E. Dixon, [George E.] beyond Fort Sumter where he intended to make an attack on the ships of the enemy off Charleston, as Lieut. Dixon's idea was to strike some of the ships laying outside the harbor as they would not be apt to have any outside guard to protect them from a torpedo boat as all the ships at anchor off Morris Island had. The *Hunley* was propelled by hand and the exertion and time it took to reach the lower harbor exhausted his men who had to turn the crank attached to the propeller shaft, there being eight in all, and when at her best could make about 3 knots. The original intention, when constructed, was to dive under a ship and tow the torpedo behind, but this idea was given up later and a spar attached to the bow as was the *David*. Lieut. Dixon's idea was to submerge his boat and strike with the boat's torpedo from below. This we advised against as the lack of power to back, and also lack of buoyancy in the *Hunley* would make his chances of coming up again doubtful, and we thought the surface attack and [the] lowering [of] his torpedo the best. And that was the conclusion he came to. After towing him down the harbor a few times we found she was very easy handling, and one night his torpedo got adrift and came under the *David* and for a time it was uncertain whether we were going up or down or both. We turned upstream and the action of the tide brought it clear, so we got it in operation once more. While working to clear his torpedo the *David* took fire in some way around the boiler and before we could extinguish it, it had burned within a ¼ of an inch of the steel cover on the outside. I reported this to Flag Officer Tucker and requested to be relieved of the duty of towing the *Hunley* down the harbor any more and was relieved of that duty. The *Hunley* took a position under Sullivan's Island so as to avoid the long time down the harbor from the city, and it was from that point that the *Hunley* started out on the night of the 17th of Feb., 1864, when she sunk the *Housatonic* and went down herself. We could not understand what caused the *Hunley* to sink unless it was [that] Lieut. Dixon submerged his boat just before striking and being below the surface, her seams started filling her with water and preventing her rising to the surface. She was a most unfortunate boat from the time she was built in Mobile to the time of her sinking the *Housatonic* off Charleston.

There were 8 lost when she went to the bottom while testing her in Mobile, and when she came to Charleston in 1863, she went to the bottom while getting ready for a trip and laying along side the wharf at Fort Johnson, while her crew under Lieut. Paine [John A. Payne] was below, caused from the wash of a passing steamer. Lieut. Paine just got out as the water passed down the open hatch. She was raised and after being put in order under Lieut. Dixon and Capt. Hunley, also of the army. She left the wharf at Charleston Oct. 15, 1863 in charge of Capt. Hunley just as Lieut. Dixon, James L. Easne, and myself watched it, and as he was standing with his head out of the hatch wanted us to join him, but we did not. The boat proceeded up the river until she was abreast of the receiving ship *Indian Chief* when she passed out of sight intending to pass under the ship and come out on the other side. After waiting awhile and not seeing anything of her, we decided she had passed up the river and it was not until later that we heard she had never come to the surface again.

She was raised some days afterwards and Lieut. Dixon informed me that Capt. Hunley and all the crew were in a bunch at the hatch, and the after valve to the water tank was still open. He regretted that he had not gone out with Capt. Hunley as he had better control of the boat and her mechanisms.

After this you would have thought Lieut. Dixon would have lost confidence in the boat, but he did not as he went to work and soon had her ready for service and secured a crew from the *Chicora* and the fort, and this last crew went to the bottom with him when Lieut. Dixon sank the *Housatonic*. It is hard to conceive of a more gallant officer or modest man that was Lieut. Geo. E. Dixon of the C.S.A. The *Hunley* never should have been submerged when making use of a torpedo, and from Lieut. Dixon's statement he was always more anxious about the lack of fresh air then anything about the boat, as after being submerged a short time [it] became very oppressive, and [he] found that drum candles caused less discomfort than any light he could use while submerged.

I am satisfied that to Lieut. Wm. T. Glassell, C.S.N., belongs the credit of making the first successful attack against an enemy ship with a steam torpedo boat as he did when he struck the USS *New Ironsides* off Charleston, S.C. on the night of Oct. 5, 1863.

> [History has proven Engineer Tomb substantially correct in his narrative, although the *Hunley* did not sink at Mobile and the attack on the *Housatonic* was carried out on the surface. The *Hunley* did sink twice before Dixon's final mission — once on August 29, 1863, when five men died, and again on October 15, when Horace Hunley and seven men lost their lives.
>
> Dixon and his crew were lost the night of February 17, 1864, when they sent the *Housatonic* to the ocean floor. Speculation abounds as to the cause of their failure to return. With the recovery of the submarine on August 8, 2000, and the recovery of Dixon and his crew's remains, that mystery may finally be solved.— Editor]

Appendix C

Reminiscences of Torpedo Service in Charleston Harbor

by *Commander William T. Glassell, CSN*

(*Southern Historical Society Papers*, vol. IV, Richmond, Va., July to December 1877, pp. 225–234)

[The following interesting paper was sent to us from the secretary of the South Carolina Historical Society. In a note that originally accompanied the paper and that the Historical Society kept, the author said that while he had written from memory, and without official reports to refer to, he believed he had given the facts in the order of their occurrence.]

I had served, I believe faithfully, as a lieutenant in the United States Navy, and had returned from China on the United States steamer *Hartford* to Philadelphia, some time in 1862, after the battles of Manassas and Ball's Bluff had been fought. I was informed that I must now take a new oath of allegiance or be sent immediately to Fort Warren. I refused to take this earth, on the ground that it was inconsistent with one I had already taken to support the Constitution of the United States. I was kept in Fort Warren about eight months, and then exchanged as a prisoner of war, on the banks of the James River.

Being actually placed in the ranks of the Confederate States, I should think that even Mr. President Hayes would now acknowledge that it was my right, if not my duty, to act the part of a belligerent.

A lieutenant's commission in the Confederate States navy was conferred on me, with orders to report for duty on the ironclad *Chicora* at Charleston. My duties were those of a deck officer, and I had charge of the first division.

On the occasion of the attack upon the blockading squadron (making the attack at night), if I could have had any influence, we should not have fired a gun, but trusted to the effect of iron rams at full speed. It was thought though, by older and perhaps wiser officers, that this would have been at the risk of sinking our ironclads together with the vessels of the enemy. I have ever believed there was no such danger to be apprehended; and if there was, we had better have encountered it, than to have made the fruitless attempt which we did, only frightening the enemy and putting them on their guard for the future.

It was my part, on that memorable morning, to aim and fire one effective shell into the *Keystone State* while running down to attack us, which (according to Captain LeRoy's report), killing twenty-one men and severely wounding fifteen, caused him to haul down his flag in token of surrender.

The enemy now kept at a respectful distance while preparing their ironclad vessels to sail up more closely. Our Navy Department continued slowly to construct more of these rams, all on the same general plan, fit for little else than harbor defense. The resources of the United States being such that they could build ten ironclads to our one, and of a superior class almost invulnerable to shot or shell, I had but little faith in the measures we were taking for defense.

Mr. Frank Lee, of the Engineers, was employed constructing torpedoes to be placed in the harbor, and called my attention to the subject. It appeared to me that this might be made an effective weapon to use offensively against the powerful vessels now being built. An old hulk was secured and Major Lee made the first experiment, as follows: A torpedo made of copper, and containing thirty or forty pounds of gunpowder, having a sensitive fuse, was attached by means of a socket to a long pine pole. To this weights were attached, and it was suspended horizontally beneath a row-boat, by cords from the bow and stern — the torpedo projecting eight or ten feet ahead of the boat, and six or seven feet below the surface. The boat was then drawn towards the hulk till the torpedo came in contact with it and exploded. The result was the immediate destruction of the old vessel and no damage to the boat.

I was now convinced that powerful engines of war could be brought into play against ironclad ships. I believed it should be our policy to take immediate steps for the construction of a large number of small boats suitable for torpedo service, and make simultaneous attacks, if possible, before the enemy should know what we were about. The result of this experiment was represented to Commodore Ingraham. I offered all the arguments I could in favor of my pet hobby. Forty boats with small engines for this service, carrying a shield of boiler-iron to protect a man at the helm from rifle-balls, might have been constructed secretly at one-half the cost of a clumsy ironclad. The Commodore did not believe in what he called "new-fangled notions." I retired from his presence with a feeling of grief, and almost desperation, but resolved to prove at least that I was in earnest. I got rowboats from my friend, Mr. George A. Trenholm, and at his expense equipped them with torpedoes for a practical experiment against the blockading vessels at anchor off the bar.

Commodore Ingraham then refused to let me have the officers or men who had volunteered for the expedition, saying that my rank and age did not entitle me to command more than one boat. I was allowed, some time after this, to go out alone with one of these boats and a crew of six men, to attack the United States ship *Powhatan* with a fifty-pound torpedo of rifle-powder attached to the end of a long pole, suspended by wires from the bow and stern, beneath the keel of the boat, and projecting eight or ten feet ahead, and seven feet below the surface.

I started out with ebb-tide in search of a victim. I approached the ship about 1 o'clock. The young moon had gone down, and every thing seemed favorable, the stars shining over head and sea smooth and calm. The bow of the ship was towards us and the ebb tide still running out. I did not expect to reach the vessel without being discovered, but my intention was, no matter what they might say or do, not to be stopped until our torpedo came in contact with the ship. My men were instructed accordingly. I did hope the enemy would not be alarmed by the approach of such a small boat so far out at sea, and that we should be ordered to come alongside. In this I was disappointed. When they discovered us, two or three hundred yard distant from the port bow, we were hailed and immediately ordered to stop and not come nearer. To their question, "What boat is that?" and numerous others, I gave evasive and stupid answers; and notwithstanding repeated orders to stop, and threats to fire on us, I told them I was coming on board as fast as I could, and whispered to my men to pull with all their might. I trusted they would be too merciful to fire on such a stupid set of idiots as they must have taken us to be.

My men did pull splendidly, and I was aiming to strike the enemy on the port-side, just below the gangway. They continued to threaten and to order us to lay in our oars; but I had no idea of doing so, as we were not within forty feet of the intended victim. I felt confident of success, when one of my trusted men, from terror or treason, suddenly backed his oar and stopped the boat's headway. This caused the others to give up apparently in despair. In this condition we drifted with the tide past the ship's stern, while the officer of the deck, continuing to ply me with embarrassing questions, gave order to lower a ship's boat to go for us.

The man who backed his oar had now thrown his pistol over-board, and reached to get that of the man next to him for the same purpose. A number of men, by this time, were on deck with rifles in hand. The torpedo was now an encumbrance to retard the movements of my boat.

I never was rash, or disposed to risk my life, or that of others, without large compensation from the enemy. But to surrender thus would not do. Resolving not to be taken alive till somebody at least should be hurt, I drew a revolver and whispered to the men at the bow and stern to cut loose the torpedo.

This being quickly done, they were directed quietly to get the oars in position and pull away with all their strength. They did so. I expected a parting volley from the deck of the ship, and judging from the speed with which the little boat traveled, you would have thought we were trying to outrun the bullets which might follow us. No shot was fired. I am not certain whether their boat pursued us or not. We were soon out of sight and beyond their reach; and I suppose the captain and officers of the *Powhatan* never have known how near they came to having the honor of being the first ship ever blown up a by a torpedo boat.

I do not think this failure was from any or want of proper precaution of mine. The man who backed his oar and stopped the boat at the critical moment declared afterwards that he had been terrified so that he knew not what he was doing. He seemed to be ashamed of his conduct, and wished to go with me into any danger. His name was James Murphy, and he afterwards deserted to the enemy by swimming off to a vessel at anchor in the Edisto River.

I think the enemy must have received some hint from spies, creating a suspicion of torpedoes, before I made this attempt. I got back to Charleston after daylight next morning, with only the loss of one torpedo, and convinced that steam was the only reliable motive power.

Commodore Tucker having been ordered to command the naval forces at Charleston, torpedoes were fitted to the bows of ironclad rams for use should the monitors enter the harbor.

My esteemed friend, Mr. Theodore Stoney, of Charleston, took measures for the construction of the little cigar-boat *David* at private express; and about this time I was ordered off to Wilmington as executive officer to attend to the equipment of the ironclad *North Carolina*. She drew so much water it would have been impossible to get her over the bar, and consequently was only fit for harbor defense.

In the meantime, the United States fleet, monitors and *Ironside*, crossed the bar at Charleston and took their comfortable positions protecting the army on Morris Island, and occasionally bombarding Fort Sumter.

The *North Carolina* being finished, was anchored near Fort Fisher. No formidable enemy was in sight, except the United States steamer *Minnesota*, and she knowing that we could not get out, had taken a safe position at anchor beyond the bar to guard one entrance to the harbor. I made up my mind to destroy that ship or make a small sacrifice in the attempt. Accordingly, I set to work with all possible dispatch, preparing a little steam tug, which had been placed under my control, with the intention of making an effort. I fitted a torpedo to her bow so that it could be lowered in the water or elevated at discretion.

I had selected eight or ten volunteers for this service, and would have taken with me one rowboat to save life in case of accident. My intention was to slip out after dark through the passage used by blockade-runners, and then to approach the big ship from seaward as suddenly and silently as possible on a dark night, making such answer to their hail and question as occasion might require, and perhaps burning a blue light for their benefit, but never stopping till my torpedo came in contact and my business was made known.

I had every thing ready for the experiment, and only waited for a suitable night, when orders came requiring me to take all the men from the *North Carolina* by railroad to Charleston immediately. An attack on that city was expected. I lost no time in obeying the order, and was informed, on arriving there, "my men were required to reinforce the crews of the gunboats, but there was nothing in particular for me to do." In a few days, however, Mr. Theodore Stoney informed me that the little cigar boat built at his expense had been brought down by railroad, and that if I could do anything with her he would place her at my disposal. On examination I determined to make a trial. She was yet in an unfinished state. Assistant-Engineer J. H. tombs volunteered his service, and all the necessary machinery was soon fitted and got in working order, while Major Frank Lee gave me his zealous aid in fitting on a torpedo. James Stuart (alias Sullivan) volunteered to go as firemen, and afterwards the service of J. W. Cannon as pilot was secured. The boat was ballasted so as to float deeply in the water, and all above painted the most invisible color, (bluish.) The torpedo was made of copper, containing about a hundred pounds of rifle powder, and provided with four sensitive tubes of lead, containing explosive mixture; and this was carried by means of a hollow iron shaft projecting about fourteen feet ahead of the boat, and six or seven feet below the surface. I had also an armament on deck of four double-barrel shotguns, and as many navy revolvers; also, four cork life-preservers had been thrown on board, and made us feel safe.

Having tried the speed of my boat, and found it satisfactory, (six or seven knots an hour) I got a necessary order from Commodore Tucker to attack the enemy at discretion, and also one from General Beauregard. And now came an order from Richmond, that I should proceed immediately back to rejoin the *North Carolina*, at Wilmington. This was too much! I never obeyed that order, but left Commodore Tucker to make my excuses to the Navy Department.

The 5th of October, 1863, a little after dark, we left Charleston wharf, and proceeded with the ebb-tide down the harbor. A light north wind was blowing, and the night was slightly hazy, but starlight, and the water was smooth. I desired to make the attack about the turn of the tide, and this ought to have been just after nine o'clock, but the north wind made it run out a little longer.

We passed Fort Sumter and beyond the line of picket-boats without being discovered. Silently steaming along just inside the bar, I had a good opportunity to reconnoiter the whole fleet of the enemy at anchor between me and the camp-fires on Morris Island. Perhaps I was mistaken, but it did occur to me that if we had then, instead of only one, just ten or twelve torpedoes, to make a simultaneous attack on all the ironclads, and this quickly followed by the egress of our rams, not only might this grand fleet have been destroyed, but the 20,000 troops on Morris Island been left at our mercy. Quietly maneuvering and observing the enemy, I was half an hour more waiting on time and tide. The music of drum and fife had just ceased, and the nine o'clock gun had been fired from the admiral's ship, as a signal for all unnecessary lights to be extinguished and for the men not on watch to retire for sleep. I thought the proper time for attack had arrived.

The admiral's ship, *New Ironsides*, (the most powerful vessel in the world) lay in the midst of the fleet, her starboard side presented to my view. I determined to pay her the highest compliment. I had been informed, through prisoners lately captured from the fleet, that they were expecting an attack from torpedo boats, and were prepared for it. I could, therefore, hardly expect to accomplish my object without encountering some danger from riflemen, and perhaps a discharge of grape or canister from the howitzers. My guns were loaded with buckshot. I knew that if the officer of the deck could be disabled to begin with, it would cause them some confusion and increase our chance for escape, so I determined that if the occasion offered, I would commence by firing the first shot. Accordingly, having on a full head of steam, I took charge of the helm, it being so arranged that I could sit on deck and work the wheel with my feet. Then directing the engineer and firemen to keep below and give me all the speed possible, I gave a double barrel gun to the pilot, with instructions not to fire until I should do so, and steered directly for the monitor. I intended to strike her just under the gang-way, but the tide still running out, carried us to a point nearer the quarter. Thus we rapidly approached the enemy. When within about 300 yards of her a sentinel hailed us: Boat ahoy! Boat ahoy! Repeating the hail several times very rapidly. We were coming towards them with all speed, and I made no answer, but cocked both barrels of my gun. The officer of the deck next made his appearance, and loudly demanded, "What boat is that?" Being now within forty yards of the ship, and plenty of headway to carry us on, I thought it about time the fight should commence, and fired my gun. The officer of the deck fell back mortally wounded (poor fellow), and I ordered the engine stopped. The next moment the torpedo struck the vessel and exploded. What amount of directed damage the enemy received I will not attempt to say.* My little boat plunged violently, and a large body of water which had been thrown up descended upon her deck, and down the smoke-stack and hatchway.

I immediately gave orders to reverse the engine and back off. Mr. Tomb informed me then that the fires were put out, and something had become jammed in the machinery so that it would not move. What could be done in this situation? In the mean time, the enemy recovering from the shock, beat to quarters, and general alarm spread through the fleet. I told my men I thought our only chance to escape was by swimming, and I think I told Mr. Tomb to cut the waterpipes, and let the boat sink. Then taking one of the cork floats, I got into the water and swam off as fast as I could.

The enemy, in no amiable mood, poured down upon the bubbling water a hailstorm of rifle and pistol shots from the deck of the *Ironsides*, and from the nearest monitor. Sometimes they struck very close to my head, but swimming for life, I soon disappeared from their sight, and found myself all alone in the water. I hoped that, with the assistance of flood-tide, I might be able to reach Fort Sumter, but a north wind was against me, and after I had been in the water more than an hour, I became numb with cold, and was nearly exhausted. Just then the boat of a transport schooner picked me up, and found, to their surprise, that they had captured a rebel.

The captain of this schooner made me as comfortable as possible that night with whiskey and blankets, for which I sincerely thanked him. I was handed over next morning to the mercy of Admiral Dahlgren. He ordered me to be transferred to the guard-ship *Ottowa*, lying outside the rest of the fleet. Upon reaching the quarter-deck of this vessel, I was met and recognized by her Commander, William D. Whiting. He was an honorable gentleman and high-toned officer. I was informed that his orders were to have me put in irons, and if obstreperous, in double irons. I smiled, and told him his duty was to obey orders, and mine to adapt myself to circumstances—I could see no occasion to be obstreperous.

I think Captain Whiting, felt mortified at being obliged thus to treat an old brother officer, whom he knew could only have been actuated by a sense of patriotic duty in making the attack which caused him to fall into his power as a prisoner of war. At any rate, he proceeded immediately to see the admiral, and upon his return I was released, on giving my parole not to attempt an escape from the vessel. His kindness,

---

*Pilot Cannon states that the injuries were of so serious a nature that extra steam-pumps were found necessary to keep her afloat, that she was towed by tug-boats to Port Royal, where they lightened and tried to repair her, but without success; thence she was towed to Philadelphia, and finally sold for old iron. W. H. H. Davis, a northern writer, makes a statement which entirely contradicts the above.—Y. S. [Y. S. was the original editor of this article. The footnote is not entirely correct.—Editor]

and the gentlemanly courtesy with which I was treated by other officers of the old navy, I shall ever remember most gratefully. I learned that my fireman had been found hanging on to the rudder-chains of the *Ironsides* and taken on board.* I had every reason to believe that the other two, Mr. Tomb and Mr. Cannon, had been shot or drowned, until I heard of their safe arrival in Charleston.

I was retained as a prisoner in Fort LaFayette and Fort Warren for more than a year, and learned while their that I had been promoted for what was called "gallant and meritorious service."

What all the consequences of this torpedo attack upon the enemy were is not for me to say. It certainly awakened them to a sense of the dangers to which they had been exposed, and caused them to apprehend far greater difficulties and dangers than really existed should they attempt to enter the harbor with their fleet. It may have prevented Admiral Dahlgren from carrying out the intention he is said to have had of going in with twelve ironclads on the arrival of his double-turreted monitor to destroy the city by a cross-fire from the two rivers. It certainly caused them to take many precautionary measures for protecting their vessels which had never before been thought of. Possibly it shook the nerve of a brave admiral and deprived him of the glory of laying low the city of Charleston. It was said by officers of the navy that the ironclad vessels of that fleet were immediately enveloped like women in hoop-skirt petticoats of netting, to lay in idle admiration of themselves for many months. The *Ironsides* went into dry-dock for repairs.

The attack also suggested to officers of the United States Navy that this was a game which both sides could play at, and Lieutenant Cushing bravely availed himself of it. I congratulate him for the eclat and promotion he obtained thereby. I do not remember the date of my exchange again as a prisoner of war, but it was only in time to witness the painful agonies and downfall of an exhausted people, and the surrender of a hopeless cause.

I was authorized to equip and command any number of torpedo boats, but it was now too late. I made efforts to do what I could at Charleston, till it became necessary to abandon that city. I then commanded the ironclad. *Fredericksburg* on James River, until ordered by Admiral Semmes to burn and blow her up when Richmond was evacuated. Leaving Richmond with the admiral, we now organized the First Naval Artillery Brigade, and I was in command of a regiment of sailors when informed that our noble old General, R. E. Lee, had capitulated. Our struggle was ended.

All that is now passed, and our duty remains to meet the necessities of the future. After the close of the war I was offered a command and high rank under a foreign flag. I declined the compliment and recommended my gallant old commander,

---

*Pilot Cannon states, that not being able to swim, when the fires were extinguished he jumped overboard and clung to the unexposed side of the David. The boat gradually drifted away from the Ironsides, without being materially injured, though a bull's-eye lantern afforded a mark to the Federal cannoneers. After drifting about a quarter of a mile, Pilot C. got aboard. Seeing something in the water he hailed, and heard, to his surprise, a reply from Engineer Tomb. Tomb got aboard, caught up the fires with the light from the lantern, got up steam, and started for the city. They were fired at several times while passing the Federal monitors and picket-boats, but escaped them unhurt, and reached Atlantic wharf at 12 P. M.—Y. S. [the original article editor].

†Pilot Cannon states, that after the war, while acting as pilot for the United States fleet, Admiral Dahlgren asserted that such was his intention, and that the attack on the Ironsides prevented its execution.—Y. S.

Commodore J. R. Tucker, as one more worthy and competent than myself to fill a high position.

In conclusion let me say: I have never regretted that I acted in accordance with what appeared to be my duty. I was actuated by no motive of self-interest, and never entertained a feeling of hatred or personal enmity against those who were my honorable opponents. I have asked for no pardon, which might imply an acknowledgment that I had been either traitor or rebel. No amnesty has been extended to me.

Bear in mind, loyal reader, these facts: I had been absent nearly two years. No one could have lamented the beginning of the war more than I did. It had been in progress nearly six months when I came home from sea. I had taken no part in it, when on my arrival in Philadelphia, only because I could not truthfully swear that I felt no human sympathy for my own family and for the friends of my childhood, and that I was willing to shed their blood and desolate their homes; and because I would not take an oath that would have been a lie, I was denounced as a traitor, thrown into prison for eight months, and then exchanged as a prisoner of war.

I may have been a fool. I supposed or believed that the people of the south would never be conquered. I hardly hoped to live through the war. Though I had no intention of throwing my life away, I was willing to sacrifice it, if necessary, for the interests of a cause I believed to be just. I was more regardless of my own interests and those of my family than I should have been. A large portion even of my paper salary was never drawn by me. Nearly every thing I had in the world was lost—even the commission I had received for gallant and meritorious conduct, and I possess not even a token of esteem from those for whom I fought to leave, when I die, to those I love.

But the time has arrived when I think it my duty to grant pardon to the government for all injustice and injury I have received. I sincerely hope that harmony and prosperity may yet be restored to the United States of America.

Appendix D

Torpedo Service in the Harbor and Water Defenses of Charleston

by General P. G. T. Beauregard

(*Southern Historical Society Papers*, vol. V, 1878, pp. 145–155)

On my return to Charleston in September, 1862, to assume command of the Department of South Carolina and Georgia, I found the defenses of those two States in a bad and incomplete condition, including defective location and arrangement of works, even at Charleston and Savannah. Several points—such as the mouths of the Stono and Edisto rivers, and the headwaters of Broad river at Port Royal—I found unprotected; though soon after the fall of Fort Sumter, in 1861, as I was about to be detached, I had designated them to be properly fortified. A recommendation had even been made by my immediate predecessor that the outer defenses of Charleston Harbor should be given up as untenable against the ironclads and monitors then known to be under construction at the North, and that the waterline of the immediate city of Charleston should be made the sole line of defense. This course, however, not having been authorized by the Richmond authorities, it was not attempted, except that the fortifications of Cole's Island—the key to the defense of the Stono river—was abandoned and the harbor in the mouth of the Stono left open to the enemy, who made it their base of operations. Immediately on my arrival I inspected the defenses of Charleston and Savannah, and made a requisition on the War Department for additional troops and heavy guns deemed necessary; but neither could be furnished, owing, it was stated, to the pressing wants of the Confederacy at other points. Shortly afterward Florida was added to my command, but without any increase of troops or guns, except the few already in that State; and, later, several brigades were withdrawn from me, notwithstanding my protest, to reinforce the armies of Virginia and Tennessee.

As I have already said, I found at Charleston an exceedingly bad defensive condition against a determined attack. Excepting Fort Moultrie, on Sullivan's Island, the works and batteries covering Charleston Harbor, including Fort Sumter, were insufficiently armed and their barbette guns without the protection of heavy traverses. In all the harbor works there were only three 10-inch and a few 8-inch Columbiads, which had been left in Forts Sumter and Moultrie by Major Anderson, and about a dozen rifle guns—un-banded 32-pounders, made by the Confederates—which burst after a few discharges. There were, however, a number of good 42-pounders of the old pattern, which I afterward had rifled and banded. I found a continuous floating boom of large timbers bound together and interlined, stretching across from Fort Sumter to Fort Moultrie. But this was a fragile and unreliable barrier, as it offered too great a resistance to the strong current of the ebb and flood tide at full moon, especially after southeasterly gales, which backed up the waters in the bay and in the Ashley and Cooper rivers. It was exposed, therefore, at such periods, to be broken, particularly as the channel-bottom was hard and smooth, and the light anchors which held the boom in position were constantly dragging—a fact which made the breaking of the boom an easy matter under the strain of hostile steamers coming against it under full headway. For this reason the engineers had proposed the substitution of a rope obstruction, which would be free from tidal strain, but little had been done toward its preparation. I, therefore, soon after summing command, ordered its immediate completion, and, to give it protection and greater efficiency, directed that two lines of torpedoes be planted a few hundred yards in advance of it. But before the order could be carried out, a strong southerly storm broke the timber boom in several places, leaving the channel unprotected, except by the guns of Forts Sumter and Moultrie. Fortunately, however, the Federal fleet made no effort to enter the harbor, as it might have done if it had made the attempt at night. A few days later the rope obstruction and torpedoes were in position, and so remained without serious injury till the end of the war.

The rope obstruction was made of two heavy cables, about five or six feet apart, the one below the other, and connected together by a network of smaller ropes. The anchors were made fast to the lower cable, and the buoys or floats to the upper one. The upper cable carried a fringe of smaller ropes, about three-fourths of an inch in diameter by fifty feet long, which floated as so many "streamers" on the surface, destined to foul the screw propeller of any steamer which might attempt to pass over the obstruction. Shortly after these cables were in position a blockade-runner, in attempting at night to pass through the gap purposely left open near the Sullivan Island shore, under the guns of Fort Moultrie and of the outside batteries, accidentally crossed the end of the rope obstruction, when one of the streamers got entangled around the shaft, checking its revolutions. The vessel was at once compelled to drop anchor to avoid drifting on the torpedoes or ashore, and afterward had to be docked for the removal of the streamer before she could again use her propeller. The torpedoes, as anchored, floated a few feet below the surface of the water at low tide, and were loaded with one hundred pounds of powder arranged to explode by concussion—the automatic fuse employed being the invention of Capt. Francis D. Lee, an intelligent young engineer officer of my general staff, and now a prominent architect in St. Louis. The fuse or firing apparatus consisted of a cylindrical lead tube with a hemispherical head, the metal in the head being thinner than at the sides. The tube was open at the lower extremity, where it was surrounded by a flange; and, when in place, it was protected against leakage by means of brass couplings and rubber washers. It was charged as follows: In its center was a glass tube filled with sulfuric acid and hermetically sealed. This was guarded by another glass tube sealed in like manner, and both were retained in position by means of a peculiar pin at the open end of the leaden tube; the space between the latter and the glass tube was then filled with a composition of chlorate of potassa and powdered loaf sugar, with a quantity of rifle powder. The lower part of the tube was then closed with a piece of oiled paper. Great care had to be taken to ascertain that the leaden tube was perfectly water-tight under considerable pressure. The torpedo also had to undergo the most careful test. The firing of the tube was produced by bringing the thin head in contact with a hard object, as the side of a vessel; the indentation of the lead broke the glass tubes, which discharged the acid on the composition, firing it, and thereby igniting the charge in the torpedo.

The charges used varied from sixty to one hundred pounds rifle powder, though other explosives might have been more advantageously used if they had been available to us. Generally four of the fuses were attached to the head of each torpedo so as to secure the discharge at any angle of attack. These firing tubes or fuses were afterward modified to avoid the great risk consequent upon screwing them in place and of having them permanently attached to the charged torpedo. The shell of the latter was thinned at the point where the tube was attached, so that, under water pressure, the explosion of the tube would certainly break it and discharge the torpedo; though, when unsubmerged, the explosion of the tube would vent itself in the open air without breaking the shell. In this arrangement the tube was of brass, with a leaden head, and made water-tight by means of a screw plug at its base. Both the shell and the tube being made independently water-tight, the screw connection between the two was made loose, so that the tube could be attached or detached readily with the fingers. The mode adopted for testing against leakage was by placing them in a vessel of alcohol, under the glass exhaust of an air-pump. When no air bubbles appeared the tubes could be relied on. Captain Lee had also an electric torpedo which exploded by concussion against a hard object; the electric current being thus established, insured the discharge at the right moment.

Captain Lee is the inventor also of the "spar-torpedo" as an attachment to vessels, now in general use in the Federal navy. It originated as follows: He reported to me that he thought he could blow up successfully any vessel by means of a torpedo carried some five or six feet under water at the end of a pole ten or twelve feet long, which should be attached to the bow of a skiff or row-boat. I authorized an experiment upon the hulk of an unfinished and condemned gunboat anchored in the harbor, and loaded for the purpose with all kinds of rubbish taken from the "burnt district" of the city. It was a complete success; a large hole was made in the side of the hulk, the rubbish being blow high in the air, and the vessel sank in less than a minute. I then determined to employ this important invention, not only in the defense of Charleston, but to disperse or destroy the Federal blockading fleet by means of one or more small swift steamers, with low decks, and armed only with "spar-torpedoes" as designed by Captain Lee. I sent him at once to Richmond, to urge the matter on the attention of the Confederate Government. He reported his mission as follows:

"In compliance with your orders, I submitted the drawing of my torpedo and a vessel with which I propose to operate them, to the Secretary of War. While he heartily approved, he stated his inability to act in the matter, as it was a subject that appertained to the navy. He, however, introduced me and urged it to the Secretary of Navy. The Secretary of War could do nothing, and the Secretary of the Navy would not, for the reason that I was not a naval officer under his command. So I returned to Charleston without accomplishing anything. After a lapse of some months I was again sent to Richmond to represent the matter to the Government, and I carried with me the endorsement of the best officers of the navy. The result was the transfer of an unfinished hull, on the stocks at Charleston, which was designed for a gunboat — or rather floating battery, as she was not arranged for any motive power, but was intended to be anchored in position. This hull was completed by me, and a second-hand and much worn engine was obtained in Savannah and placed in her. Notwithstanding her tub-like model and the inefficiency of her engine, Captain Carlin, commanding a blockade-runner, took charge of her in an attack against the *New Ironsides*. She was furnished with a spar designed to carry three torpedoes of one hundred pounds each. The lateral spars suggested by you, Captain Carlin declined to use, as they would interfere very seriously with the movements of the vessel, which, even without them, could with the utmost difficulty stem the current. The boat was almost entirely submerged, and painted gray like the blockade runners, and, like them, made no smoke, by burning anthracite coal. The night selected for the attack was very dark, and the *New Ironsides* was not seen until quite near. Captain Carlin immediately made for her; but her side being oblique to the direction of his approach, he ordered his steersman, who was below deck, to change the course. This order was misunderstood, and, in place of going the 'bow on' as was proposed, she ran alongside of the *New Ironsides* and entangled her spar in the anchor-chain of that vessel. In attempting to back the engine hung on the center, and some delay occurred before it was pried off. During this critical period Captain Carlin, in answer to threats and inquiries, declared his boat to be the *Live Yankee*, from Port Royal, with dispatches for the admiral. This deception was not discovered until after Carlin had backed out and his vessel was lost in the darkness."

Shortly after this bold attempt of Captain Carlin, in the summer of 1863, to blow up the *New Ironsides*, Mr. Theodore Stone, Dr. Ravenel, and other gentlemen of Charleston, had built a small cigar-shaped boat, which they called the *David*. It had been specially planned and constructed to attack this much-dreaded naval Goliath, the *New Ironsides*. It was about twenty feet long, with a diameter of five feet at its middle, and was propelled by a small screw worked by a diminutive engine. As soon as ready for service, I caused it to be fitted with a "Lee spar-torpedo" charged with seventy-five pounds of powder. Commander W. T. Glassell, a brave and enterprising officer of the Confederate States Navy, took charge of it, and about eight o'clock one hazy night, on the ebb tide, with a crew of one engineer, J. H. Tomb; one fireman, James Sullivan; and a pilot, J. W. Cannon; he fearlessly set forth from Charleston on his perilous mission — the destruction of the *New Ironsides*. I may note that this ironclad steamer threw a great deal more metal, at each broadside, than all the monitors together of the fleet; her fire was delivered with more rapidity and accuracy, and she was the most effective vessel employed in the reduction of Battery Wagner.

    The *David* reached the *New Ironsides* about ten o'clock P.M., striking her with a torpedo about six feet under water, but fortunately for that steamer she received the shock against one of her inner bulk-heads, which saved her from destruction. The water, however, being thrown up in large volume, half-filled her little assailant and extinguished its fires. It then drifted out to sea with the current, under a heavy grape and musketry fire from the much alarmed crew of the *New Ironsides*. Supposing the *David* disabled, Glassell and his men jumped into the sea to swim ashore; but after remaining in the water about one hour he was picked up by the boat of a Federal transport schooner, whence he was transferred to the guard ship *Ottowa*, lying outside of the rest of the fleet. He was ordered at first, by Admiral Dahlgren, to be ironed, and in case of resistance, to be double ironed; but through the intercession of his friend, Captain W. D. Whiting, commanding the *Ottawa*, he was released on giving his parole not to attempt to escape from the ship. The fireman, Sullivan, had taken refuge on the rudder of the *New Ironsides*, where he was discovered, put in irons and kept in a dark cell until sent with Glassell to New York, to be tried and hung, as reported by Northern newspapers, for using an engine of war not recognized by civilized nations. But the government of the United States has now a torpedo corps, intended specially to study and develop that important branch of the military service. After a captivity of many months in Forts Lafayette and Warren, Glassell and Sullivan were finally exchanged for the captain and a sailor of the Federal steamer *Isaac Smith*, a heavily-armed gunboat which was captured in the Stono river, with its entire crew of one hundred and thirty officers and men, by a surprise I had prepared, with field artillery only, placed in ambuscade along the river bank, and under whose fire the Federal gunners were unable to man and use their powerful guns. Captain Glassell's other two companions, Engineer Tomb and Pilot Cannon, after swimming about for a while, espied the *David* still afloat, drifting with the current; they betook themselves to it, re-lit the fires from its bull's-eye lantern, got up steam and started back for the city; they had to re-pass through the fleet and they received the fire of several of its monitors and guard-boats, fortunately without injury. With the assistance of the flood tide they returned to their point of departure, at the Atlantic wharf, about midnight, after having performed one of the most daring feats of the war. The *New Ironsides* never fired another shot after this attack upon her. She remained some time at her anchorage off Morris Island, evidently undergoing repairs; she was then towed to Port Royal, probably to fit her for her voyage to Philadelphia, where she remained until destroyed by fire after the war.

Nearly about the time of the attack upon the *New Ironsides* by the *David*, Mr. Horace L. Hunley, formerly of New Orleans, but then living in Mobile, offered me another torpedo-boat of a different description, which had been built with his private means. It was shaped like a fish, made of galvanized iron, was twenty feet long, and at the middle three and a half feet wide by five deep. From its shape it came to be known as the "fish torpedo-boat." Propelled by a screw worked from the inside by seven or eight men, it was so contrived that it could be submerged and worked under water for several hours, and to this end was provided with a fin on each side, worked also from the interior. By depressing the points of these fins the boat, when in motion, was made to descend, and by elevating them it was made to rise. Light was afforded through the means of bull's-eyes placed in the man-holes. Lieut. Payne, Confederate States Navy, having volunteered with a crew from the Confederacy Navy, to man the fish-boat for another attack upon the *New Ironsides*, it was given into their hands for that purpose. While tied to the wharf at Fort Johnston, whence it was to start under cover of night to make the attack, a steamer passing close by capsized and sunk it. Lieut. Payne, who at the time was standing in one of the man-holes, jumped out into the water, which, rushing into the two openings, drowned two men then within the body of the boat. After the recovery of the sunken boat Mr. Hunley came from Mobile, bringing with him Lieutenant Dixon, of the Alabama Volunteers, who had successfully experimented with the boat in the harbor of Mobile, and under him another naval crew volunteered to work it. As originally designed, the torpedo was to be dragged astern upon the surface of the water; the boat, approaching the broadside of the vessel to be attacked, was to dive beneath it, and, rising to the surface beyond, continue its course, thus bringing the floating torpedo against the vessel's side, when it would be discharged by a trigger contrived to go off by the contact. Lieutenant Dixon made repeated descents in the harbor of Charleston, diving under the naval receiving ship which lay at anchor there. But one day when he was absent from the city Mr. Hunley, unfortunately, wishing to handle the boat himself, made the attempt. It was readily submerged, but did not rise again to the surface, and all on board perished from asphyxiation. When the boat was discovered, raised and opened, the spectacle was indescribably ghastly; the unfortunate men were contorted into all kinds of horrible attitudes; some clutching candles, evidently endeavoring to force open the man-holes; others lying in the bottom tightly grappled together, and the blackened faces of all presented the expression of their despair and agony. After this tragedy I refused to permit the boat to be used again; but Lieutenant Dixon, a brave and determined man, having returned to Charleston, applied to me for authority to use it against the Federal steam sloop-of-war *Housatonic*, a powerful new vessel, carrying eleven guns of the largest caliber, which lay at the time in the north channel opposite Beach Inlet, materially obstructing the passage of our blockade-runners in and out. At the suggestion of my chief-of-staff, Gen. Jordan, I consented to its use for this purpose, not as a submarine machine, but in the same manner as the *David*. As the *Housatonic* was easily approached through interior channels from behind Sullivan's Island, and Lieutenant Dixon readily procured a volunteer crew, his little vessel was fitted with a Lee spar torpedo, and the expedition was undertaken. Lieutenant Dixon, acting with characteristic coolness and resolution, struck and sunk the *Housatonic* on the night of February 17, 1864; but unhappily, from some unknown cause, the torpedo boat was also sunk, and all with it lost. Several years since a "diver," examining the wreck of the *Housatonic*, discovered the fish-boat lying alongside of its victim.

From the commencement of the siege of Charleston I had been decidedly of the opinion that the most effective as well as least costly method of defense against the powerful iron-clad steamers and monitors originated during the late war, was to use against them small but swift steamers of light draught, very low decks, and hulls iron-claded down several feet below the water-line; these boats to be armed with a spar-torpedo (on Captain Lee's plan), to thrust out from the bow at the moment of collision, being inclined to strike below the enemy's armor, and so arranged that the torpedo could be immediately renewed from within for another attack; all such boats to be painted gray like the blockade-runners, and, when employed, to burn anthracite coal, so as to make no smoke. But unfortunately, I had not the means to put the system into execution. Soon after the first torpedo attack, made, as related, by the *David* upon the *New Ironsides*, I caused a number of boats and barges to be armed with spar-torpedoes for the purpose of attacking in detail the enemy's gunboats resorting to the sounds and harbors along the South Carolina coast. But, the Federals having become very watchful, surrounded their steamers at night with nettings and floating booms to prevent the torpedo boats from coming near enough to do them any injury. Even in the outer harbor of Charleston, where the blockaders and their consorts were at anchor, the same precaution was observed in clam weather.

The anchoring of the large torpedoes in position was attended with considerable danger. While planting them at the mouth of the Cooper and Ashley rivers (which form the peninsula of the city of Charleston), the steamer engaged in that duty being swung around by the returning tide, struck and exploded one of the torpedoes just anchored. The steamer sank immediately, but, fortunately, the tide being low and the depth of water not great, no lives were lost. In 1863–4, Jacksonville, Florida, having been evacuated by the Confederates, then too weak to hold it longer, the Federal gunboats frequently ran up the St. John's river many miles, committing depredations along its banks. To stop these proceedings I sent a party from Charleston under a staff officer, Captain Pliny Bryan, to plant torpedoes in the channels of that stream. The result was the destruction of several large steamers and cessation of all annoyance on the part of the others. In the bay of Charleston and adjacent streams I had planted about one hundred and twenty-five torpedoes and some fifty more in other parts of my department. The first torpedoes used in the late war were placed in the James river, below Richmond, by General G. R. Raines, who became afterward chief of the Torpedo Bureau. Mr. Barbarin, of New Orleans, placed also successfully a large number of torpedoes in Mobile bay and its vicinity.

To show the important results obtained by the use of torpedoes by the Confederates and the importance attached, now, at the North to that mode of warfare, I will quote here the following remarks from an able article in the last September number of the Galaxy, entitled, "Has the Day of Great Navies Past?" The author says: "The real application of submarine warfare dates from the efforts of the Confederates during the late war. In October, 1862, a 'torpedo bureau' was established at Richmond, which made rapid progress in the construction and operations of these weapons until the close of the war in 1865. Seven Union ironclads, eleven wooden war vessels, and six army transports were destroyed by Southern torpedoes, and many more were seriously damaged. This destruction occurred, for the most part, during the last two years of the war, and it is suggestive to think what might have been the influence on the Union cause if the Confederate practice of submarine warfare had been nearly as efficient at the commencement as it was at the close of the war. It is not too much to say, respecting the blockade of the Southern ports, that if not altogether broken up, it would have been rendered so inefficient as to have command no respect from European powers, while the command of rivers, all important to the Union forces as bases of operations, would have been next to impossible."

"Think of the destruction this infernal machine effected, and bear in mind its use came to be fairly understood, and some system introduced into its arrangement, only during the last part of the war. During a period when scarcely any vessels were lost, and very few severely damaged by the most powerful guns then employed in actual war, we find this long list of disasters from the use of this new and, in the beginning, much despised comer into the arena of naval warfare. But it required just such a record as this to arouse naval officers to ask themselves the question, 'Is not the day of great navies gone forever?' If such comparatively rude and improvised torpedoes made use of by the Confederates caused such damage and spread such terror among the Union fleet, what will be the consequence when skillful engineers, encouraged by governments, as they have never been before, diligently apply themselves to the perfecting of this terrible weapon? The successes of Confederates have made the torpedo, which before was looked on with loathing—a name not to be spoken except contemptuously—a recognized factor in modern naval warfare. On all sides we see the greatest activity in improving it."

I shall now refer briefly to the use in Charleston harbor of rifle-cannon and iron-clad floating and land batteries. In the attack on Fort Sumter, in 1861, these war appliances were first used in the United States. When I arrived at Charleston, in March of that year, to assume command of the forces there assembling and direct the attack on Fort Sumter, I found under construction a rough floating battery made of palmetto logs, under the direction of Captain Hamilton, an ex–United States naval officer. He intended to plate it with several sheets of rolled iron, each about three-quarters of an inch thick, and to arm it with four 32-pounder carronades. He and his battery were so much ridiculed, however, by the State government. He came to me in great discouragement, and expressed in vivid terms his certainty of success, and of revolutionizing future naval warfare as well as the construction of war vessels. I approved of Captain Hamilton's design, and having secured the necessary means, instructed him to finish his battery at the earliest moment practicable. This being accomplished before the attack on Fort Sumter opened, early in April I placed the floating battery in position at the western extremity of Sullivan's Island to enfilade certain barbette guns of the fort which could not be reached effectively by our land batteries. It therefore played an important part in that brief drama of thirty-three hours, receiving many shots without any serious injury. About one year later, in Hampton Roads, the *Virginia*, plated and roofed with two layers of railroad iron, met the *Monitor* in a momentous encounter, which first attracted the attention of the civilized world to the important change that iron-plating or "armors" would thenceforth create in naval architecture and armaments. The one and a half to two-inch plating used on Captain Hamilton's floating battery has already grown to about twelve inches thickness of steel plates of the best quality, but together with the utmost care, in the effort to resist the heaviest rifle-shots now used. About the same time that Captain Hamilton was constructing his floating battery, Mr. C. H. Steven, of Charleston, (who afterward died a brigadier-general at the battle of Chickamauga), commenced building an iron-clad land battery at Cumming's Point, the northern extremity of Morris Island and the point nearest to Fort Sumter — that is, about thirteen hundred years distant. This battery was to be built of heavy timbers covered with one layer of railroad iron, the rails well-fitted into each other, presenting an inclined, smooth surface of about thirty-five degrees to the fire of Sumter; the surface was to be well greased and the guns were to fire through small embrasures supplied with strong iron shutters. I approved also of the plan, making such suggestions as my experience as an engineer warranted. This battery took an active part in the attack and was struck several times; but excepting the jamming and disabling one of the shutters, the battery remained uninjured to the end of the fight.

From Cumming's Point also, and in the same attack, was used the first rifled cannon fired in America. The day before I received orders from the Confederate Government, at Montgomery, to demand the evacuation or surrender of Fort Sumter, a vessel from England arriving in the outer harbor, signaled that she had something important for the Governor of the State. I sent out a harbor boat, which returned with a small Blakely rifled-gun, of two and a half inches diameter, with only fifty rounds of ammunition. I placed it at once behind a sand-bag parapet next to the Steven battery, where it did opportune service with its ten-pound shell while the ammunition lasted. The penetration of the projectiles into the brick masonry of the fort was not great at that distance, but the piece had great accuracy, and several of the shells entered the embrasures facing Morris Island. One of the officers of the garrison remarked after the surrender, that when they first heard the singular whizzing, screeching sound of the projectile, they did not understand its cause until one of the unexploded shells being found in the fort the mystery was solved. As a proof of the rapid strides taken by the artillery arm of the service, I shall mention that two years later the Federals fired against Fort Sumter, from nearly the same spot, rifle projectiles weighing three hundred pounds. Meantime I had received from England two other Blakely rifled cannon of thirteen and a quarter inches calibre. These magnificent specimens of heavy ordnance were, apart from their immense size, different in construction from any thing I had ever seen. They had been bored through from muzzle to breech; the breech was then plugged with a brass block extending into the bore at least two feet, and into which had been reamed a chamber about eighteen inches in length and six in diameter, while the vent entered the bore immediately in advance of this chamber. The projectiles provided were shells weighing, when loaded, about three hundred and fifty pounds, and solid cylindrical shots weighing seven hundred and thirty pounds; the charge for the latter was sixty pounds of powder. The first of these guns received was mounted in a battery specially constructed for it at "The Battery," at the immediate mouth of Cooper river, to command the inner harbor. As no instructions for their service accompanied the guns, and the metal between the exterior surface of the breech and the rear of the inner chamber did not exceed six to eight inches, against all experience in ordnance, apprehensions were excited that the gun would burst in firing with so large a charge and such weight of projectile. Under the circumstances it was determined to charge it with an empty shell and the minimum of powder necessary to move it; the charge was divided in two cartridges, one to fit the small rear chamber and the other the main bore. The gun was fired by means of a long lanyard from the bomb-proof attached to the battery; and, as apprehended it burst at the first fire, even with the relatively small charge used; the brass plug was found started back at least the sixteenth of an inch, splitting the breech with three of four cracks and rendering it useless.

With such a result I did not attempt, of course, to mount and use the other, but assembled a board of officers to study the principle that might be involved in the peculiar construction, and to make experiments generally with ordnance. The happy results of the extensive experiments made by this board with many guns of different caliber, including muskets, and last of all with the other Blakely, was that if the cartridge were not pressed down to the bottom of the bore of a gun, and a space were thus left in rear of the charge, as great a velocity could be imparted to the projectile with a much smaller charge and the gun was subject to less abrupt strain from the explosion, because this air-chamber, affording certain room for the expansion of the gases, gave time for the inertia of the heavy mass of the projectile to be overcome before the full explosion of the charge, and opportunity was also give for the ignition of the entire charge, so that no powder was wasted as in ordinary gunnery. When this was discovered the remaining Blakely was tried from a skid, without any cartridge in the rear chamber. It fired both projectiles, shell and solid shot, with complete success, notwithstanding the small amount of metal at the extremity of the breech. I at once utilized this discovery. We had a number of 8-inch Columbiads (remaining in Charleston after the capture of Sumter in 1861) which contained a powder-chamber of smaller diameter than the caliber of the gun. The vent in rear of this powder-chambers, leaving the latter to serve as an air-chamber, as in our use of the Blakely gun. They were then rifled and banded, and thus turned into admirable guns, which were effectively employed against the Federal iron-clads. I am surprised that the new principle adapted to these guns has not been used for the heavy ordnance of the present day, as it would secure great economy in weight and cost. The injured Blakely gun was subsequently thoroughly repaired, and made as efficient as when first received.

In the year 1854, while in charge as engineer of the fortifications of Louisiana, I attended a target practice with heavy guns by the garrison of Fort Jackson, on the Mississippi river, the object fired at being a hogshead floating with the current at the rate of about four and a half miles an hour. I was struck with the defauts of trailing or traversing the guns—42-pounders and 8-inch Columbiads—and with the consequent inaccuracy of the firing. Reflecting upon the matter, I devised soon afterward a simple method of overcoming the difficulty by the application of a "rack and lever" to the wheels of the chassis of the guns; and I sent drawings of the improvement to the Chief of Engineers, General Totten, who referred them, with his approval, to the Chief of Ordnance. In the course of a few weeks the latter informed me that his department had not yet noticed any great obstacle in traversing guns on moving objects, and therefore declined to adopt my invention. When charged in 1861 with the Confederate attack on Fort Sumter, I described this device to several of my engineer and artillery officers; but before I could have it applied I was ordered to Virginia to assume command of the Confederate force then assembling at Manassas. Afterward, on my return to Charleston in 1862, one of my artillery officers, Lieutenant-Colonel Yates, an intelligent and zealous soldier, applied this principle (modified, however) to one of the heavy guns in the harbor with such satisfactory results that I gave him orders to apply it is rapidly as possible to all guns of that class which we then had mounted. By April 6, 1863, when Admiral Dupont made his attack on Fort Sumter with seven monitors, the *New Ironsides*, several gunboats and mortal boats, our heaviest pieces had this traversing apparatus adapted to their chassis, and the result realized fully our expectations. However slow or fast the Federal vessels moved in their evolutions, they received a steady and unerring fire, which at first disconcerted them, and at last gave us a brilliant victory—disabling fire of the monitors, one of which, the *Keokuk*, sunk at her anchors that night. It is pertinent for me professionally to remark that had this Federal naval attack on Fort Sumter of the 6th of April, 1863, been made at night, while the fleet could have easily approached near enough to see the fort—a large, lofty object, covering several acres—the monitors, which were relatively so small and low on the water, could not have been seen from the fort. It would have been impossible, therefore, for the latter to have returned with any accuracy the fire of the fleet, and this plan of attack could have crumbled under the enormous missiles, which made holes two and a half feet deep in the walls, and shattered the latter in an alarming manner. I could not then have repaired during the day the damages of the night, and I am confident now, as I was then, that Fort Sumter, if thus attacked, must have been disabled and silenced in a few days. Such a result at that time would have been necessarily followed by the evacuation of Morris and Sullivan's Islands, and, soon after, of Charleston itself, for I had not yet had time to complete and arm the system of works, including James Island and the inner harbor, which enabled us six months later to bid defiance to Admiral Dahlgren's powerful fleet and Gilmore's strong land forces.

Chapter Notes

Preface

1. Harris Ball, "Tomb's 'Sub' was a Torpedo Boat," *Jacksonville Journal*, June 5, 1974.
2. Robert A. Taylor, *Rebel Storehouse: Florida in the Confederate Economy*, Tuscaloosa: University of Alabama Press, 1995, pp. 21–22.
3. *Ibid.*
4. Richard N. Current, *Encyclopedia of the Confederacy*, New York: Simon & Schuster, 1993, vol. 2, p. 589.
5. Ronald N. Prouty, "War Comes to Tampa Bay," *Tampa Bay History*, 1988, vol. 10, num. 2, p. 36.
6. Current, p. 268.
7. Tom H. Wells, *The Confederate Navy: A Study in Organization*," Tuscaloosa: The University of Alabama Press, 1971, p. 108.

Introduction

1. Raimondo Luraghi, *A History of the Confederate Navy*, Annapolis: Naval Institute Press, 1996, pp. 101–102.
2. *Ibid.*, p. 104.
3. *Official Records of the Union and Confederate Navies in the War of the Rebellion*, Washington, DC: Government Printing Office, 1884–1927, series II, vol. 1, pp. 514–515.

Chapter 1

1. Secretary of State William H. Seward and Congressman Thaddeus Stevens, both radical Republicans in the Lincoln government.
2. Tomb is mistaken concerning the *Conestoga*. According to official records, the two steamers were the USS *Tyler* and the USS *Lexington*.
3. This engagement took place near Lucas Bend, Missouri.
4. The Union vessels were the *Richmond*, 22 guns; the *Preble*, 10 guns; the *Water Witch*, 4 guns; and the *Vincennes*, 20 guns

Chapter 2

1. Engineer Henry Fagan was severely burned in a tragic accident on May 27, 1863, when the boiler of the CSS *Chattahoochee* exploded. He died three days later.
2. James Morris Morgan, *Recollections of a Rebel Reefer*, New York: Houghton Mifflin, 1917, pp. 61–62.
3. *Ibid.*, p. 65.
4. *Ibid.*, pp. 68-69.
5. 6,976 Confederate soldiers were taken prisoner when Island No. 10 surrendered.
6. Charles W. Read, "Reminiscences of the Confederate States Navy," *Southern Historical Society Papers*, May 1876, vol. 1, pp. 337–339.
7. *Dictionary of American Naval Fighting Ships*, "Confederate Forces Afloat," 1970, vol. VI, pp. 263–264.
8. *Official Records of the Union and Confederate Navies in the War of the Rebellion*, Washington, DC: Government Printing Office, 1884–1927, series 2, vol. 1, p. 520.
9. *ORN*, series I, vol. 18, pp. 289–292.
10. Charles F. McIntosh was from Virginia and was a former commander in the U.S. Navy. Mortally wounded when Farragut's ships fought their way past the forts below New Orleans, he died on May 17, 1862.
11. Lieutenant Kennon resigned from the Confederate Navy in December 1861 in order to serve in the Louisiana State Navy. He was re-commissioned into the C.S. Navy on August 20, 1862.
12. *ORN*, series I, vol. 18, pp. 332–335.

13. A. F. Warley, "The Ram *Manassas* at the Passage of the New Orleans Forts," *Battles and Leaders of the Civil War*, vol. 2, New York: The Century Company, 1884–1888, p. 90.

Chapter 3

1. *Dictionary of American Naval Fighting Ships*, "Confederate Forces Afloat," 1970, vol. VI, p. 322.
2. *Official Records of the Union and Confederate Navies in the War of the Rebellion*, Washington, DC: Government Printing Office, 1884–1927, series I, vol. 18, pp. 333–334.
3. J. Thomas Scharf, *History of Maryland*, 1879, vol. 3, p. 523.
4. James H. Tomb, *Prison Life at Fort Warren, Boston Harbor*, "Confederate Veteran," vol. 21, January 1913, p. 110.
5. *Official Records Navy*, series I, vol. 13, p. 163. Washington, DC: Government Printing Office, 18XX.

Chapter 4

1. Tom H. Wells, *The Confederate Navy: A Study in Organization*, Birmingham: University of Alabama Press, 1971, p. 165.
2. David P. Werlich, *Admiral of the Amazon: John Randolph Tucker*, Charlottesville: University of Virginia Press, 1990, pp. 3–257.
3. J. Thomas Scharf, *History of the Confederate States Navy*, New York: Rogers & Sherwood, pp. 670–671.
4. William H. Parker, *Recollections of a Naval Officer*, New York: Charles Scribner's Sons, 1883, p. 308.
5. *Register of Officers of the Confederate States Navy 1861–1865*, Washington, DC: U.S. Navy Department, 1931.
6. *Ibid.*
7. *Official Records of the Union and Confederate Navies in the War of the Rebellion*, Washington, DC: Government Printing Office, 1884–1927, series I, vol. 13, pp. 579–581.
8. *ORN*, series I, vol. 13, pp. 581–582.
9. *ORN*, series I, vol. 13, pp. 622–623.
10. *ORN*, series I, vol. 14, p. 638.

Chapter 5

1. John S. Barnes, *Submarine Warfare: Offensive and Defensive*, New York, GP Putnam and Sons, 1868, pp. 58–60.
2. P. G. T. Beauregard, "Torpedo Service in the Harbor and Water Defenses of Charleston," *Southern Historical Society Papers*, vol. V, April 1878, p. 145.
3. J. Thomas Scharf, *History of the Confederate States Navy*, New York: Rogers & Sherwood, 1887, p. 754.
4. *Ibid.*, p. 227.
5. *Ibid.*, pp. 227–228.
6. David C. Ebaugh, "David C. Ebaugh on the Building of the *David*," *South Carolina Magazine*, January 1953, p. 23.
7. William T. Glassell, "Reminiscences of Torpedo Service in Charleston Harbor," *Southern Historical Society Papers*, 1877, vol. 4, pp. 230–235.

Chapter 6

1. *Dictionary of American Naval Fighting Ships*, "Confederate Forces Afloat," 1970, vol. VI, p. 258.
2. *Register of Officers of the Confederate States Navy 1861–1865*, Washington, DC: U.S. Navy Department, 1931.
3. *Official Records of the Union and Confederate Navies in the War of the Rebellion*, Washington, DC: Government Printing Office, 1884–1927, series I, vol. 14, pp. 423–426.
4. *Register of Officers*.
5. Stephen D. Wise, *Lifeline of the Confederacy*, Columbia: University of South Carolina Press, 1988, pp. 152–153.

Chapter 7

1. *Official Records of the Union and Confederate Navies in the War of the Rebellion*, Washington, DC: Government Printing Office, 1884-1927, series I, vol. 15, pp. 334–335.
2. *Ibid.*, pp. 356–357.
3. *Ibid.*, pp. 358–359.
4. *Ibid.*, p. 405.
5. James H. Tomb, "Submarines and Torpedo Boats," *Confederate Veteran*, April 1914, p. 168

Chapter 8

1. *Official Records of the Union and Confederate Navies in the War of the Rebellion*, Washington, DC: Government Printing Office, 1884–1927, series I, vol. 15, p. 29.
2. E. B. Long, *The Civil War Day by Day*, New York: Da Capo Press, 1971, p. 600.
3. Major General William J. Hardee from the Army of Tennessee fame had replaced General Beauregard as commander of the Department of South Carolina, Georgia, and Florida.
4. *ORN*, series I, vol. 16, p. 506.
5. The USS *Water Witch* was captured in Ossabaw Sound, Georgia, on June 3, 1864, in a daring boat-boarding attack led by Lt. Thomas P. Pelot, who gave his life in the action. She was taken into the Confederate States Navy as the CSS *Water Witch* and was placed under the command of Lieutenant William W. Carnes. It was planned to take her to Savannah for a special assignment but she remained at White Bluff, Georgia, until December 19, 1864, when she was burned to prevent capture.

Chapter 9

1. *Official Records of the Union and Confederate Navies in the War of the Rebellion*, Washington, DC: Government Printing Office, 1884-1927, series I, vol. 16, p. 284.
2. *Ibid.*, pp. 514–515

Chapter 10

1. *Official Records of the Union and Confederate Navies in the War of the Rebellion*, Washington, DC: Government Printing Office, 1884-1927, series I, vol. 16, p. 514.
2. Charleston was evacuated on February 17–18, 1865.
3. This took place on May 20, 1865

Chapter 11

1. *Official Records of the Union and Confederate Navies in the War of the Rebellion*, Washington, DC: Government Printing Office, 1884-1927, series I, vol. 14, p. 427.
2. *Ibid.*, vol. 15, pp. 20–21.
3. *Ibid.*, pp. 358–359. There are some differences here between Tomb's memoirs and the *ORN*.
4. *Ibid.*, p. 358.
5. *Ibid.*, pp. 10–11.
6. *Ibid.*, p. 12.
7. *Ibid.*, pp. 12–13.
8. *Ibid.*, pp. 13–14.
9. *Ibid.*, pp. 16
10. *Ibid.*, pp. 16–17.
11. *Ibid.*, p. 17.
12. *Ibid.*
13. *Ibid.*, pp. 17–18.
14. *Ibid.*, p. 18.
15. *Ibid.*, pp. 18–19.
16. *Ibid.*, pp. 19–20.
17. *Ibid.*, p. 20

Chapter 12

1. *Official Records of the Union and Confederate Navies in the War of the Rebellion*, Washington, DC: Government Printing Office, 1884–1927, series I, vol. 15, pp. 334–335.
2. *Ibid.*, p. 335.
3. *Official Records Navy*, series I, vol. 16, p. 514. Washington, DC: Government Printing Office, 18XX.
4. *Ibid.*
5. *Ibid.*, p. 515.
6. *Ibid.*, p. 464.
7. *Ibid.*, p. 463.
8. *Ibid.*, p. 510

Chapter 13

1. Paraphrased from www.atwar.com, "War of the Triple Alliance, 1864–1870."
2. *The World Book Encyclopedia*, "Argentina," Chicago: Field Enterprises Education Corp., vol. 1, p. 624.
3. M. W. Williams, *The Brazilian Empire: Myths and Histories*, E. V. de Costa, 1985, p. 685.
4. Paraphrased from www.ads.x10.com, "Francisco Solano López."

Chapter 14

1. Narrative from the Brazilian Naval Archives.
2. Many of the Brazilian ironclads were in effect direct copies of Confederate ironclads.
3. Thomas T. Moebs, *Confederate States Navy Research Guide*, Williamsburg, VA: Moebs Publishing Company, 1991, pp. 246–247.

Chapter 15

1. James H, Tomb, Letter in the "Tomb Family Papers," Chapel Hill: Wilson Library, University of North Carolina.
2. Tomb Family Papers.

Bibliography

Ball, Harris. "Tomb's 'Sub' was a Torpedo Boat." *Jacksonville Journal*, June 5, 1974.
Beauregard, P. G. T. "Torpedo Service in the Harbor and Water Defenses of Charleston." *Southern Historical Society Papers*, vol. V, April 1878.
Campbell, R. Thomas. *Fire and Thunder: Exploits of the Confederate States Navy*. Shippensburg, PA: White Mane Publishing Co., 1997.
_____. *Gray Thunder: Exploits of the Confederate States Navy*. Shippensburg, PA: White Mane Publishing Co., 1996.
_____. *Southern Fire: Exploits of the Confederate States Navy*. Shippensburg, PA: White Mane Publishing Co. Inc., 1997.
_____. *Southern Thunder: Exploits of the Confederate States Navy*. Shippensburg, PA: White Mane Publishing Co., 1996.
Current, Richard N. *Encyclopedia of the Confederacy*. 4 volumes. New York: Simon & Schuster, 1993.
Dictionary of American Naval Fighting Ships. "Confederate Forces Afloat." Vol. VI. Washington, DC: Government Printing Office, 1970.
Durkin, Joseph T. *Confederate Navy Chief: Stephen R. Mallory*. Chapel Hill: University of North Carolina Press, 1954.
Ebaugh, David C. "David C. Ebaugh on the Building of the *David*." *South Carolina Magazine*, January 1953.
Glassell, William T. "Reminiscences of Torpedo Service in Charleston Harbor." *Southern Historical Society Papers*, 1877.
Johnson, Robert U., and Clarence C. Buell, ed. *Battles and Leaders of the Civil War*. 4 vols. New York: The Century Company, 1887–88.
Jones, Virgil C. *The Civil War at Sea*. 3 volumes. New York: Holt, Rinehart, and Winston, 1960–1962.
Long, E. B. *The Civil War Day by Day*. New York: Da Capo Press, 1971.
Luraghi, Raimondo. *A History of the Confederate Navy*. Annapolis, MD: Naval Institute Press, 1996.
Melton, Maurice. *The Confederate Ironclads*. New York: A. S. Barnes and Co., 1968.
Moebs, Thomas T. *Confederate States Navy Research Guide*. Williamsburg, VA: Moebs Publishing Company, 1991.
Morgan, James Morris. *Recollections of a Rebel Reefer*. New York: Houghton Mifflin, 1917.
Official Records of the Union and Confederate Navies in the War of the Rebellion. Washington, DC: Government Printing Office, 1884–1927.
Parker, William H. *Recollections of a Naval Officer*. New York: Charles Scribner's Sons, 1883.
Prouty, Ronald N. "War Comes to Tampa Bay." *Tampa Bay History*, 1988, vol. 10, num. 2.
Read, Charles W. "Reminiscences of the Confederate States Navy." *Southern Historical Society Papers*, vol. I, May 1876.

Register of Officers of The Confederate States Navy 1861–1865. Washington, DC: U.S. Navy Department, 1931.
Scharf, J. Thomas. *History of the Confederate States Navy.* New York: Rogers & Sherwood, 1887.
_____. *History of Maryland.* 1879, vol. 3.
Silverstone, Paul H. *Warships of the Civil War Navies.* Annapolis, MD: Naval Institute Press, 1989.
Stern, Philip Van Doren. *The Confederate Navy: A Pictorial History.* New York: Bonanza Books, 1962.
Still, William N., Jr. *Confederate Shipbuilding.* Columbia: University of South Carolina Press, 1987.
_____. *Iron Afloat.* Nashville, TN: Vanderbilt University Press, 1971.
Taylor, Robert A. *Rebel Storehouse: Florida in the Confederate Economy.* Tuscaloosa: University of Alabama Press, 1995.
Tomb, James H. "Prison Life at Fort Warren, Boston Harbor," *Confederate Veteran* vol. 21, January 1913.
_____. "Submarines and Torpedo Boats," *Confederate Veteran,* April 1914.
The War of the Rebellion: A Compilation of the Official Records of the Union and Confederate Armies, 130 volumes. Washington, DC: Government Printing Office, 1880–1901.
Warley, A. F. "The Ram *Manassas* at the Passage of the New Orleans Forts," *Battles and Leaders of the Civil War,* vol. 2. New York: The Century Company, 1884–1888.
Wells, Tom Henderson. *The Confederate Navy: A Study in Organization.* Tuscaloosa: University of Alabama Press, 1971.
Werlich, David P. *Admiral of the Amazon: John Randolph Tucker.* Charlottesville: University of Virginia Press, 1990.
Williams, M. W. *The Brazilian Empire: Myths and Histories.* E. V. de Costa, 1985.
Wise, Stephen D. *Lifeline of the Confederacy.* Columbia: University of South Carolina Press, 1988.
The World Book Encyclopedia. "Argentina." Chicago: Field Enterprises Education Corp., vol. 1.

Index

Abbott, Lt. T. 58
Ables, James 121
Aikin Landing, VA 51
Amazon, CSS 97, 101
Amazonas 145, 146
Andersonville, GA 111, 113
Araguarí 145
Argo 113, 114
Arpa 142, 146, 152, 153, 159
Atlanta, CSS 91
Atlanta, GA 111
Augusta, GA 93–96, 99, 103, 105, 107, 111, 131

Bahia 149, 151, 152
Barboso, Capt. 140, 142
Barroso, Adm. Francisco 145, 146
Battle of Riachuelo 145
Beauregard, Gen. Pierre G. T. 65, 72, 78, 87, 88, 116, 127
Beberibé 145
Belmont, MO 21
Belmonte 145, 146
Benton Hotel, St. Louis, MO 164
Bishop, Carpenter T. H. 125
Bloem, Commander 160
Borchert, Lt. George 51, 52
Borchert, Henry 51
Bowling Green, KY 21
Bragg, Gen. Braxton 93–95
Brazil 149, 151, 152
Brent, Comdr. Thomas W. 91
Brier Creek 102–104

Brock, Asst. Engr. Samuel 25, 29, 30, 34, 42
Brockington, Mastr. Mate Samuel L. 96, 97, 100, 102, 104, 105, 113, 130–132
Brown, Comdr. Isaac N. 109
Brown, Gov. Joseph 94, 102
Brown, Maj. 94, 95
Bruguez, Col. José Maria 145
Buenos Aires, Argentina 134, 136, 137, 157, 159, 162
Bureau of Orders and Detail 107
Burke, Pilot William 76, 81, 82, 115

Cairo, IL 21–23
Calhoun, CSS 12–14, 25
Camp Chase 52
Cannon, Pilot J. W. 71, 75, 84, 90, 116–118, 126, 168
Carnes, Lt. William W. 97, 131
Carter, Lt. Jonathan H. 14
Catskill, USS 78, 79
Charleston, CSS 71, 109, 131
Charleston, SC 52, 53–64, 75, 76, 96, 101, 107, 108, 118, 165
Chattahoochee, CSS 44
Chicora, CSS 53, 54, 56–63, 66, 67, 79, 109, 131
Church Flats 86, 87, 118, 120
Clareta 136

Clark, Engr. Hugh 59, 60, 81, 87
Columbus, GA 44, 111
Columbus, KY 20, 22, 25
Conestoga, USS 22
Cooper, Gen. Samuel 127
Cooper River 93
Corrientes, Argentina 134, 159
Coste, Pilot A. 84, 118
Coxetter, Capt. Louis M. 108, 129
Craven, Ens. 90
Cumberland Gap 21
Cumming's Point, SC 79

Dahlgren, Rear Adm. John A. 74–75, 78, 102, 120, 122, 123, 126
Dantzler, Lt. Col. O. M. 129
Darcy, Chief Engr. John J. 131
David, CSS 65–75, 79, 83, 84, 88, 90, 92, 93, 107, 109, 116–118, 120, 126, 128, 129, 165, 168
Davis, Pres. Jefferson 25
Davis, Sgt. 94, 95
de Lamar, Lt. Victor 142, 144, 151, 159
Dent, Asst. Engr. John H. 25, 29, 33, 40–42, 51, 52, 76, 82
Dillon, Capt. David 101, 102
Dimick, Col. Justin E. 44, 46, 48, 49

Dixon, Lt. George E. 83, 84, 128, 129, 168
Dom Pedro II (Emperor) 137, 138, 139, 158, 161, 162
Dougherty, Mdshp. H. H. 11, 20, 21
Drewry's Bluff, VA 81
Duncan, Col. Johnson K. 20
Duqucron, Capt. Augustus 88
Duro, R.M.S. 161, 162

Eason, James 53, 57, 128
Ebaugh, David C. 68, 93
Echebani, Pilot 151
Elliott, Maj. Stephen, Jr. 63
Evergreen Cemetery, Jacksonville 165

Fagan, Asst. Engr. Henry 25, 29, 38, 41, 42, 44, 51
Farragut, Adm. David G. 15, 35, 37, 43
Fernandina, FL 52
Fingal 91
Fister, Lt. Thomas D. 25, 29, 30
Florence, SC 52
Fort Columbus 46
Fort Delaware 51
Fort Jackson 14, 15, 23, 34, 35, 43
Fort Johnson 63
Fort La Fayette 75
Fort McHenry 48
Fort Pillow 33–35
Fort St. Philip 14, 15, 34, 35, 42, 43
Fort Sumter 62, 63, 66, 72, 79, 83, 109, 115, 129
Fort Warren 42–44, 49, 50, 51, 75
Fry, Gen. Birkett D. 96, 99, 101, 104–106, 130
Fry, Lt. Joseph 13, 14

Gen. Polk, CSS 25, 32, 33
Gen. Quitman 35
Georgia Central Railroad 94
Gibbs, Col. Cooper 111
Glasgow, Scotland 91
Glassell, Lt. William T. 58–61, 66, 67, 68, 70, 71, 116, 117, 121–123, 126, 131, 132, 168
Gorgas, Brig. Gen. Josiah 109
Grant, Gen. Ulysses S. 20

Green, Sarah J. 163
Griswoldville, GA 94
Guayara 153, 154
Gwathney, Capt. Washington 11, 12, 15, 17, 20, 22, 23, 24, 35, 43

H. L. Hunley, CSS 53, 83, 84, 128, 129, 168
Haines, Act. Mstr. Edward L. 78
Hampton Roads, VA 50
Handy, Comdr. Robert 24
Hardee, Maj. Gen. William J. 96
Harriet Lane, USS 41
Harris, Lt. Frank M. 41, 48, 50, 57
Harris, Rep. William G. 48
Hatteras Island, NC 46
Head of the Passes 14, 15, 24, 35
Helen 81, 82
Hickman, KY 21
Hollins, Capt. George N. 22, 24, 25, 30, 35
Holt, Mdshp. Henry C. 11
Housatonic, USS 129
Howard, Mayor Charles 48
Howard, Frank K. 48
Howell, Capt. 99
Huger, Capt. Thomas B. 13, 25, 38, 40
Hunley see *H. L. Hunley*, CSS
Hunter, Capt. William W. 96, 105–107, 129–132

Ignácio, Vice Adm. Joaquim 160
Iguatemi 145
Ingraham, Capt. Duncan N. 57, 58, 66, 67
Ipiranga 145, 146
Island No. 10 25, 27
Ivy, CSS 12–14, 24, 25, 31, 35

Jackson, CSS 11–13, 17, 20–25, 35
Jacksonville, FL 111, 112, 165
Jacobi, Prof. Meritz Hermann von 65
James River, VA 50, 53
Jeff Davis 108
Jefferson City, LA 43
Jejuí 145, 146
Jequitinhonha 145, 146
Johnson, Capt. 162

Johnson, Engr. C. 115
Johnson, Mstr. Mate Andrew W. 131
Jones, Lt. Catesby ap R. 44, 48
Jones, Maj. Gen. Samuel 93, 96, 111, 112, 131
Jordan, Asst. Engr. Charles W. 25
Jordan, Brig. Gen. Thomas 119
Joseph H. Toone 24
Juno, CSS 76–82, 84, 87, 115

Kane, George P. 48
Kendrick, Fireman 29, 30, 38
Kennard, Lt. Joel S. 99, 105–107, 130
Kennon, Lt. Beverley 37, 41
Kepper, Capt. 142
Key West, FL 43, 44
Keystone State, USS 58–61
Kilpatrick, Gen. Judson 93
Knickerbocker 50

Landis 41
Lawless, Fireman James 84, 118
Lee, Capt. Francis D. 65, 67, 68, 71, 87, 119, 120
Lee, Gen. Robert E. 107
Lee, Capt. Sidney S. 106, 107, 130
Leesburg, CSS 97, 99, 100, 105, 130
Lexington, USS 22
Lily Bell 137
Lincoln, Pres. Abraham 11
Livingston, CSS 24, 25
Long, Sec. John D. 164, 165
López, Francisco Solano 133, 134, 139, 140, 144, 145, 152, 155, 157, 158
Louisiana, CSS 34, 35, 37–43

Mackay, Capt. E. R. 88
Magill, Dr. 48
Mallory, Sec. Stephen R. 108, 132
Manassas, CSS 12–14, 24, 25, 35, 39, 41
Mano House, St. Louis, MO 163
Marquês de Caxias 134, 160
Marquês de Olinda 145, 146
Mato Grosso 133

Index

Maurepas, CSS 25, 32
McBlair, Comdr. William 91
McCown, Maj. Gen. John 30
McGary, 1st Lt. Charles P. 11
McIntosh, Capt. Charles F. 37
McPherson, Maj. 48, 49
McRae, CSS 12–14, 24, 25, 28–32, 35, 38, 41, 42
Mearin 145
Memphis, TN 21, 27, 34
Memphis, USS 84, 117, 118, 120
Mercedita, USS 58
Meza, Cmndr. Pedro Inácio 145, 146
Mississippi, CSS 43
Mississippi River 21, 35
Mitchell, Capt. John K. 34, 35, 37, 41, 42
Mitre, President Bartolomé 133, 134, 136
Montevideo, Argentina 136, 159
Morgan, Mdshp. James Morris 25, 30, 31
Morris Island, SC 61, 66, 68, 71, 72, 79, 91, 120

Nahant, USS 91
Neteroy 159
New Ironsides, USS 68, 70–72, 74, 75, 83, 93, 116, 120, 121, 124, 125, 132, 165
New Madrid, MO 25, 27–30
New Orleans, CSS 25
New Orleans, LA 20–23, 34, 35, 43, 98
New York, NY 113, 136
North Carolina, CSS 72
North Edisto River, SC 79, 84, 87, 117

Oil City, PA 134, 135
Otey, John M. 121
Ottowa, USS 74

Paducah, KY 20
Page, Commodore Thomas J. 152, 153
Palace of San Christobal 137
Palmetto State, CSS 55–58, 60, 61, 109
Paraguari 145, 146
Paraguay River 134, 139, 142, 145, 152
Paraná River 134, 146, 157

Parker, Lt. William H. 58
Parnaíba 145, 146
Parry, Lt. 51
Patrick Henry, CSS 53, 81
Patterson, Master R. O. 86, 87
Payne, Pilot Thomas R. 59, 60
Pensacola, FL 43
Petersburg, VA 54
Petrel 82
Philadelphia, PA 113, 114, 134
Philpot, Pilot T. N. 99–101, 105
Pillow, Brig. Gen. Gideon J. 20, 22
Pirabebé 145
Polk, Maj. Gen. Leonidas 20, 25
Pontchartrain, CSS 25, 32
Pope, Capt. John 24, 35
Pope, Gen. John 25, 28
Porcher, Lt. Philip 76, 77, 81, 82, 115
Port Royal, SC 76, 91, 113
Porter, Ens. B. H. 79
Porter, Comdr. David D. 35, 42
Porter, Constructor John L. 56
Porto Alegre, Brazil 160
Powhatan, USS 67
Presidente 159

Race, Capt. 136
Ravenel, Dr. St. Julien 68, 81
Read, Lt. Charles W. 25, 28, 30, 31, 33, 38–40, 42
Rhode Island, USS 43, 49
Richmond, USS 24
Richmond, VA 51, 52
Rio de Janeiro 149, 151
Rio de Janeiro, Brazil 137, 159, 161
Rio Grande do Sul 133, 159
River Defense Fleet 35
Rochelle, Capt. James H. 109
Rowan, Capt. S. C. 122

St. Amecota 157
St. Espiqade 137
St. Marys 113
Salto Oriental 145, 146
Sampson, CSS 76, 97, 131
Savannah, GA 52, 53, 91, 96, 101, 102
Savannah River 96, 97, 130

Sayler's Creek 54
Scemps, Charles 121
Scott, Rep. T. Parkin 48
Shell Bluff Battery, GA 96, 98, 100, 101, 104, 105, 130
Silvado, Capt. 149
Simmons & Co. 113
Sinclair, Comdr. Arthur 43
Stevenson, James A. 14
Stoney, Theodore 68, 71, 81, 84, 117, 120, 121
Stoney Landing 68
Sullivan, Fireman James 70, 71, 116, 117, 126, 168
Sullivan's Island 63
Sumter, CSS 13
Swamp Angel 61

Tacuari 145, 146
Tallahassee, FL 111
Tamandaré 140, 142, 143, 144, 152
Tamandaré, Adm. Joaquim 146, 152, 153
Tattnall, Capt. Josiah 91
Telfair, Mdshp. David A. 12
Tift, A. F. 43, 91
Tift, N. 43, 91
Tilton, Maj. 96
Tiptonville, TN 31, 32
Tomb, Chief Engr. James H. 25, 67, 68, 71, 72, 74, 75, 83, 84, 87, 90, 107, 108, 115–126, 128–132, 163, 165, 168
Tomb, James H. 163
Tomb, William V. 163
Trenholm, George A. 67
Tucker, Master Charles D. 76, 115
Tucker, Capt. John R. 53, 57, 59, 60, 66, 68, 71, 72, 78, 79, 81, 83, 84, 87, 91, 96, 108, 109, 111, 116–119, 122, 128, 131, 132, 165
Tuscarora, CSS 24, 27
Twiggs, Gen. David E. 98
Tyler, USS 22

Varuma, USS 41
Vicksburg, MI 27, 34
Vincennes, USS 24
Virginia, CSS 56

W. Burton 42
Wabash, USS 88, 90, 115, 118, 123

Wainsborro, GA 105
Wallis, Rep. Severn T. 48
War of the Triple Alliance 133
Ward, Surgeon John 12, 20, 23
Warfield, Rep. Henry M. 48
Warley, 1st Lt. Alexander F. 13, 14, 24, 41
Warsaw Sound, GA 91
Weechawken, USS 91
Welles, Sec. Gideon 121
Wells, Asst. Engr. W. S. 165
Whiting, Comdr. William D. 74, 75
Whittle, Lt. William C. 41
Williams, Engineer George 12, 22
Williamson, Col. 104
Wilmington, NC 72, 81
Wilson, Lt. John A. 129
Worrison, Maj. 99

Ybera 145
Ygureí 145
Young, Maj. Gen. Pierce M. B. 105, 107, 130

www.ingramcontent.com/pod-product-compliance
Lightning Source LLC
Chambersburg PA
CBHW081556300426
44116CB00015B/2907